The Female Form

Women Writers and the Conquest of the Novel

Rosalind Miles

Routledge & Kegan Paul
London and New York

First published in 1987 by
Routledge & Kegan Paul Ltd
11 New Fetter Lane, London EC4P 4EE

Published in the USA by
Routledge & Kegan Paul Inc.
in association with Methuen Inc.
29 West 35th Street, New York, NY 10001

Set in 10/11pt Baskerville
by Columns of Reading
and printed in Great Britain
by Billings & Sons Ltd, Worcester

© *Rosalind Miles 1987*

Library of Congress Cataloging in Publication Data

Miles, Rosalind.
The female form.
Bibliography: p.
Includes index.
1. English fiction—Women authors—History
and criticism.   2. English fiction—20th century—
History and criticism.   3. Women and literature—
Great Britain.   I. Title.
PR116.M54   1987   823'.009'9287   86–33871

British Library CIP Data also available

ISBN 0–7102–1008–6

FOR MY MOTHER
who first taught me the joy of a
good book

Contents

	Preface	ix
1	Writers and women writers	1
2	Finding a voice	20
3	Lady novelists and honorary men	35
4	The feminine novel	50
5	The battle lines	64
6	Moral themes	88
7	The sex war	111
8	Man the enemy	132
9	Free women	148
10	Loving women	177
11	Female, human, gifted, white and black	193
	Bibliography	209
	Index	219

Preface

Who can deny that the novel is unique among literary forms in owing its birth, survival, and success at every stage as much to women writers as to men? Yet we are still in a situation where one very recent survey of the novel could include only Jane Austen and Daphne du Maurier as female practitioners, and where another, discussing the fifty greatest novelists since Rabelais, could name only one woman (see Chapter 5 for a discussion of these and other examples of this extraordinary process of denial and annihilation). I wrote this book to assert the supremacy of the role of women writers in the evolution of the modern novel, and to review some of the reasons why this simple fact seems to need restating again and again and again.

This exploration led inevitably to a consideration of the many complex issues surrounding women's writing from its earliest days. It is clear that not enough recognition has yet been given to the courage and resource of the pioneer women novelists, facing as they did a two-fold task – for in addition to the struggle to write undertaken by any writer, they also had to fight a much deeper and usually unacknowledged battle within the predominantly masculine novel tradition, first to find a permitted place, and second to find a voice that could make itself heard. A very great deal of effort was expended throughout the nineteenth century and beyond to reclaim the novel form as a vehicle for exploring their own distinctively female experiences and preoccupations.

Given the number of exciting innovations in women's writing in recent years, any critical observations have to be in the nature of an interim report. This stunning explosion of female talent has created a new wave of women writers, most of whom are only beginning to realise their potential, and who will go further in directions as yet unimagined. There is also much work for women writers still to do in continuing to explore the intimate aspects of their lives as women; as daughters, as mothers, in sexual relations with men, and with each other, or as women alone: besides the

ix

ongoing challenge of mapping those areas of experience still under
patriarchal taboo.

For there is another crucial sense in which the novel is '*the
female form*'. For centuries women readers have turned to it to
help them make sense of their lives. The task of interpretation of
women's experience cannot be left to male writers alone, however
sympathetic they may be. The female perspective, expressed
through women's writing of all kinds, is more than a valuable
corrective to an all-male view of the universe. For women readers,
it is a lifeline.

For me the chance to renew acquaintance with some of the
founding mothers of the modern novel, and to meet a number of
those who have recently joined the sisterhood of women writers,
has been a delight and privilege above anything I imagined when I
began. I have tried to share some of this by allowing the writers to
speak for themselves as much as possible, in order to give readers
the texture and flavour of the originals. With the same aim of
minimising the barriers between reader and text I have broken
with contemporary practices of footnoting, which seems to me to
have reached epidemic proportions; all references will be found
either incorporated into the text, or in the Bibliography at the back
of the book.

For their help in tracking down often difficult or obscure
material, my thanks are due to the librarians of the Bodleian,
Oxford, the Birmingham Reference Library, and the British
Library. Such a study as this must, however, necessarily be
selective, and some of the new developments considered here, like
the growth of black and lesbian women's writing, merit much fuller
treatment. *The Female Form* sets out to pursue an argument rather
than to provide an encyclopaedic survey – but I hope that novel-
fanciers will not find too many of their favourite authors missing.
Finally, if this book sends even one of its readers back to the source
and inspiration of these pages, the novelists themselves, my work
will have been fully rewarded.

The lines on page 189 are reprinted by permission of New York
University Press from *The Hand That Cradles the Rock* by Rita Mae
Brown (Copyright © 1971 by New York University).

Rosalind Miles
Corley Hall
Corley

CHAPTER 1

Writers and women writers

My profession is literature; and in that profession there are fewer experiences for women than in any other, with the exception of the stage – fewer, I mean, that are peculiar to women. For the road was cut many years ago – by Fanny Burney, by Aphra Behn, by Harriet Martineau, by Jane Austen, by George Eliot – many famous women, and many more unknown and forgotten, have been before me, making the path smooth, and regulating my steps. Thus, when I came to write, there were very few material obstacles in my way. Writing was a reputable and harmless occupation. The family peace was not broken by the scratching of a pen. No demand was made on the family purse. For ten and sixpence one can buy paper enough to write all the plays of Shakespeare – if one has a mind that way. Pianos and models, Paris, Vienna and Berlin, masters and mistresses, are not needed by a writer. The cheapness of writing paper is, of course, the reason why women have succeeded as writers before they have succeeded in other professions.

> Virginia Woolf, 'Professions for Women',
> *The Death of the Moth* (1942)

If human beings were not divided into two biological sexes, there would probably be no need for literature. And if literature could truly say what the relations between the sexes are, we would doubtless not need much of it then, either. . . . It is not the life of sexuality that the novel cannot capture; it is literature that inhabits the very heart of what makes sexuality problematic for us speaking animals. Literature is not only a thwarted investigator but also an incorrigible perpetrator of the problem of sexuality.

> Barbara Johnson, *The Critical Difference* (1981)

The question of sex difference has had a unique relation to the

1

novel throughout its history. As Ellen Moers observed in *Literary Women* (1977, p. ix), 'literature is the only intellectual field to which women, over a long stretch of time, have made an indispensable contribution.' Within this wide field women and the novel have been particularly important to one another, as the novel has been the only literary form in which women have participated in numbers large enough to make their presence felt, or to which they have contributed on anything like equal terms with men. It has been the preferred form for women writers almost since women began to write, and it has been the chosen medium through which in recent years women have investigated and published those aspects of their lives as sexual beings that have not previously been acknowledged by art or society.

When we say 'women writers', then, the phrase is generally taken to mean 'women novelists'. For reasons only recently being addressed by feminist criticism, women have yet to make any substantial impact in large numbers on any other literary form. Where they have tried, their work has been ignored, or routinely downgraded to a special subsection created especially for women. Neither Emily Brontë, known to her contemporary admirers as 'a Baby God', nor Emily Dickinson, can be dismissed as 'a woman poet', or worst of all 'poetess'. But very few women have been able to follow them as poets, and even today Emily Brontë's authorship is still debated in terms of the vexatious 'woman question'; even, indeed, by those who seek to dismiss this question from consideration – see Inga-Stina Ewbank's study of the Brontë sisters, *Their Proper Sphere* (1966, p.155):

> Whether she was a perfect woman or not, the art of Emily Brontë makes us see that there is an order of creative genius where the sex of the possessor ceases to matter. The only vital 'woman question' in her case is: why are there no women poets like her?

There are, indeed, a whole series of problems for the critic in the fact that so very few women in the history of literature have been accorded the status of major poet. Margaret Homans crisply stressing in *Women Writers and Poetic Identity* (1980, p.7) that 'nothing is inherently female', points to women's continued subjugation to social ideals of womanhood, none of which included writing: 'the same literary atmosphere that made it difficult for women to become poets must also have made it – and still makes it – difficult for readers to appreciate those who did succeed.'

It was formerly argued that women writers would take to writing poetry when they outgrew their historical handicap of being late starters, and managed to catch up with the men. Virginia Woolf thought this way; she saw the woman novelist as the woman artist in embryo. Female writing she thought of as necessarily evolving in the direction of poetry, and the woman writers as needing only some traditionally masculine privileges and freedoms to enable her to make up the distance between male and female accomplishment. In her famous pronouncement of 1929 she wrote:

> Give her another hundred years . . . give her a room of her own and five hundred a year, let her speak her mind and leave out half that she now puts in, and she will write a better book one of these days. She will be a poet . . . in another hundred years' time. (*A Room of One's Own*, p. 142).

But this is historically fallacious, and cannot be supported from evidence. Poets, of either sex, are not novelists who, like the Alchemist's base metals in Ben Jonson's play, 'would be gold, if they had time'.

At all events it must be observed that over fifty of Virginia Woolf's hundred years have passed without bringing forth 'the female Shakespeare'. But there are not so many male writers challenging for this title in recent times. Historical and cultural factors determine the form and medium through which the creative impulse finds its expression, and not merely sexual mores. With the torrents of words released daily through books, newspapers, television, and other mass media of communication, the twentieth century is incontrovertibly an age of prose; just as the eighteenth century was in England, and for not dissimilar reasons, since the novel form has a similar relevance to our needs now as it had in the era that developed it. The novel is pre-eminently the twentieth-century form, *the* contemporary mode for writers today; and most writers adopt it for that reason, whether they are male or female.

Leaving women poets, it is no more encouraging to consider the question of women dramatists, who have been even more thin on the ground. Aphra Behn shines virtually alone and rather dimly down the centuries to the present day, ignored by the British national theatre companies until the belated but successful revival of *The Rover* in 1986 (see Fidelis Morgan's *The Female Wits 1660–1720*, 1981, for an account of Behn and her sister-dramatists of the time). Even the 'emancipated' twentieth century can only boast a handful of women playwrights like Lillian Hellman, Ann Jellicoe, Shelagh Delaney, Pam Gems, Louise Page, and Caryl Churchill, while a number of other very promising women are known for one play only.

Despite late twentieth-century pieties, women are still very far from attaining that level of socio-cultural, educational, and economic advantage enjoyed by men. They are also still under pressure to conform to traditional concepts of womanly behaviour, to be self-effacing, supportive, and unjudging, and to invest all their efforts in their man's success rather than their own. Writing a novel is a far less assertive act than making a play. It calls for no further action or input from others to realise it, while the drama by contrast is a collaborative act and a public medium. The act of making a play is a deliberate laying-claim to enjoying visibility and taking up space. As a further obstacle, access to this space has always been in the hands of men, who have shown as much enthusiasm for admitting women as they have for any other challenge to male hegemony. Novel writing, however, is compatible with the conventional requirement of women that they should keep their heads down.

Finally, in considering the stifled potential of women poets and dramatists, how many women writers have simply been lost to view? A huge amount of female literary talent has always been channelled away from public forms of writing. The creative drive has found its outlet in surreptitious, unacknowledged, or 'unimportant' productions. Women have for centuries been among the most prolific and accomplished of letter-writers and diarists, but despite the cult success of Anais Nin, these activities were not defined as writing in the real sense, and are only now being reclaimed for full consideration. Women's writing in general has a knack of failing to satisfy the critical criteria of the male canon, and is faulted on these grounds of genre; women's novels are called autobiographical, women's autobiographies stigmatised as novelistic, if not novelettish – see Mary McCarthy's *Memories of a Catholic Girlhood* (1957) and Maxine Hong Kingston's *The Woman Warrior: Memoirs of a Girlhood Among Ghosts* (1975). Other women have directed their energies, or had them directed, into the sub-genres or foothills of the literary mountain range. Their subsequent pre-eminence in the fields of detective fiction or children's stories, for example, have then ensured that these are kept as low-status genres, more badly paid and lowly rated than anything comparable written by a man.

Then there is the basic physiological act of creation, which art has assumed as its own central metaphor. Women who can give birth to babies are creative by sheer force of nature, without having to pick up a pen or sweat over a typewriter. And since men in general have found it convenient that women should undertake the burden of childcare while they wrote the plays and poems, many women must have been encouraged to feel like the mother of the

Gracchi, who rebuked a boastful female visitor adorned with jewels with the statement that her children were her jewels and all the adornment a woman needed.

For all these reasons and many more besides, the novel then has engrossed the attention of women writers to the virtual exclusion of any other art form. This fact has been of substantial significance to all who work in this area. The sex of a novelist is always in question somewhere, sometime, in the course of the critical response – the sex of a woman novelist, that is. Whatever a woman produces as a writer, she is still judged as a woman. Roland Barthes, in *Mythologies* (1972), examined a photograph of a group of women novelists which appeared in the magazine *Elle*. Every single one of the seventy writers represented was described as 'Jacqueline Lenoir, two daughters, one novel; Marina Grey, one son, one novel; Nicole Dutreuil, two sons, four novels'; and so on.

Nor should it be assumed that this heightened consciousness of women writers as women first and writers a long way second, only occurs at the level of magazine journalism. For the last hundred years or so the awareness of a woman writer's sex has been so important as to form the basis of any committed critical observation. This tension originated with the origins of the novel in the eighteenth century, and was an entrenched practice by the nineteenth, when many women had to deny or disguise their female identity in the struggle to secure a fair hearing for their writings. The nature of the process at work here is perfectly illustrated by the fact that this was actually a reversal of the eighteenth-century practice, when male authors had to masquerade as females to get their novels published.

As Dale Spender irrefutably demonstrates in her copious and polemical *Mothers of the Novel* (1986), the 'lady novelist' initially picked up her pen and staked out the novel as female territory *before* her male colleague. But a funny thing happened to her on the way to posterity. As Dale Spender expresses it, 'we have a splendid but suppressed tradition of women writers . . . Jane Austen is presented as a solitary figure and starting point of women's literary achievement.' The denial of women's writing by the opinion-makers of succeeding ages has been deliberate, systematic, and massive in scale:

Of the approximately two thousand novels that were written during the eighteenth century, only a very few have been preserved and passed on in the literary canon. This in itself is no cause for complaint. But when to this is added the information that about half these novels were written by women, and *all* of them have since failed the test of greatness, then explanations are required. (p. 119)

Dale Spender's work is based on and endorsed by that of other women scholars. Janet Todd's *Dictionary of British and American Women Writers 1660–1800* (1984) lists nearly five hundred names, while Lina Mainiero's *American Women Writers* (1979–81) runs to four large volumes. But by the nineteenth century, the idea that the novel was man's 'proper sphere' was so entrenched that the very idea of a 'lady novelist' was enough to arouse suspicion, scorn, surprise, or roguish gallantry on all sides. Considerable interest was aroused by the hope of spotting a female hand at work, as Dickens did with George Eliot's *Scenes from Clerical Life* (1857). Masculine opinion combined to produce an impression of the woman writer as an aberration; the philistine gibe of W. S. Gilbert in *The Mikado* at the 'lady novelist' as a 'singular anomaly' who could well be spared from the cultural scene both illustrated the entrenched prejudices of the operetta's audiences and confirmed their limitations of taste.

This was nothing new. Dale Spender notes that 'from the advent of the first woman novelist we have a value system which automatically places women's concerns, and the literature which reflects them, in a subordinate position' (p. 58). Where woman is deemed inferior, nothing she can do will reverse that judgment. 'It is the value attached to the sex, and not to the writing, which is primarily responsible for women's exclusion from the literary heritage':

Women novelists are not consigned to the low status category of romantic fiction because of either the quality of their experience or the quality of their writing. Far more important as the deciding factor is their sex. Numerous studies have been undertaken on everything from essay writing to publisher's rejection slips and academic editors' partiality, which suggests that the sex determines the status of the writer, and as Philip Goldberg found, many years ago, the same piece of writing is judged to be *mediocre* when thought to flow from the pen of Joan Smith and *impressive* when thought to be the work of John Smith. Not that it is always necessary to set up 'experiments' to detect this practice in operation. From the 1840s onwards, when females began to adopt male pseudonyms, women writers have been aware that, in principle, male authors get a fairer hearing and a better reception. Which is why women have taken various steps to avoid the inferior connotations of their sex. (p. 164)

These elements of denial, denigration, and simple surprise in the masculine response to women writers have been noticeable even in the tributes of admirers. Max Beerbohm was apparently unaware of any contradictions co-existing in his sweeping assessment of Ouida: 'Ouida is essentially feminine, as much *une femme des femmes* as Jane Austen or "John Oliver Hobbes", and it is indeed remarkable that she should yet be endowed with force and energy so exuberant and indefatigable' (*English Critical Essays, Twentieth Century*, ed. Phyllis M. Jones, 1933, p. 179).

This sense of the strangeness of women writers has persisted, a suspicious unease lurking under the veneer of admiration. Beerbohm's antique surprise was echoed by Anthony Burgess: 'It is rarely that one finds such a variety of gifts in one contemporary woman writer – humour, poetry, the power of the exact image, the ability to be both hard and compassionate, a sense of place, all the tricks of impersonation and, finally, a historical eye' (*The Novel Now*, 1967, p. 95). It would seem that the possession of all these gifts has been rare in any writer since Shakespeare went back to Stratford, but that does not decrease Burgess's surprise at finding a *woman* of such capacity.

Many would concede that the sense of sex difference was strong in the past, but feel that on the whole, things are different now. The idea of the 'lady novelist', like the phrase itself, has a whiff of stale elegance and misplaced chivalry about it. The days are gone in which a male critic could no more bring himself to dispraise a lady's novel than he could express dislike of her bonnet. Those familiar with Norman Mailer's critique of Mary McCarthy in *Cannibals and Christians* (1967), and his general response to his female critics in *The Prisoner of Sex* (1971), will be aware that they are gone indeed; Mailer proved that he could bring himself to the entire critical gamut that lies between the left hook and the right cross.

And for all this, the part-playful, part-hostile nineteenth-century distinction of women writers as 'lady novelists' has stayed very much alive. Consciousness of sex difference is as marked as ever it was. The distinction, however, has become hallowed as 'writers' and 'women writers', the phrase still operating to confine creative women to a pejorative subsection of the real thing, the great world of literature. This process was well illustrated in the literary pages of the *Guardian* of 25 January 1986, where the readers were informed 'Hilary Bailey reviews new fiction', while lower down on the page 'Christian McEwen reviews women writers'. A letter from Gaby Weiner in the same week wittily drew attention to the internal contradictions and downright silliness of this categorisation:

I am at a loss to understand why, in this week's Books Page, there should be a section subtitled 'women writers' . . . the odd thing is that there are two other women reviewed on the page, Marilyn French and Emma Tennant. Why were they left out of the women's section? Aren't they really women? Or is it the case that when women writers become successful they become discernible from other 'women' writers and so qualifying for honorary membership of the male literary elite?

These sex-based critical processes are of particular importance to women writers, since they are disadvantaged by these hidden assumptions and unacknowledged criteria. The process is deftly exposed by Ivy Compton-Burnett in *Men and Wives* (1931); the initiated will observe a characteristic Compton-Burnett joke in the deliberate use of the author with whom she has herself most frequently been linked:

'What do you think of Miss Jane Austen's books, Jermyn?' said Dominic – 'if I may approach so great a man upon a comparatively flimsy subject.'
'Our row of green books with the pattern on the backs, Rachel?' said Sir Percy with a sense of adequacy in conversation. 'Very old-fashioned, aren't they?'
'What do the ladies think of the author, the authoress, for she is of their own sex?' said Dominic.
'I have a higher standard for greatness,' said Agatha, 'but I don't deny she has great qualities. I give her the word great in that sense.'
'You put that very well, Mrs Calkin,' said Dominic. 'I feel I must become acquainted with the fair writer.'
'That is a great honour for her!' said Geraldine. (p. 94)

Note that the reader of this is not only made aware of the writer's sex in the abstract – Jane Austen was a 'lady novelist' – but is also shown how it conditions each individual's response in terms of his or her own sex. As Dominic illustrates, a certain type of man approaches a woman's novel as if it were a woman, flirtatiously, but not forgetting the demands of chivalry. Ivy Compton-Burnett throughout her work nudges her readers into the realisation of the part their own sex plays in their response to a writer, in the establishing of the dialogue of any fiction between creator and recipient; although true to her sybilline persona she never called herself anything more flamboyantly sexual than 'I. Compton-Burnett'.

Mary Ellmann has also registered her ironic amusement at this process when, in dealing with a woman writer, 'criticism embarks, at its happiest, upon an intellectual measuring of busts and hips' (*Thinking About Women*, 1968, p. 29). At a more profound level, Patricia Meyer Spacks argues in *Contemporary Women Novelists* (1977, p. 1), sexual politics dominate discussions of writers who present themselves vividly and unmistakably as women. This proceeds inevitably from a wider cause:

Twentieth-century views of contemporary women novelists reflect the same dilemmas as twentieth-century views of women in general . . . sociologists, psychoanalysts, anthropologists – as well as literary critics – have trouble agreeing exactly what difference sex makes. The fundamental quandary remains: is the woman novelist a special breed?

Sex difference is of course only part of the basic equipment which each writer brings to the task of being a novelist. It may not be a major conditioning influence; social class, with all its contingent effects upon education, leisure, self-esteem, and life expectations, is clearly an enormous thing to come to terms with, and in all its potential refinements likely to affect as many facets of the novelist's production as merely being male or female does. And even in what we think of as the more rigidly structured society of the nineteenth century, Parson Austen's daughter led a very different life from Parson Brontë's, only a few years earlier. It is the distinctive setting of the life that will shape the fiction – Charlotte's from its first years so full of the standard horrors of Victorian everyday life, and of unbearable blows so continuously borne, Jane's existence so apparently undisturbed.

This last, though, like Ivy Compton-Burnett's claim to have led a life so uneventful that there was nothing to put in a biography, must be deceptive. Elizabeth Sprigge's authorised version, *The Life of Ivy Compton-Burnett* (1973), clearly showed up the nature of this deception but was all too reticent to indicate its extent; see Hilary Spurling's *Secrets of a Woman's Heart: The Later Life of Ivy Compton-Burnett* (1984). All lives are eventful, unless we make the mistake of excluding all but terminal or sensational acts from view. Drama and significance are extrinsic qualities which Jane Austen understood as well as any other writer how to produce; see the memorable and justly famous scene at the end of chapter XVIII of *Mansfield Park*, when the illicit thespians are electrified by these simple monosyllables: 'My father is come! He is in the hall at this moment.' Sir Thomas is here fully embodied in the minds of all what he has been in Fanny's fearful apprehension all along, the threatening masculine principle of vengeance and punishment. It is the measure of his moral progress in the novel that he is permitted to shake off his association with the novel's other egotistic and destructive males, and develop an adherence to that area of the emotional action in which Edmund links with Fanny in his apparently passive virtue. But the virtue of Fanny and Edmund is only superficially unimpressive. Both have the moral courage to stand by an 'undesirable' decision – and both are subjected to severe trials, emotionally and sexually – Mary Crawford, Edmund's personal *lamia*, has as much power to disturb and distort his life as her brother has over Fanny. All the key episodes in Jane Austen readily lend themselves to analysis in terms of a variety of significances; it seems likely that the full sexual implications of her writing have not yet been uncovered.

Nevertheless a parson's daughter will obviously lead a different life from a parson's son, and sex difference has been vital, if unacknowledged, in conditioning attitudes, both of the writer towards characters and themes, and of the readers towards the writer. There seems to be an inescapable ambivalence in all approaches to this subject. The sex of a writer may be something we never consider, but it is also something we never forget. We may not think of 'George Eliot' as a lady novelist (though possibly the subliminal effects of the masculine name should not be underestimated; such pressures seem to be at work in the case of Stevie Smith whose deliberately intersex name leads many of those who do not know to think her male). But do we think of Jane Austen in this way? Virginia Woolf?

The great artists may illustrate the absurdity and pettiness of such classification, but they seem to be able to do little to undermine it. It is the more ironic that there has never been any basis shown for establishing or continuing such a division. Various studies have appeared which could be expected to tackle the question of whether or not there is such a thing as a distinctively 'feminine style'. Marjory Bald's *Women-Writers of the Nineteenth Century* (1923), Muriel Masefield's *Women Novelists from Fanny Burney to George Eliot* (1934), and more recently Vineta Colby's *The Singular Anomaly* (1970), are among books which considered women writers in a group, as if their sex must have some significance, or provide some common factor to their work, and then made no attempt to discover what it could be. The usual form is to announce their intention to treat their subjects not as sexual beings, but as 'authors only', and the illogic of a procedure which undermines their central premise of selection goes unnoticed.

They may have been deterred, however, by contemplating the difficulties of those who have tried. The critics who have made the attempt upon this north face of commentary predictably find themselves perpetuating existing concepts of contemporary behaviour rather than illuminating the secrets of mental activity:

The new woman, the feminine novelist of the twentieth century, has abandoned the old realism. She does not accept *observed* revelation. She is seeking, with passionate determination, for that Reality which is behind the material, the things that matter, spiritual things, ultimate Truth. And here she finds man an outsider, wilfully blind, purposely indifferent. Not that her own conceptions, or definitions, are yet by any means definite or clearly formulated. Speaking generally, I think one may say that she is striving to see and express, all that part of life and humanity which formal Religion once claimed to interpret. (R. Brimley Johnson, *Some Contemporary Novelists, Women*, 1920, pp. xiv–xv)

The new women, on closer inspection, proves to be our old friend, the Angel at the Hearth. How difficult it is for all women except witches and whores to shake off this time-honoured female role of custodian of the moral values, sensitive to 'the things that matter'! Social notions of appropriate role behaviour vitiate this as a critical attempt to discern thematic preoccupations.

One of the few critics of the past to make a genuine effort to isolate and describe the specifically female qualities of women's writing was W. L. Courtney. His comments in *The Feminine Note in Fiction* (1904) amply illustrate his inherited prejudices. He asserts that there does exist 'a distinctively feminine style in fiction', 'of a type peculiarly its own'. This style is inferior to that achieved by male novelists, since the female writer cannot transcend the limits of the immediate: 'the beginning of a woman's work is generally the writing of a personal diary' – 'would it be wrong to say that a woman's heroine is always a glorified version of herself?' She is further restricted by the narrowness of her perception and understanding; 'a passion for detail is the distinguishing mark of nearly every female novelist' (little things please little minds, perhaps?). Women's novels are deficient in construction, since their authors cannot take the broad view; the female intellect cannot strain so far; 'it is the neutrality of the artistic mind which the female novelist seems to find it so difficult to realise.' Naturally, difficulties of tone result: 'the female author is at once self-conscious and didactic.' Women writers should stick to their little

squares of ivory; Courtney sees the female genius as expressed best
in the 'novels of manners' like Jane Austen's. Women can be equal
or indeed superior at 'miniature-work', but inferior on the 'large
canvas'. Women should also recognise that their essential nobility
is best shown not in writing but in their readiness to subordinate
and sacrifice themselves to duty.

Courtney's uninformed condescension and failure of objectivity
can most charitably be seen as the unquestioned and undigested
assumptions of his time. Anthony Burgess has no such historical
figleaf with which to cover his naked attitudes. In his study *The
Novel Now* (1967), Burgess restricts the entire range of women
novelists to one chapter, coyly entitled '*Yin* and *Yang*'. Note the
Lawrentian flavour of his summary of the 'big contemporary
theme' of women writers:

> Woman has a sexual need of man, but she objects to having this
> need; she wants to reject man, but she cannot, and so she seeks
> to dominate him, though a great deal of her sexual fulfilment
> must derive from being dominated. *Yin* and *Yang* are tangled up
> together, and the literary expression of the female dilemma is
> often harsh, sensational, explosive. (p. 122)

It is difficult to conceive of a pronouncement upon women writers
which could contrive so well to be unfair simultaneously to Iris
Murdoch and to Alice Walker, to Anita Brookner and to Keri
Hulme. But this is not meant to be unflattering. 'Harsh,
sensational, explosive', are all terms of praise in Burgess's critical
vocabulary; all good qualities are masculine and all masculine
qualities good. Hence 'guts' is both a term of high approbation and
the chief indication that a masculine controlling intelligence (?) is
at work (women for the purposes of this metaphor being
understood as devoid of the standard viscera). Burgess's stereotyped
notions of women writers are further revealed by his conclusion:

> We have tended to regard clarity and common sense as
> essentially feminine properties in the novel – Alice in a land of
> male jabberwocks. Some of our traditionalists among women . . .
> have made our sweating male experimentalists look gauche and
> uncomfortable. But, if the art of the novel is to progress, there
> will have to be sweat and discomfort. The *Yin* cannot have all its
> own way. (pp. 129–30)

This passage contains a series of belittling assumptions – women
writers are all Jane Austens if not Alices in Wonderland – and it is

informed throughout by that primitive sense of superiority which is not assailable by rational processes. By some extension of what is usually admiringly referred to as masculine logic, a sweating, struggling male novelist is not only the owner of this land in which the women wander, Alice-like; his effort alone represents the future of the novel, in his 'sweat and discomfort' lies the creative effort. (See again how these physical manifestations are not only abrogated to the male, as if women never sweat or struggle, but are also held up as criteria of excellence, demonstrations of potency and the capacity to become deeply involved in the struggle for mastery over the brute inertia of the raw material – sexual analogy again.)

But the defensive note in the last line clearly points up the embattled nature of Burgess's thinking. The novel is masculine territory, where men must keep control. In a very real sense, both the novel and the words out of which it is made are female, created and existing only for men's pleasure and use. So to Norman Mailer in *Cannibals and Christians* (1967), the novel is 'the Great Bitch'; writing is fucking and mastering her, good writing is 'making her squeal': 'Man, I made her moan.' David Lodge made a similar claim to masculine sexual possession in *The Language of Fiction* (1966): 'Fiction is never virgin: words come to the writer already violated by other men.' The French structuralist Jacques Derrida was not only speaking for the nation of lovers when he identified the pen with the penis on the virgin page. But the American writer William Gass found solace in a more domestic metaphor when he gave his version of the *Boys' Own* definition of the creative act:

> Ordinary language ought to be like the gray inaudible wife who services the great man: an ideal engine, utterly self-effacing, devoted without reminder to its task . . . it demands to be treated as a thing, inert and voiceless. (*Fiction and the Figures of Life*, 1971, p. 93)

So Burgess's '*Yin*' must not expect to call the tune. Nor must females break out of their traditional compound. Doris Lessing, one of the few women writers who seem to Burgess through their aggression, drive, and scope to approximate to a 'masculine' rather than to a 'feminine' mode, is handled with a mixture of the reproachful, the sarcastic, and the dismissive. Writing of Anna, the heroine of *The Golden Notebook* (1962), he says:

> Her conception of herself as a 'free woman' leads her to say some hard things about male arrogance, crassness, sexual impotence

and incompetence, and her own sexual frustrations (which are, of course, to be blamed on men) fill up a good part of one notebook. She is intelligent, honest, burning with conviction, but she ends up as a bit of a bore. So for that matter does Mrs Lessing's own experiment. (p. 100)

Who will be surprised to learn that among Burgess's other pet aversions top of the list comes Brigid Brophy – 'Brigid Brophy has won herself a small reputation in recent years as one of our leading shrews'?

Burgess is an extreme case, but he is not alone in his attitudes. Many critics feel vaguely that there is something odd or threatening about women writers: 'Who's afraid of Virginia Woolf?' is apparently a key question of our time. Edward Albee's anti-feminism is treated fully by Katharine Rogers in her study of misogyny in literature, *The Troublesome Helpmate* (1966); what is interesting here is that he found Virginia Woolf a particularly appropriate peg to hang his preoccupations on. It shows, too, that hostility towards intelligent females is not simply the idiosyncrasy of the old fogey still fostering ancient grudges against suffragettes and bluestockings. It seems to be rediscovered by every generation of creative men, as a logical extension of the assumption that literary creation is itself a masculine art, a process of exploring and mastering the feminine, unconscious mass of life and material. Hence any woman who tries this and succeeds in it contradicts the unacknowledged laws of kind – it should not be in the nature of the beast to behave so. Lord David Cecil has remarked in conversation how frequently people comment unfavourably upon Jane Austen's unmarried state and childlessness. It is felt to be unfortunate that she did not marry, while we should more reasonably consider it unfortunate, on the basis of their matrimonial records, that Dickens, Hardy, or Tolstoy did.

Criticism seems to have had to come to terms with women writers in every new age, treating each fresh generation of women writers as if they were the first of their sex to pick up the pen. It is not the least interesting aspect of women's writing that its very existence has continually to be explained (away?). As Patricia Meyer Spacks observed in *Contemporary Women Novelists* (p. 1):

Critical discussion of women writers seems even now at a primitive stage, though women have written a large proportion of published novels ever since the genre first developed in the eighteenth century. . . . Conceivably the relative invisibility of women writers reflects special difficulty in dealing with them.

How this feels from the point of view of one on the receiving end was deftly satirised by Alison Lurie in *Real People* (1969, pp. 30–1):

> I suppose I was irritated by Nick because he interrupted a conversation about my book, which Leonard turns out to have read. And even more because of the way he did it.
>
> NICK: You a writer? Hey, Baxter, pass the salt. Yeah, I thought you looked like a lady writer.
>
> That looks harmless written down, but it wasn't; it was coarse and dismissive.
>
> Of course, it's been said before, though not in that tone of voice. What's occasionally meant (and sometimes also said) is that I look a little like pictures of Virginia Woolf – a less fine drawn, less neurasthenic, middle-class American version. (Pictures of me, on the other hand, seldom catch any such resemblance, perhaps because the camera adds another ten pounds to the ten I must already have on her.) Somebody asked once if that was why I decided to become a writer. 'Not at all,' I replied indignantly. 'Long before I even *heard* of VW, I wanted to be a writer.' Quite true, but so do a lot of young girls. And who can say it didn't influence me when I found out? Standing in the library stacks at Smith, with Daiches' biography open in my hand, feeling a deep sentimental shock of recognition . . .
>
> When people in Westford say I look like a writer, though, my first reaction is to check my stockings for runs, my hands for ink – because that's what they usually mean. They've seen, or imagined they've seen, some flaw in my disguise as the conservatively attractive, well-dressed wife of an insurance executive. Which isn't a disguise anyhow, but half of the truth.
>
> A lady writer. And why should I mind that, anyway? Do I mind being a writer? Or being a lady?

As this shows, both critical and authorial comment repeatedly raises and tries to answer the question, 'Why do women write novels?' The conventional historical answer has been that the rise of the novel was roughly contemporary with the emancipation of women; motive and opportunity coincided. Hazel Mews, in *Frail Vessels* (1969), drew attention to the fact that women novelists first appeared in any numbers or quality during the years of revolutionary upheaval at the beginning of the nineteenth century, after Mary Wollstonecraft's *Vindication of the Rights of Woman* had appeared in 1792. Mews comments cautiously:

It seems at least probable that the upheaval in old ways of thought in the minds of women should provide some release of power for works of the imagination, the response of the women writers matching the dynamic of the transitional changes that confronted them. (pp. 5–6)

Ivy Compton-Burnett has already similarly linked the development of women's writing in the twentieth century with the devastating cataclysm that marked its opening years. Speaking of becoming established as a novelist in the period after the First World War, she attributed women's success starkly to a far more horrific social convulsion than female emancipation:

> . . . the men were dead, you see, and the women didn't marry so much because there was no one for them to marry, and so they had leisure, and, I think in a good many cases they had money, because their brothers were dead, and all that would tend to writing, wouldn't it, being single, and having some money, and having the time – having no men, you see. (Kay Dick, *Ivy and Stevie*, 1971, p. 7).

This seems to imply that she felt that women of her time owed most of their prominence to the massive male mortality without which they would have been overwhelmed by the men in one way or another. Or perhaps the suggestion is rather that women need some external event of great reverberance to awake them from their long sleep of history to the fullness of their potential – Eve's dream of truth?

In recent years sustained and serious attempts have been made to come to grips with the whole question of femininity and masculinity, and their relation to creativity. Mary Ellmann attempted to analyse sex difference as expressed through difference of tone between men and women writers (ch. IV, pp. 148–74). She argued that the 'male' mode contains and conveys authority, weight, rationality, knowledge, and control. By opposition the 'female' mode is intuitive, formless, subtle, over-intense ('shrill' has been the word used to derogate this quality in women's writing). Mary Ellmann sees this as a false dichotomy, originating early in the nineteenth century when women first began to publish not only as novelists but as what we now call 'intellectuals'. This provoked in consequence a male response which codified its own utterance in the more commanding terms, both in definition and in defence.

This opposition tends to stereotype production; some women 'repeat the ritual gestures of sensibility, just as some men repeat those of authority', and never find their own voice. It could be added that these modes are not necessarily adopted according to sex. Many women writers, especially in the nineteenth century, sought and achieved the masculine mode, and its stylistic correlative, the rhetorical stance. Similarly many men have tried to avoid the external view, the public posture that this implies, and have chosen instead the equivocations of irony, the interior dialogue, the subjective flow. This is discussed at length in Lisa Appignanesi's *Femininity and the Creative Imagination* (1973). She sums up part of her argument as follows:

Feminine, then, as a term of literary description would suggest an art of which the two distinguishing features are interiorisation and the conscious creation of mystery either around or within the work of art. The long historical insistence on the otherness of woman, her core of feminine mystery, makes her the natural focus for an art which finds no fruitful material in what it considers the prose of ordinary life and which seems to transcend the configurations of a known reality. (p. 15)

As Virginia Woolf had noted, 'a woman's writing is always feminine; at its best it is most feminine; the only difficulty lies in defining what we mean by feminine.' In 1975 Sydney Janet Kaplan took the struggle for meaning a stage further:

When I use the term 'feminine consciousness' here, I hope the reader understands that I am using it in a rather special and limited way. I use it not simply as some general attitude of women towards their own femininity, and not as something synonymous with a particular sensibility among female writers. I am concerned with it as a literary device: a method of characterisation of females in fiction ... I am not using 'feminine consciousness' even so broadly as to take in the full range of any given woman's consciousness in a novel, but only those aspects of it which are involved with her definition of self as a specifically feminine being. That is why I use the adjective 'feminine' to modify 'consciousness' rather than 'female'. The latter simply refers to the biological condition of being a woman; the former connotes characteristics which, though usually ascribed to women, derive not only from their physical makeup but from a combination of physical traits and socially based attitudes about what constitutes 'femininity'. After all, there is a difference between a 'female body' and a 'feminine figure'. The first is fact, the second opinion. When considering 'feminine consciousness' one must never forget all the ways in which the beliefs of the author about what constitutes femininity of mind have gone into the structuring of consciousness of any given female character. (*Feminine Consciousness in the Modern British Novel*, p. 4)

Complex as this is, its painstaking method penetrates further into the heart of this confusion of sex difference than the attitudinising of earlier critics. The extreme difficulty of resisting the tyranny of the unfelt sexual stereotype is readily apparent on all sides. Virginia Woolf, with an unexpected and now dated coyness, once opined that 'Fiction is a lady; and a lady who has somehow got herself into trouble,' a concept which Mailer's 'Great Bitch', for all its crudity, only updates. The use of male and female to delineate (or, as here, to expropriate) areas of activity or sensibility in literature, has been standard practice for so long that even the sharpest intellect will hardly be free of its influence. Consider the following reflections on the contemporary novel by Mary McCarthy:

> The fictional experiments of the twentieth century went in two directions: sensibility and sensation. To speak very broadly, the experiments in the recording of sensibility were made in England (Virginia Woolf, Katherine Mansfield, Dorothy Richardson, Elizabeth Bowen, Forster), and America was the laboratory of sensation (Hemingway and his imitators, Dos Passos, Farrell). The novel of sensibility was feminine, and the novel of sensation was masculine. . . . The effect of these two tendencies on the subject matter of the novel was identical. Sensation and sensibility are the poles of each other, and both have the effect of abolishing the social. Sensibility, like violent action, annihilates the sense of character. (*On the Contrary*, 1962, pp. 275–6)

The novel here is seen as doing what every individual artist must do, that is, coming to terms with those areas of experience which we all find in apposition within ourselves and call male and female. The artist as hermaphrodite matches himself against the hermaphroditic potential of this most subtle and flexible of fictional forms. But equally interesting here in McCarthy's comment is the illustration of how easy it is even for an intelligent and highly critical woman to accept unquestioned any rationalisations of male commentators.

Given this routine denial to women of all that does not fall within the paradigm of 'femininity' or 'womanhood', it is hardly surprising that women writers in the past have not been able either confidently to create new traditions, or even to hang on to what had been achieved. As Elaine Showalter stresses in her magisterial *A Literature of Their Own: British Women Novelists from Brontë to Lessing* (1977, pp. 11–12), 'each generation of women writers has found itself . . . without a history, forced to rediscover the past anew, forging again the consciousness of their sex.' It was in this spirit that Adrienne Rich, who won the American National Book Award for *Diving into the Wreck* (1973), a work exploring women's anger among other things, accepted the prize 'on behalf of all the women whose voices have gone and still go unheard in the patriarchal world . . . '

It is this silence, unwilled, and all too often enforced, that women's writing has always sought to combat. Recovering the lost tradition, while finding the individual voice, has involved rediscovering in every generation the terms of confrontation with the dominant masculine world. Yet in no sense is the writing that these women produced in response to their subordination to be seen as reactive or second-class. On the contrary, from their inferior position, women novelists succeeded in capturing the heights. Singly and in numbers they have established the novel as the female form. As writers they have repeatedly demonstrated their outstanding mastery of it; as readers they have continuously turned and returned to it for the vital task of making sense of their experience as women, and harmonising the often unbearably painful conflicts of their lives. And all this they have achieved in the face of long-standing, deep-rooted hostility and denial. For all these reasons the struggle to understand the process and the productions of women's writing must be pursued with all the vigour we can muster. In the words of Hélène Cixous:

> It is important to *define* a feminine practice of writing, and this is an importance that will remain, for this practice will never be theorised, enclosed, encoded – which doesn't mean that it doesn't exist . . . ('The Laugh of the Medusa', 1976)

CHAPTER 2

Finding a voice

I see my self-consciousness in terms of battling with myself to let go of something . . . I had fought through very difficult emotional tasks in order to allow myself to say: 'OK, as weird as this is, *this* is how truly I feel. Therefore, if I write anything else, it would be a lie . . . ' In other words, my self-consciousness has nothing really to do with other people. It has to do with whether or not I'm going to confront what I'm feeling.

Ntozake Shange, *Black Women Writers at Work*,
ed. Claudia Tate (1985), p. xvii

As soon as I started selling women's magazine stories I could afford a half-day babysitter or something equivalent to do the drudge work . . . the wonderful thing about these stories is that I can do them by perspiration, not inspiration – so I can work on them while Frieda [her daughter] is playing in the room.

Sylvia Plath (1960) in *Letters Home*, ed. Aurelia Schober Plath
(1975), pp. 402–3

One of the major questions concerning women's writing is not *why* they write, a non-issue which has been done to death in the past – but *how* they manage to do so in the face of all the difficulties and disadvantages they endure simply by virtue of being born female. How each individual woman makes her escape from the traditional world-wide culture of female subordination effected first through paternal domination and later through married life and child-bearing, and the exclusion from work, is something that has never been fully considered. Yet its relevance not only to the women who write, but to what and when they write, and how much – not to mention its relevance to the whole question of women's literary achievement and to those who do not escape, therefore do not write – is immeasurably important.

Among major impediments to women's prospects of becoming writers was the problem of literacy. When Fanny Burney made novel-writing a respectable profession for women with her sensationally successful *Evelina*, it was no coincidence that her mother and stepmother were two of the only three women in King's Lynn who could read and write (the other was herself). Fanny Burney's first novel was prophetically subtitled 'A Young Lady's Entrance into the World'. But even in an age where education, like so much else in the society of the time, was almost entirely class-based, a 'young lady' had far less chance of becoming literate than a young gentleman. And as for those born to be 'women' rather than 'ladies', their chances of literacy were virtually nil.

Women were also much less likely to have either of the two vital aids to creativity that Virginia Woolf insisted on as essential, financial independence and privacy ('a room of her own and five hundred a year'). These have not been felt as female needs even by women themselves. Generations of her admirers have smiled at James Austen-Leigh's account of his aunt Jane scribbling away at a desk in the family sitting-room, alert for the creak of the hall door which was her signal to slip her papers unobtrusively together before the visitor entered; equally compelling is the insight into Mrs Gaskell's domestic management, as she wrote on the dining-room table from a seat that commanded, through three open doors, views of different areas of her house. But do we ever stop to wonder how under such circumstances these women produced anything at all, let alone work of sustained quality and quantity? Mrs Humphry Ward seems fortunate in comparison to have been able to share the study of her enlightened husband.

But she still had a husband, who expected her to behave like a wife. Where men writers could count on the domestic services of a partner without even having to think about it, women had to struggle with the burden of the domestic management and the guilt that it induced, even when living with men who might have been thought intelligent and enlightened. Consider Katherine Mansfield's 1913 description of her life with Middleton Murry, and measure this against the writing lost while she washed dishes as he sat around griping:

> . . . the house seems to take up so much time if it isn't looked after with some sort of method. I mean . . . when I have to clear up twice over or wash up extra unnecessary things I get frightfully impatient and want to be working. So often this week, I've heard you and Gordon talking while I washed dishes. Well, someone's got to wash dishes and get food, otherwise – 'There's nothing in the house but eggs to eat'. Yes, I hate hate *hate* doing

these things that you accept just as all men accept of their
women. I can only play the servant with a very bad grace
indeed. It's all very well for females who have nothing else to
do . . . and then you say I am a tyrant, and wonder because I get
tired at night! The trouble with women like me is – they can't
keep their nerves out of the job in hand – and Monday after you
and Gordon and Lesley have gone I walk about with a mind full
of ghosts of saucepans and primus stoves and 'Will there be
enough to go round?' . . . and you calling (whatever I am doing)
'*Tig*, isn't there going to be tea? It's five o'clock' as though I were
a dilatory housemaid.

I loathe myself today. I detest this woman who 'superintends'
you and rushes about, slamming doors and slopping water – all
untidy with her blouse out and her nails grimed. I am disgusted
and repelled by the creature who shouts at you. 'You might at
least empty the pail and wash out the tea leaves!' Yes, no
wonder you 'come over silent'. (*Katherine Mansfield: Letters and
Journals*, ed. C. K. Stead, 1981, pp. 43–4)

Marriage has in general posed a major threat to the flowering of
female talent. In the nature of the institution women are required
to surrender that autonomy essential to the practice of any art.
Singleness by contrast is usually blessed; in Ivy Compton-Burnett's
Men and Wives (1931) a childless woman advises a girl who chooses
the life of a single poet rather than that of a married woman, 'a
selfish life is a lovely life, darling.' The advent of marriage and all
its consequences, especially in the ages before contraception,
threatened a woman with the possibility of a physical death like
Charlotte Brontë's, or a mental, emotional, and spiritual invasion
and destruction.

Zelda Fitzgerald is a poignant case-study here. She wrote all her
life, and particularly in her youth was a tireless diarist and letter-
writer, nursing literary ambitions of her own. But Scott Fitzgerald
regarded their entire life together, and her written accounts of it, as
'his' material. Nancy Milford, in *Zelda Fitzgerald: A Biography*
(1970) has demonstrated the extent of Scott's plagiarism of Zelda's
writing for his own work, and his inability to see her as a writer in
her own right.

Inevitably, then, Zelda's one serious attempt to launch herself as
a novelist provoked a catastrophic reaction from Scott. He felt that
Zelda's use of incidents from their life in her only novel, *Save Me the
Waltz* (1932), was an unscrupulous descent and a betrayal of the
meaning of their marriage. It was this act of Zelda's, rather than
the infidelity which the novel celebrates, that brought about the

final death of Scott's love. Scott also felt passionately that the
flowering of whatever talent his wife possessed was due entirely to
'*the greenhouse of my money, and my name, and my love*' (Milford, p. 271).
Comparisons are pointless, and who could wish to sacrifice
anything that Scott himself wrote in favour of some hypothetical
contribution from Zelda? But other women writers have been more
fortunate in their choice of the matrimonial greenhouse, and it is
suggestive of the continuous willed disaster of Zelda's life that,
having some literary talent of her own, she tried to bloom in the
'greenhouse' kept by the most distinguished writer of their entire
generation.

When they have married, women writers have tended towards
men who have loved and served their geniuses, who have been able
to accept constructively and on the whole gracefully the role of
'Mr Siddons'. Otherwise the marriage has proved less durable than
the woman's talent (though writers as different as Dorothy Parker
and Carson McCullers divorced and then remarried men who
could live neither with nor without their clever wives). On one
occasion at least the man proved to be the midwife to the woman's
talent; George Henry Lewes certainly assisted George Eliot, to put
it no higher, towards the definitive expression of her varied gifts as
well as lending her his first name, and Edmund Wilson is similarly
credited with directing Mary McCarthy's transition from criticism
to fiction, reputedly by locking her up till she had done something
'creative'. As this apocryphal story suggests, the Svengali element
is not entirely absent; Virginia Woolf dreaded what she called the
'beak' of Leonard's critical comment, but awaited his verdict on all
her new productions as among the most important of all the
opinions she was likely to receive; she invariably sought not only
his advice but also relied on his practical help with the revising,
editing, and even punctuation of her work. Such unselfishly
supportive husbands are, however, very much the exception rather
than the rule.

If marriage is a trap for a woman, how much more are children
the enemies of her promise? It is hardly coincidental that among
women writers the greatest and most distinctive have often been
childless: Jane Austen, the three Brontës, George Eliot, Virginia
Woolf, Ivy Compton-Burnett, Iris Murdoch, Stevie Smith, Anita
Brookner. In *Silences* (1978, p. 31), Tillie Olsen drew up her own
list of women writers who were free from the distractions of a
family: Willa Cather, Ellen Glasgow, Gertrude Stein, Edith
Wharton, Virginia Woolf, Elizabeth Bowen, Katherine Mansfield,
Isak Dinesen, Katherine Anne Porter, Dorothy Richardson, Henry
Handel Richardson, Susan Glaspell, Dorothy Parker, Lillian

Hellman, Eudora Welty, Djuna Barnes, Anais Nin, Ivy Compton-Burnett, Zora Neale Hurston, Elizabeth Madox Roberts, Christina Stead, Carson McCullers, Flannery O'Connor, Jean Stafford, May Sarton, Josephine Herbst, Jessamyn West, Janet Frame, Lilian Smith, Iris Murdoch, Joyce Carol Oates, Hannah Green, Lorraine Hansberry.

Amongst others a picture of relative childlessness comes through, with women writers tending to avoid childbearing where they could not get out of it altogether. Katherine Mansfield, despite the often-repeated sentimentalism about her longing for children, miscarried of her first pregnancy through an 'accident' while heaving a heavy trunk from a high wardrobe, and used her faithful friend 'L.M.'s' savings to abort her second – for an account of this moving and previously undisclosed incident, see the fascinating *Katherine Mansfield: The Memories of L.M.* (1971, pp. 64–5).

This is not to suggest that physical and artistic creation are necessarily antithetical. The links between them in each individual are highly personal. Margaret Drabble has stated that for her, physical and mental creativity are linked; she wrote her first, second, and third novels while awaiting the birth of her first, second, and third children. Conversely the successful novelist Susan Hill observed that she lost all desire to write novels after the birth of her first child. In general, however, the hand that rocks the cradle will have a reduced amount of time and energy left for pounding the typewriter. In creating the preconditions for literary work, it has usually been necessary for women to emulate men as far as they could, in limiting or regulating their domestic commitments. Otherwise they are condemned to the fate of Margaret Walker, who took thirty years to write her great novel of slavery, *Jubilee* (1965). In *How to Suppress Women's Writing* (1983, p. 140), Joanna Russ cites one woman's painfully ironic reflection on this theme: 'I was able to snatch a few precious days in the month of January in which to write undisturbed. But . . . when shall I ever be so fortunate again as to break a foot?'

These, then, are the disadvantages of the woman's life. It is not, though, a picture of unrelieved misery, frustration and enslavement. There have been suggestions that certain aspects of a woman's life were positively conducive to novel-writing. Virginia Woolf expressed it like this:

> . . . all the literary training that a woman had in the early nineteenth century was training in the observation of character, in the analysis of emotion. Her sensibility had been educated for centuries by the influence of the common sitting-room. People's

feelings were impressed on her, personal relations were always before her eyes. (*A Room of One's Own*, p. 100)

Margaret Drabble again has made a similar point about the twentieth century; women, she feels, have plenty of experience of daily life, and 'novels are about daily life'. But men have 'daily lives' too. This statement links with the widespread assumption that women rely more than men on the basis of disguised autobiography in their writing. It is a tendency deliberately played upon by Mary McCarthy when she declared herself to be the sexually adventurous heroine of her short story 'The Man in the Brooks Brothers Shirt'; though Sarah Harrison in *Hot Breath* (1985), her witty spoof of an adulterous 'lady novelist', found it prudent to deny any connection with her heroine.

Plainly the writer's own lived and felt experience will form the inalienable matrix of creation. But women's writing is not inherently more autobiographical than men's. Take Doris Lessing's account, in the very largely autobiographical *Martha Quest*, of how Martha embarks on her career as a writer:

> For a few days then she dreamed of herself as a writer. She would be a free lance. She wrote poems, lying on the floor of her room; an article on the monopoly press; and a short story about a young girl who. . . . This story was called 'Revolt'. (Part IV, ch. 2)

Has literature no examples of male writers who began their work with stories about a young man who . . . ? We need think no further than the portraits of artists as young man and young dog delineated by James Joyce and Dylan Thomas; and there is always Proust to quash any suggestion that women have better memories for detail than men. Writers have better memories than other people; that is all.

There remains, however, the theory that women writers are those who have succeeded in turning certain potentially restrictive aspects of those lives to advantage. Margaret Drabble has claimed that it is easier for a woman, freed from the tyranny of economic necessity to work and provide which cramps the lives of most men, to find or make the time to write. She has also, like other women, stressed the point made by Virginia Woolf, that it is a cheap and unobtrusive career to embark on, free from the demands for expensive paints or instruments. Several women who have won world-wide respect as writers originally contemplated other art-forms as the vehicle for their talents; Carson McCullers for many years subordinated her writing to a deep commitment to music, and others tried their hand at painting. This is described, again by Doris Lessing in *Martha Quest* (IV, 2), with the irony of hindsight (note the echo of Virginia Woolf):

> She remembered that as a child she had had a talent for drawing. She made a sketch there and then of the view of the park from her door; it really wasn't too bad at all. But the difficulty with being a painter is that one must have equipment. Ah, the many thousands of hopeful young writers there are, for no better reason than that a pencil and writing pad takes up less room than an easel, paints, and drawing boards, besides being so much less expensive.

Arguably the urge to paint is not strong enough. The young Martha is rather struck with the notion of 'being a painter' than driven by the compulsion to express herself in *this* medium and no other. Martha is drawn with resentful urgency simply to claim for herself what she sees as the 'masculine' free life of the artist; her use of the masculine image of the free 'lance' is significant, particularly as this ideal is defined in Martha's instance by comparison with the especially odious and restricted life of the South African white woman.

But there is something of wider application to all women writers here, the sense of settling for less. Could it be that this process, so characteristic of female behaviur, is responsible for the generalised underachievement of women across the whole of the artistic spectrum? Or is it just that consciousness of masculine prejudice that makes women stick to something they can hide under their embroidery if need be? Virginia Woolf insisted that creative women are always 'impeded by the extreme conventionality of the other sex'. This may be interpreted as a general social prejudice, rather than as an exclusively masculine one: nonconformist men have had as much to put up with from philistines and bullies as women have. But there still remains the irreducible difference between a man's life and a woman's, between the contribution of men to the various art-forms, and that of women. How is the feminist critic to come to terms with these facts?

It seems to me that women's contribution to art must be assessed in relation to their opportunities as a sex, which at best have usually been, and remain, inferior to the best offered to men. Paradoxically in view of the harshly anti-feminist temper of the Middle Ages, the Paston women, whose letters so well reveal their literary as well as their commercial and human abilities, were better off than any of their male serfs in this respect. Those women who wrote wrote, as men did, in the contemporary and available literary modes. If they showed an inevitable bias towards the literary fashions currently prevailing, again, so did the men. It is not so much writing habits which have altered to admit women into the literary arena by way of the novel, as educational and social ones. As society evolved from the medieval model, aristocratic women lost the educational advantage they had had at a time when education and culture were almost totally class-based in distribution. Nor were they advantaged as large numbers of men were by the cultural development of the nineteenth century which substantially replaced class by sex as the criterion for educational opportunity; or through the establishing of the public schools, which reinforced the interaction of the two. Opportunity is a fine thing, and the majority of women simply never received theirs.

Yet a century and upwards of free public education has taken some effect. Thousands of women are now writers who would previously have thronged with the ranks of the illiterate. What use are they making of these relatively new freedoms in the struggle to find their voice? Paradoxically, as new women, they have turned in great numbers to one of the oldest of literary forms, that of romance. The spirit of romance, its characters, themes, and motifs, constitute a vitally influential element of contemporary fiction and of modern women's writing in particular.

What is romance? Any definition of the term has to encompass its two key elements: adventure, and love. Its practitioners strive to hold on to its former high style and dignity; as romantic novelist Anne Maybury explains, 'the trouble with "romance" is that it has moved away from its original meaning. True romance is not something gentle and rose-tinted, it is Arthurean, Brontëan, full of action, desire, tension. Unfortunately it has taken on an entirely different meaning, and has become a word to giggle over.' Her sister-novelist in the romance tradition Hermina Black agrees: 'Romance not only supplies a need, but expresses a truth. The romantic novel points to an idea, and is worthy of respect.'

Romantic fiction of any and every kind has always been a prime target of men's humour, disrespect, and satire, as this parody by James Joyce in *Ulysses* (1922, p. 346), indicates:

There was an innate refinement, a languid queenly *hauteur* about Gerty which was unmistakably evidenced in her delicate hands and higharched instep. Had kind fate but willed her to be born a gentlewoman of high degree in her own right and had she only received the benefit of a good education Gerty MacDowell might

easily have held her own beside any lady in the land and have
seen herself exquisitely gowned with jewels on her brow,
patrician suitors at her feet vying with one another to pay their
devoirs to her. Mayhap it was this, the love that might have
been, that lent to her softly featured face at whiles a look, tense
with suppressed meaning, that imparted a strange yearning
tendency to the beautiful eyes a charm few could resist. Why
have women such eyes of witchery?

The female reaction to the sneers of the boys has been
predictable. Both as readers and as writers they have turned in
large numbers to the consolations of romance, and have sought
comfort and reassurance among the lower reaches of this ancient
and venerable literary form. They have tended to abandon the
larger issues, and have taken refuge in soothing dreams of happy
marriage, exotic adventures, the one true love, and life among the
wealthy. Some women writers tapped this vein of longing with
beady-eyed calculation, and grew rich on the proceeds – the
Victorians and Edwardians were particularly ready to reward the
purveyors of such stuff, as the careers of Marie Corelli, Ouida, and,
later, Elinor Glyn will testify. But they all seem to have believed
wholeheartedly in what they were doing. Even the wonderful
Mrs Amanda M'Kittrick Ros, the queen of overblown romance
writing and the female prose answer to the ineffable McGonagall,
derived her potency, not to mention her receipts, from her ability
to produce such passages as this without a glimmer of humour or
self-consciousness. In this extract from her inimitable *Irene
Iddesleigh* (1897, p. 47), Sir John reproaches the divine Irene, who
has, not to put too fine a point upon it, married him for his money:

I, you see, am tinged with slightly snowy tufts, the result of a
stifled sorrow and care concerning you alone; and on the
memorable day of our alliance, as you are well aware, the black
and glossy locks of glistening glory crowned my brow. There
dwelt then, just six months this day, no trace of sorrow or
smothered woe – no variety of colour where it is and shall be so
long as I exist – no furrows of grief could then be traced upon
my visage. But alas! now I feel so changed! And why?
Because I have dastardly and doggedly been made a tool of
treason in the hands of the traitoress and unworthy! I was
enticed to believe that an angel was always hovering around my
footsteps, when moodily engaged in resolving to acquaint you of
my great love, and undying desire to place you upon the highest
pinnacle possible of praise and purity within my power to bestow!

I was led to believe that your unbounded joy and happiness were never at such a par as when sharing them with me. Was I falsely informed of your ways and worth? Was I duped to ascend the ladder of liberty, the hill of harmony, the tree of triumph, and the rock of regard, and when wildly manifesting my act of ascension, was I to be informed of treading still in the valley of defeat?

Am I, who for nearly forty years was idolised by a mother of untainted and great Christian bearing, to be treated now like a slave? Why and for what am I thus dealt with?

The popularity of these women writers and the craving for romance are not merely the preoccupation of odd individuals, but a flowering of a long-standing tradition based on a deep human need. The female character-type of romantic aspiration is classically rendered and shrewdly exposed by Hardy in his portrait of Eustacia Vye in chapter VII, book I, of *The Return of the Native* (1878). This young woman is developed entirely through her emotions and presented in a moral and intellectual vacuum. She is never shown working, indeed she avoids anything remotely mundane in her determination to avoid compromising her self-image – a poignant comparison with the working girl Marty (an echo of the biblical Martha) in *The Woodlanders* (1887) is inevitable. Hardy does not spare the exposure of the other side of Eustacia's romantic nature, her shopgirl dreams of Paris, her idleness, her aspirations to be fashionable, in short all the tawdry underslip of her glamorous outward show. There is, too, a light but consistent irony directed at her reliance upon paraphernalia, her telescope and her hourglass – she has a watch, but prefers the archaism, the evocation of a vanished but more romantic era.

But not only in character terms can the continuance of the traditions be seen. The lure of romance is inherent in the novel form from its origins in the eighteenth century, and what has passed for serious fiction in the twentieth is often only a glorified and modishly revamped version of this staple. In part this may be attributed to the continuing adherence to the older fictional modes, a consequence of the stress on former styles of presenting external reality. Women writers as different as Pearl Buck and Bertha Ruck carried on the tradition of books which provide a good solid read, constructed with a beginning, a middle, and an end, and offering some adventure, some love, and much reassurance. This type of fiction has its place, not only in the long history of English writing, but also in the hearts and minds of very many of the reading public. It is not, however, much, if anything, more than the extension of various historical precedents, and only a whisker divides it, at its worst, from 'romance' in the pejorative, the soothing and sentimental, sense of the term.

This is in fact for women writers a particular danger, an ever-open trap. There are many examples of the debasing of real issues to the 'weak-sided' type of production mocked by Keats, even in the work of women writers whose reputations in their own day were not merely respectable but towering. A classic case is that of Elizabeth Bowen, whose death in 1972 brought her fleetingly back into a limelight which she had not enjoyed for many years. Her gift lay in the evocation of the romance of class. In one of her main works, *The House in Paris* (1935), the parents of the heroine are described with approbation as 'not only good to the poor, but kind to the common, tolerant of the intolerant'. Theirs is a 'world of grace and intelligence, in which the Boer War, the war, and other fatigues and disasters had been so many opportunities to behave well'. This philosophy is also expressed in their attitude to their daughter's marriage, which is, naturally, synonymous with her entire destiny:

> Karen then saw that in [her mother's] view a woman's real life began only with marriage, that girlhood amounts to no more than a privileged looking on. Her own last four years showed up as rather aimless; it was true that her painting lately had been half-hearted; she seemed to have lost sight of her ambition. There is more art in simply living, Mrs Michaelis said. Karen was glad to fall back on her mother's view of things. (p. 60)

Inevitably Karen becomes involved with a man whom she has been brought up to regard as 'a person who will not do'. Max is French, Jewish, has 'no family', and horror of horrors, *works for a living*, in a bank. Her mother greets the suggestion of their marrying with the opinion, 'It would be horrible if it were a fact' (note the well-bred subjunctive). The author then outlines the way in which a subtle parent deals with a daughter in this situation:

> Not seeking husbands yet, they have no reason to love socially. This natural fleshly protest against good taste is broken down soon enough; their natural love of the cad is outwitted by their mothers. Vulgarity, inborn like original sin, unfolds with the woman's nature, unfolds ahead of it quickly and has a flamboyant flowering in the young girl. Wise mothers do not nip it immediately; that makes for trouble later; they watch it out. (p. 99)

A similar set of unexamined social assumptions underlies the work of Rosamond Lehmann, though her subject-matter and technique are not otherwise comparable with those of Elizabeth Bowen. *The Weather in the Streets* (1936) seems to take Bowen's thesis a stage further when its heroine is shown as actually undertaking an affair with a 'man who will not do'. Rollo is disqualified not through any want of background, which is impeccable, as his name is chosen to indicate, but through the primary impediment of an existing marriage. The novel is divided into two sections of first-person narrative and two of third-person, and these movements are designed to coincide with and to convey the development of the love affair. First-person narrative indicates when things are beginning and going well, while the retreat into third-person denotes the heroine's withdrawal, as the affair withers and shrinks, into the emotional condition of listlessness and nervous inertia in which she began. There is also use of a sort of stream-of-consciousness device. But strip the story of its fashionable fleshing down to the bare bones, and it is revealed as yet another saga of sensitive girl versus romantic irresistible sod, a game that was old when Byron played it. No matter how artfully done, it is still the same basic formula, the romance as before.

Even in the harsh world of post-war austerity and realism, or perhaps as an unconscious antidote to it, Enid Bagnold's *The Loved and the Envied* (1951) shows how easily even an experienced and respected writer could succumb to the pull of the old romance formula. The heroine who is described by the title is beautiful, eternally youthful, quite irresistible, and happily surrounded by an assortment of other cliché characters – the silent but devoted lover, the hideous aunt who determines that her niece's beauty shall be her revenge on the world of men, the fortune-hunting gigolo in pursuit of the plain daughter, all these set against various arrogant aristocrats, faithful servants and wily peasants.

The assurance of the style in this novel is very marked. But it in no way distracts attention from the poverty of the material and its blatant appeal to the romance of class. Nearly all the characters are endowed with titles, land, money, social position, or at the least some cachet of talent or charm. The significance of money in the novel's scale of values emerges from its importance in the conclusion, where the heroine, having worked through a husband and a daughter in the course of the novel, is left with a vast inheritance to renew her function and to take her into the happy-ever-after of the reader's envious fantasy.

And so it goes on. One of the most successful of later practitioners in this field was Elizabeth Jane Howard, who, despite her disparagement of 'this childish equation of money with caste' in *The Sea Change* (1959), devotes most of her time in that novel to showing us precisely how and why it works. Her theme is not that money is caste, but that it will surely command the blessings and perquisites of it, or else operate very well in place of it. Her rich though humbly born playwright jets between London, New York, and a Greek holiday island; the lucky reader is treated to all the trappings of the romantic travelogue:

> We drive to Phaleron, past dusty squares where people drink orange soda under shrill strings of lights threaded through the tired trees: down one long narrow street which had at its end and above us the Acropolis, radiant in the full dress of floodlighting – out on to a wide highway where one notices chiefly the evening sky with land dark below it pollinated with lights. We turn on to a road which has the harbour on our left – the waters have still a dull sheen on them from the sun – like golden oil. There are a few boats anchored and an air of gentle desertion, but to our right, cafés, booths, restaurants are strung out with irregular bursts of cheap savage light and violent music. As we climb, the curve of Phaleron is below us to our left; pretty, laid out with beady lights like a doll's bay which blots out as we plunge into the quiet town above it. (p. 231)

Meanwhile two women, one old and sensitive, one young and fresh, circulate around the sixty-year-old writer. His wife is shown as loving her husband and dead child too much, and suffers from heart trouble, both symbolic and real – her role is defined as 'not doing anything particular, but just being someone'. Being it elegantly and graciously, of course – *Aida* on the radiogram, drinks at the ready, and always, always, the faultless sartorial effect: 'She was wearing a long dress of some finely pleated material – a very dark blue – bare on one shoulder and caught on the other by a swag of wonderful pearls . . . her face and all her skin had the most astonishing radiance, and her hair looked as though there was moonlight on it.' The echo of F. Scott Fitzgerald's *The Great Gatsby* (1925) both here and elsewhere only heightens the discrepancy between this and genuinely fine romance writing.

It is interesting to observe that among the effects sought by this type of writing is the stimulation of nostalgia, the wistful feeling that they don't write about women like that any more, when in fact they do. Of course they do; the genre is indestructible. An example of the 1960s model, updated in certain details but unchanged as to the reliable central formula, is Elizabeth Jenkins's *Honey* (1968).

This is yet another story of a breathlessly beautiful, quite irresistible female character. The novel offers itself as a piece of realistic writing, down to the trendy documentary-style observation, of clothes, houses, and domestic details. Yet at the core of this 'realism' moves our old friend, La Belle Dame Sans Merci, the fantasy figure of the beautiful woman who cannot fail, but cannot love: 'Wherever she was, some man was at hand, begging to be allowed to spend his money on her' – 'Every man who saw Honey was strongly attracted by her.' Really? This book could have been a better novel had its centre been shifted from the meaningless Honey to the other family which it deals with, the Cresswells. This family too is rendered cloying by having in its midst as wife and mother another super-female in a different way, the 'superb cook' stereotype. But theirs is at least a convincing story of normal family interaction, unlike the stale dream which is Honey.

As these examples suggest, the lure of romance and the pull of all the old forms and devices are very hard to resist. Novelist Mary Wesley has been commended by critics for the 'satisfying surge of malice' and 'sharp bite' of her style and themes. Her novel *The Vacillations of Poppy Carew* (1986) takes in a jilting lover, a father's funeral, and a range of other satiric moments as Mary Wesley's comic gift brilliantly exposes the clichés of stock emotions through her cool, sharp, acid heroine. Yet Poppy still has to be gifted not only with her native wit, but with a pretty face and a large fortune to boot; and finally she is paired off with a tall, dark and handsome husband in a capitulation to the best traditions of romance which serves to undermine everything that the author has previously set up.

In their efforts to find the personal voice within the public tradition, it is essential that women writers learn to manage romance in a less dated and more imaginative way. For the form itself is of primary importance to all women. In a persuasive and well-researched study, *Reading the Romance* (1984), one of a number of exciting new approaches to this subject (see Bibliography), Janice Radway spells out its significance. Attacking the various demeaning myths of romance which have prevented the possibility of any serious consideration until recently, she argues that women use romance as a means of dealing with their ingrained fear of masculine domination, which romance domesticates and tames. Even to read romance fiction, she suggests, with its stress upon relationships, and the escape into emotional adventure, love, and tenderness that it offers, is a protest against patriarchy. To continue with it is a refutation of the tyranny of patriarchal taste and aesthetic values, and a rejection of the reader's circumscribed role. These points are taken up by Eileen Fallon in her comprehensive survey, *Words of Love* (1984, pp. xv–xvi):

> Romances have been a significant aspect of female experience for more than two centuries, and generations of women have found pleasure and delight in *the one literary genre that belongs especially to them*. All romances tell their tales with a heroine at the centre, even when part of the story is narrated from a male point of view. All romances provide models of heroines who confront those female aspects of culture – love, emotion, commitment – that are so rarely explored in mainstream fiction. Systematic analysis of this neglected genre can provide us with valuable information about the experience of women in our culture.
>
> Romances may be unrealistic, but they do not devalue human emotion nor do they treat love and domesticity as if they were insignificant adjuncts to the universal issues of human life. In a culture where only male experience is a fully acceptable subject for public discussion, women's experience exists only on the periphery: in soap operas during daylight hours despite the rapidly increasing numbers of working women, in mainstream novels that are reviewed as 'women's books' or not at all, in women's magazines that ghettoise female experience as if it were all cooking and cleaning and child care . . . (Italics inserted)

The patriarchal culture in which we all struggle to lend some meaning to our lives has yet to credit women's experience, women's fears and fantasies with any real significance. Neither are they ever taken to have any wider relevance, any purchase on the human condition at large. But romance as a form offers a time-tried yet constantly self-renewing medium for the exploration of these very issues. Women writers must order, interpret, dramatise and heighten these events and preoccupations of women's lives, because if one thing is certain, it's that the boys won't. Romance has long done duty as an alternative reality for the powerless and forgotten – Charlotte Brontë's dazzling success with it in *Jane Eyre* amply illustrates its power and potential. As women writers master the form of the novel, at their and the reader's peril do they neglect that form within the novel which is women's and women's alone.

CHAPTER 3

Lady novelists
and honorary men

It is important to see the female literary tradition in . . . relation
to the wider evolution of women's self-awareness and to the ways
in which any minority group finds its direction of self-expression
relative to the dominant society.
Elaine Showalter, *A Literature of Their Own* (1977), p. 11

Because the greatest differences between men and women were
enacted on the social stage, and because characters in nineteenth-
century novels obey and disobey the same rules of conduct that
their creators lived by, the novel is logically the first place to look
for signs of sexual identity in literature.
Margaret Homans, *Women Writers and Poetic Identity* (1980), p. 6

The struggle of women writers for their right to claim space within
the novel, to make their voices heard, has had a long and complex
history. Although at its origins in the eighteenth century very
largely a land ruled by women, in the nineteenth century the novel
became a primary site of the kind of debates and conflicts which
were also taking place in the society at large. Chief among these
was the perennial topic of male domination, for which good new
reasons have always had to be reinvented in every age, enlivened at
this point by the growing clamour of women for votes, property rights,
human recognition, and autonomy as free-standing individuals.
Women writers' bold, wide-ranging and convincing deployment of
the form of the novel to rehearse these issues and to work out their
own way of relating to them constitutes another illustration of their
ease with it, and its appropriateness to their creative and cultural
needs.

The developments of the nineteenth century were to be crucial
both for women who were writing, and for the novel itself. These
two, although deeply, almost symbiotically intertwined, are
nevertheless distinct, since the woman writer's experience is
inevitably dissociated from that of a member of the dominant

culture. For this reason, Elaine Showalter has argued, in consideration of women writers it is essential to dispense with the conventional *evolutionary* notion of literary periods, and replace it with the idea of separate stages in women's literary history, stages which mark the growth in women's consciousness as feminine, feminist, and female:

> First, there is a prolonged phase of *imitation* of the prevailing modes of the dominant tradition, and *internationalization* of its standard of art and its views on social roles. Second, there is a phase of *protest* against these standards and values, and *advocacy* of minority rights and values, including a demand for autonomy. Finally there is a phase of *self-discovery*, a turning inward freed from some of the dependency of opposition, a search for identity. (*A Literature of Their Own*, 1977, p. 13)

We might add that these stages are not to be seen as succeeding one another, or even as historically distinct. Within the staggering scope of the nineteenth century's intellectual progression, it was possible for individual women to be living their lives and pursuing their work at different stages from one another, in terms of their own perceptions of their sex, their writing, and their relation to the society around them. Some were in the 'feminine' phase, paradoxically so called since it demanded an ability to work within and master all the dominant and preferred masculine modes, while others raised their voice in protest and struggled not towards honorary manhood, but away from it in the direction of a distinctively female identity.

All these developments appear in microcosm in the extraordinary world of nineteenth-century women's writing; and by the end of it, nothing could ever be the same again. Certain of the changes which had major and ongoing effects in terms of women's self-perception and awareness of their role and task as writers proceeded not from any intellectual or theoretical impulse but from essentially practical development on the ground. This was the era, for instance, which first saw women turning to the writing of novels as a job. Aphra Behn is often held up as the first female professional writer in the classic definition, that she supported herself by her writing, but it was not until the nineteenth century that women writers existed in any numbers as professionals, and even as hacks. Then the stories multiply of women resorting to writing to support their families. Novel-production becomes a kind of genteel cottage industry in the central decades of this century; Mrs Frances Trollope, mother of Anthony, turned out 115 volumes of fiction, commentary, and poetry, and she by no means holds the record. Dorothy Parker cast a typically beady gaze upon this tradition of the phenomenally competent and productive woman writer in 'A Pig's-Eye View of Literature':

> The pure and worthy Mrs Stowe,
> Is one we all are proud to know
> As mother, wife and authoress –
> Thank God, I am content with less!

Harriet Beecher Stowe is assured of her small corner in literary history, but most of these amazingly industrious and profilic women have not held their own with time as their more gifted sisters have. Who now recalls Lucas Malet, Gertrude Atherton, Voynich, or Miss Mary Wilkins, in comparison with George Eliot? But they are, in almost all respects, far more typical of their period than she was.

Does this mean, because women were writing novels in such vast numbers, and in that sense keeping up with male writers, that there was then established a 'feminine tradition' in novel writing? Raymond Williams has stated his belief that in the nineteenth century the work of women writers was invaluable in keeping alive and reaffirming the needs and terms not simply of a woman's world, but in certain vital ways a human world. But again, this is imply a picture of what is itself a Victorian stereotype of womanhood, the lady with the lamp, the guardian of true values, ceaselessly and unobtrusively about her task of disseminating sweetness and light. Williams himself agrees that the achieved mode of society was a masculine one, and any female productions had necessarily to conform to the externally imposed requirements not only of a masculine society at large, but more immediately to the terms of male publishers, critics, and editors. It is often asserted that as women were excluded from the social and political functioning of the dominant and shaping masculine world, so they expressed themselves creatively through the novel. This is true up to a point, but the point is a vital one; they were not allowed to express themselves *as women*.

Again, such truth as there is in Williams's statement applies only to certain specific women writers of the time. Most readers would agree that *Middlemarch* expresses, particularly towards its close, an ascending series of moments which are little short of sublime; and George Eliot consistently displays in her writing a fullness of humanity if any writer does. But she herself never committed the narrow sectarian fault of attributing this to her femininity, or saw herself as founding or contributing to a specifically female tradition of writing. There was no attempt to avoid the oppressive contemporary difficulties of women – 'A woman must choose meaner things, because only meaner things are offered to her' – and at times her characters speak of the humiliations of women with a bitterness which it is tempting to regard as personal:

> You are not a woman. You may try – but you can never imagine what it is to have a man's force of genius in you, and yet to suffer the slavery of being a girl. To have a pattern cut out – '. . . this is what you must be; this is what you are wanted for; a woman's heart must be of such a size and no larger, else it must be pressed small, like Chinese feet; her happiness is to be made as cakes are, by a fixed receipt'. (*Daniel Deronda*, 1876, book VII, ch.I)

But this was only one of any number of themes as far as George Eliot was concerned, and she always sought to be free of any close involvement with the feminist movement of her time, either in life or in literature. So while she contributed substantially to the foundation of Girton College, she remained tepid about female suffrage. And although her work must surely escape any classification as 'woman's writing', she was sensitive about and strict towards 'Silly Novels by Lady Novelists', in the title of her famous essay. At no point in her work does George Eliot ever address her reader in anything that sounds like a woman's voice. What she strives for, and perfectly accomplishes, is the 'masculine' mode, that of the detached, educated, omniscient outsider. She writes as an honorary male, largely assuming the values and processes of the male-created and -dominated society of her time. Her sympathy for women and keen sense of their wrongs is an important element in her writing; but it is hardly more than might have been expressed by any thoughtful man of her age.

It is easier to make out a case for Charlotte Brontë as the founding or Great Earth Mother of a feminine tradition in the nineteenth century. Ironically, it was she and not George Eliot who strenuously asserted the principle of authorial anonymity and independence: 'To you I am neither man nor woman – I come before you as author only. It is the sole standard by which you have a right to judge me – the sole ground on which I accept your judgment' (*The Brontës, Their Lives, Friendships and Correspondence*, ed. T. J. Wise and J. A. Symington, Oxford, 1932, III, 11). But the taut rhythms and defensive stance of this plainly show that Charlotte knew, for herself if not for all women, that the impersonal equals the impossible.

Charlotte's work has lent itself to feminist exegesis first because of the centrality of females in her thought. All her novels can crudely be summed up as dealing with a woman in search of her identity. This search is interpreted more widely and fluently than had previously seemed possible for heroines of English fiction; independence, its definition and accomplishment (still a major feminist theme today), is worked through with an obsessive passion which can still startle and persuade. There is a perennial relevance in her heroines' attempts to define their identity, and in the stress, particularly through Lucy Snowe in *Villette*, on the importance of work in establishing even a tenuous self-esteem. In *Shirley* (1849), her picture of her sister Emily, she has created a novel which, as Hazel Mews puts it, 'can almost be regarded as an artificially contrived vehicle for the expression of Charlotte Brontë's views on the intellectual and emotional privations of women'.

It is also through her female characters that Charlotte outlines her concept of the entire operation of loving, feeling, suffering, and aspiring. Her men may clench their fists, furrow their brows, and even *in extremis*, send love-calls through time and space to the beloved woman, as Rochester does. But all this is externally observed, and at times strikes the reader as contrived. Charlotte's deepest and most authoritative communication of genuine human feeling is invariably expressed through women; in her fiction, only the women have full souls.

But it is not simply that Charlotte deals in a detailed and convincing way with feminist themes, nor that she chooses women to bear her main thematic burdens. Much of the tension of her fiction, like that of her sisters, arises from the clash between her heroines' compulsion towards self-fulfilment and their neurotic attraction towards masochism and self-sacrifice. The impulse to struggle is matched evenly with the urge to submit. As *Jane Eyre* is her best-known story, it may seem that the message to resist the St John Rivers of this world would have come through loud and clear to women readers. But his is only one form of masculine dominance, a bloodless negation of the sexual principle which Jane, despite the airy symbolic associations of her surname, cannot bear to have forced upon her. Is it in any sense an option for the ideal of female freedom that Charlotte at the end of the novel consigns her heroine to the arms of the dark and dominant Rochester, maimed and tamed, it is true, but still recognisably the same thrilling brute who stalks so potently through the fiction and fantasy of all the Brontë sisters?

Perhaps Jane's freedom is no more than this, the right to choose who is to dominate her. In any case, her union with Rochester, not to mention the obligatory appearance of the beautiful offspring, while satisfactory in terms of the conventions of the fiction, cannot help but produce the same kind of disappointment as the ending of *Middlemarch*. There, as all Dorothea's moral, emotional and intellectual aspirations come to centre on marrying Will Ladislaw, who can help asking, is this all? Is all the struggle and suffering, all the intense effort and loss of peace, merely to be seen as apprenticeship to marriage? Was it really the most that nineteenth-century women could hope for, the right to gain the man whom they could love and live with? Certainly there are occasions in her fiction when Charlotte is prepared to offer not only marriage but doglike submission as the apotheosis of her heroine's emotional career; consider the climax of *Shirley*, where the male narrator, Louis, again rather like Will Ladislaw in *Middlemarch*, is sufficiently enthused by the strength of a rich woman's love for him to bring himself to overlook 'gold and her station':

'My pupil,' I said.
'My master,' was the low answer. (Ch. 36)

Low indeed. Nor are things improved by subsequent references to the man as the woman's 'keeper'. This persistent hinting at the need to submit as a main aspect of female nature, together with odd glimpses of hysteria, morbid excess of feeling, and masochism, have also strengthened Charlotte's claim to be among the first writers in a feminine, if not feminist, tradition. This element of Charlotte's work has retained its relevance and power of suggestion into the twentieth century. Jean Rhys, herself noted for her preference for masochistic and damaged heroines, the walking wounded of the sex war, mined *Jane Eyre* for the story of Rochester's first wife in *Wide Sargasso Sea* (1966). This novel reworks and reconditions the relationship between the two in a way which comments ironically on Charlotte's emphasis of treatment. Charlotte uses mad Bertha not only as a Gothic mystery element of her novel and eventually its explanation: her other principal function is to obtain sympathy for Rochester, and to reinforce the picture of him as a man betrayed and abused by women – Bertha's mental decay is linked with the faithlessness of Céline Varens and the self-seeking of Blanche Ingram as examples of what Jane rescues and cleanses him from. Charlotte focuses on the man, and like the other former loves of Rochester, Bertha is a flat character who never engages the reader's interest or sympathy.

Jean Rhys reverses this. She gives us a Bertha (rehabilitated under the less damning name of Antoinette) who has been a lifelong victim of a male-dominated society. Jean Rhys reminds us, as Charlotte does not, that a blasted and hopeless marriage happens to two people. This haunting and painful story, charting Antoinette's involvement, suffering, and despair, is not simply the story that Charlotte chose not to write. It is one she could not have written, and perfectly illustrates her inability to achieve a genuinely feminist standpoint. For her writing, like her society, is fundamentally male-oriented. Even her heroines' much-vaunted freedom is defined in masculine terms; her successful women are always those who can take on the 'man's world' according to its own rules, and survive. They fight with traditionally masculine weapons of courage and self-assertion for the masculine rights of liberty and work. Nowhere in Charlotte's fiction is there any attempt to challenge these assumptions of her society in ways which insist on appropriately *feminine* modes of self-expression. It is significant that when, in *Villette*, she nerved herself to bring about an ending which would have left her heroine without a man, having to face the world on her own, she bowed ultimately to her father's intervention in favour of the more conventional conclusion.

Ultimately, then, Charlotte always supports the conventional assumptions in her use of the traditional theme of the woman's need of man. More influential, however, has been her management of the classical form of romance as the vehicle for her ideas, her consistent efforts to create that remote and strange world which appeals to its readers on the less than conscious level, dealing with deeply-felt needs and urges, and at its highest attaining almost the status of myth. In Charlotte's fiction there are no literal monsters, maidens in chains, and chests of gold and jewels. But the experience of love is the voyage through the foreign land where the stranger wanders lost and afraid. Other people, the unpredictable convolutions of their personalities and the hidden and often threatening secrets of their psyches, constitute the demon-haunted caverns, the pagan temples, and the dragon-infested forests.

Romance conventions also dictate her characters' fondness for what might unsympathetically be interpreted as posturing, and her attraction to extremes of language and situation. It is the romance element in Charlotte's work which either enslaves or alienates her reader; individuals will either thrill to the claim she makes through her characters that self-discovery is the major creative act of the individual, that she is giving us 'not "a story" but the truth', in Karl Kroeber's phrase; or else they will resist what strikes them as overstated and even absurd. Taken with the reflex masculine contempt for women, women's writing, and romance, that will then produce such attitudes as this of Nicholas de Jongh:

Charlotte Bronte's *Jane Eyre*, whatever great claim the Leavises have made for it, is pre-eminently an erotic fantasy for woebegone young ladies, a moral fairy tale drenched in the juices of romantic melodrama from which poor plain Jane emerges rich, married and blissful after the fires of suffering. Barbara Cartland as much as D. H. Lawrence is Charlotte's heir. (*The Guardian*, 25 July 86)

In fact it indicates precisely the nature and extent of Charlotte's gift that she was able to work in the romance tradition with such range, subtlety, and abandon; but her potency derives from her recapturing the old rather than building the new. Far from directing the novel into the uncharted waters of the feminist revolution, Charlotte was the writer who accomplished its decisive link with one of the oldest and most magical of fictional forms.

Charlotte's achievement in bringing the modern novel into romance, or romance into the novel, did have one effect of peculiar importance for the development of women's writing as a whole. It assisted the division of women's writing into two genres, the 'honorary male' mode, as exemplified by George Eliot, in which the writer largely assumes the standards and values of the masculine society, and the 'feminine' mode dealing with romance themes in a muted romance form, which concentrates on, and comes to define, woman's 'proper sphere'. Romance traditionally depends upon involving the reader in a subjective experience. It offers imaginative release at the price of objectivity and detachment; but as it usually features centrally an *ideal* of behaviour, it deals in instruction as well as escapism. Its happy ending is a conscious artistic attempt to make a stand against the misery and messiness of realism by the brief satisfaction of desires and hopes which cannot be accommodated within the real life of organised society. In earlier romance (Spenser, Sidney, Shakespeare) both men and women alike experience these fairy lands and their demands and dangers. Charlotte's almost exclusive concentration on women led imperceptibly to a situation in which romance becomes *the* female form, the form chosen for fiction written by, for, and about women.

This process is further reflected in the degeneration of the word 'romance' itself. Once evocative of all that was wonderful and strange, it has decayed in modern usage into signifying a story whose stress is upon love and a female's emotional development, with marriage as the ultimate destiny and solution. In defiance of its parent form, modern 'true love romance' tends to play down and to exclude disturbing material, concentrating on the exaltation of the familiar and the enhancing of the ordinary. A. S. Byatt, in

Degrees of Freedom (1965), has said that the function of this type of romance is 'to console'; it seems plain that it is also intended to offer women situations and models that bear a strong, direct relation to their lives as they experience them. The young girl is constantly urged to settle for the plain boy next door; the wife is warned against the dangers of getting dissatisfied with her dull and worthy husband. At the same time the appetite for the remote and the exciting is satisfied with material concentrating upon foreign holidays, the past (Regency times seem especially suited to glamorous treatment), or even simply 'life in London'; but whatever the location or ambience, however intense the flirtation with the strange and exotic, including the heady new unfamiliarity for women of being a 'single' or 'career' girl, romance will always stress love and the discovery of a partner as a woman's major task of emotional self-discovery, and as invariably exalt monogamous heterosexual marriage as a woman's true destiny.

Modern romance is, as this suggests, very much the province of women writers. The particular blend of yearning, suffering, compromising, and self-comforting is inextricably tied to the quality of female lives, of both readers and writers. As a consequence, by the social rule that dictates that as soon as an activity becomes largely a female one, men will increasingly cease to practise it, male writers have on the whole abandoned romance, except where they have seen it as a chance to make a great deal of money as the price for 'going downmarket'.

This interesting historical development, with its important related side-effects for both women and men writers, was largely accomplished in the nineteenth century as a result of the fiction of Charlotte Brontë. Hers was not the only formative influence, nor was it purely the problem of her lifetime. Jane Austen was conscious of having inherited a tradition whose limits and limitations she accepted only up to a certain point. Hers may seem to be the archetypal 'romance fiction'. The truth universally acknowledged that a single man in possession of a good fortune must be in want of a wife, depends on a sardonic awareness of all the single girls out there desperately in want of a husband. Marriage in all its variations is the cornerstone of her moral and imaginative structures, so much so that it may seem that she accepts quite uncritically the social prescriptions of her time. The impression is reinforced by a consideration of the extent to which Jane Austen internalised and even elevated the fiscal obsessions of her contemporaries. In his essay 'Fiction and the Analogical Matrix', in *The World We Imagine* (1969), Mark Schorer showed through detailed evaluation that Jane Austen's novels all have 'a stylistic base derived from commerce and property, the counting house and the inherited estate'. This metaphorical substructure is so pervasive that we find even the most dead of metaphors or most colourless of figures of speech being vitalised to contribute to the overall effect. Significantly, too, 'moral qualities are persistently put in economic figures'.

But a subtler reading of Jane's fiction shows how consistently she queries and even reverses the agreed social assumptions. She never makes her good characters break conventions with a genuine moral basis, but has no patience with the Bingleys' feeling in *Pride and Prejudice* that Elizabeth should not walk alone through muddy fields to her sick sister's bedside. Through Mrs Elton, with her lamentable absence of 'elegance of mind', she shows in *Emma* how the pursuit of conventional delicacy can itself become a coarse vulgarism. She endorses, too, through her main characters, marriages which are not really so acceptable or respectable. Elizabeth and Darcy in *Pride and Prejudice* are not a good *social* match, and Darcy could have done much 'better' in conventional terms; Jane Austen's picture of the de Bourghs shows her view of this 'better' marriage and stresses the importance of ignoring extrinsic considerations.

The same is true of Emma and Knightley, Fanny and Edmund. The orthodox 'romance' pairings are carefully drawn in for us – Emma and Frank Churchill, Edmund and Mary, Fanny and Henry – in order precisely to illustrate their inadequacy and to invite us to reject them as possibilities. Many times in her work Jane Austen leads us to reject the romantic expectation in favour of the moral and human dimension. It is only as Emma awakes from her Sleeping Beauty trance that we get to know and like her as a human being. Her diminution in the social scale of the novel – coming to tolerate the Coles family, and realising her inferiority to Miss Bates – is matched by her growing in the moral one. At the conclusion of the novel the reader is intended to feel that the village has lost a princess, but Knightley has gained a person.

Nor does the handsome prince do any better in Jane Austen's hands. In *Pride and Prejudice* the power of this deceptive old ideogram is conveyed through the brilliance of Wickham's initial impact on Elizabeth, on women in general, and on men too. Jane Austen has not succeeded in her aim unless the reader is strongly taken with him too, for we are intended to share with Elizabeth in her disillusion as the charm wears thin and the glitter drops away and she realises that she is in fact dealing not with a handsome prince but with a toad after all. Benwick in *Persuasion* is not so sternly handled – he has not offended like Wickham – but his stance as the ideal faithful lover of poetry and romance is never taken seriously: it is gently tolerated as a phase he will come through, as indeed he does.

Persuasion is Jane Austen's most interesting work in this context: this novel most strongly and feelingly asserts the supremacy of individual need over social and conventional requirements. On this occasion the 'right' marriage, and how wrong it would have been, are fully shown in the younger Musgraves' ménage, and the theme is re-echoed in the treatment of Frank Elliot's worthlessness, as well as in the demonstration, through Wentworth's success, of how right the 'wrong' marriage could have been. In treating the reawakening of an affection which if only slumbering in Anne's heart is quite cold in Wentworth's, Jane Austen set herself her most difficult task; but this theme also enabled her to make some of her sharpest and most derogatory comments on the hollowness of rank and position.

That Jane Austen was herself aware of the discrepancy between what was expected and what she produced is clear from one of her rare surviving observations upon the practice of fiction, in which she mocked the current notion that even if women do not write in a certain way, they definitely ought to. Here is her 'Plan of a novel according to hints from various quarters':

> Early in her career, the heroine must meet with the hero: all perfection, of course, and only prevented from paying his addresses to her by some excess of refinement. Wherever she goes somebody falls in love with her, and she receives repeated offers of marriage, which she refers wholly to her father, exceedingly angry that *he* should not be the first applied to. Often carried away by the anti-hero, but rescued either by her father or the hero. Often reduced to support herself and her father by her talents, and work for her bread; continually cheated, and defrauded of her hire; worn down to a skeleton, and now and then starved to death. (James Austen-Leigh, *Memoir of Jane Austen*, 1870, p. 164)

This is clearly the archetypal 'woman's novel', the characteristic social details of the period notwithstanding. The paramount assumption is that the heroine's entire significance, not to mention future life, must be centred upon a man. Equally axiomatic is the heroine's irresistibility. This summary also hints at the sado-masochistic element present in most fiction of this type: the heroine has to suffer, to be at the mercy of a ruthless male, in order to stimulate and satisfy that unhealthy area of sexual fantasy, both male and female, which needs inequality as its pivot. The 'woman's novel', by, for, and about a woman, is defined here with such wit and point that we can only regret that Jane Austen never wrote it.

Women writers have always been under the pressure of masculine society, even when they were as much loved and admired as Jane was. But it is in Charlotte's fiction that we see these pressures at work most clearly. Certainly she felt as a woman – there is a poignant adolescent fantasy in the way in which her plain awkward heroines are at last rewarded with the 'best' men – but she shaped her fictions as a man of her time would have done. She crystallises contemporary preoccupations about the 'woman question' and in so doing automatically reflects the residual misogyny or at least distrust of certain types of woman which was widespread in her time.

This feeling is even more evident among the numerous less talented women writers of the nineteenth century. These tend to endorse the values of their male-dominated society strenuously, even at times hysterically. Most Victorian women writers, for instance, punish aberrant females quite sadistically: there was a savage hostility to emancipated women, the 'girl of the period', in Mrs Eliza Lynn Linton's phrase. Mrs Humphry Ward's heroine in *The Marriage of William Ashe* (1905) is a late example of a recurrent figure, the girl who through smoking, flirting, and leaving her husband for another man, brings on herself betrayal, degradation, and a suitably painful death by disease. Mrs Linton reserved an even more horrid fate as an awful warning for her suffragette heroine in *The One Too Many* (1894); she marries a policeman, truly a fate worse than the fate worse than death. This attitude was not only confined to women: Henry James's *Daisy Miller* (1879) offers another example.

Even the humane Mrs Gaskell exhausted her capacity for daring simply by dealing with an unmarried mother sympathetically in *Ruth* (1853). But despite the rare authorial empathy it was not to be expected that such a girl could live and thrive. Ruth's offence has to be expiated by suffering, at the close of which she dies, though not quite so gruesomely as the young wife who is only guilty by association with her husband's wild life in *The History of David Grieve* (grieve – grief), which Mrs Humphry Ward published in 1892.

It is sobering to contemplate the ardour with which these women embodied in their fiction the imposed social attitudes of the dominant sex. Women writers were more influential even than men in keeping other women in a carefully defined and rigidly restricted place. Their colonisation by male supremacists was complete; they policed each other. Even the high-powered and fiercely capable Mrs Linton, who felt perfectly confident that any novel of hers could hold its own with *Adam Bede* and *Jane Eyre*, with *East Lynne* thrown in as the ultimate referent, was thrown into paroxysms of submissiveness by the masculine censure of her publisher, Blackwood:

> I am so very sorry you did not like it! Could I not alter it to suit you? Indeed, indeed I am teachable and grateful for criticism, kindly (if not illnaturedly) bestowed, and have very little literary selfwill in the way of holding to my own against the advice of wiser and more experienced people. . . . If I could but interest such a man as yourself I could fear nothing and would gladly farm out my talent to his guidance and to his advantage as well as my own. (Letter dated 22 April 1863, Blackwood MSS, no. 4183, National Library, Edinburgh)

More significant in terms of contemporary events was the almost universal opposition among these women writers to female suffrage. All were in the firing-line of the battle of the sexes at its inception. They were all actively involved with the question of woman's role, and their struggles to get to grips with it have a disheartening relevance today. Their work plainly shows the alternating competition with and submission to men, the heart-searchings about marriage as a valid form of union between the sexes, the desperate hunger for education, for function, and the feeling that they should reach and assist other women, which are major themes of women writers today.

But like Charlotte Brontë they were feminine but not feminists. No woman writer of any name or distinction threw her weight behind the cause of votes for women, though it is interesting how many of the suffragettes discovered hitherto unsuspected writing skills in the course of the struggle. Sylvia Pankhurst, for instance, was the author of *The Suffragette* (1912), and *The Suffragette Movement* (1931); others like Isa Craig, Mrs Jameson, Marion Wallace-Dunlop, Lady Morgan, and Harriet Martineau gave as much time and energy to the struggle for women's rights as they did to their writing. Most women writers actively disapproved, Mrs Linton attacking the movement with all the intemperance of her ill-governed nature, and Mrs Humphry Ward proving so effective in the anti-suffrage league that she is personally credited with retarding emancipation by some years.

Occasionally the note of protest against the *status quo* which is to be observed in odd places throughout Victorian women's writing breaks out into unmistakable bitterness. Mrs Sarah Stickney Ellis, whose *Women of England, Wives of England, Mothers of England,* and *Daughters of England* were very popular in the second half of the nineteenth century, maintains a surprisingly sardonic tone towards her subject-matter and records this protest against the prevalent conventions of young women's behaviour: 'Whatever may be said in novels on the subject of beauty in tears, seems to be rendered null and void by the circumstance of marriage having taken place between the parties' (*The Women of England,* 1839, pp. 225–6). This is a recurrent theme with Mrs Ellis; she sees young women as cruelly deluded and unprepared for life:

> . . . it seems an ungracious task to attempt to rouse them from their summer dream . . . were it not that the cry of utter helplessness is of no avail in rescuing from the waters of affliction, and the plea of ignorance unheard upon the far-extending and deep ocean of experience. (pp. 17–18)

But there is not much to be built upon the fleeting criticism, the suppressed complaint. Throughout this period of history the social standards, and the controls which enforced them, were as rigid and effective as at any point in human experience. Small wonder that women laid to their hearts the only female alternatives as propounded by Ruskin in *The Ethics of the Dust, Ten Lectures to Little Housewives on the Elements of Crystallization* (1866), p. 196 – 'You must be either house-Wives or house-Moths; remember that. In the deep sense, you must either weave men's fortunes, and embroider them; or feed upon, and bring them to decay.'

Far from opening up for women a brave new world, novel-writing in the nineteenth century was even interpreted as in itself an ideal way of demonstrating the qualities of female excellence as defined at that time. Many women wrote only as an extension of their wifely or maternal role, to assist or support their families, slaving away devotedly at the literary equivalent of the Song of the Shirt; others felt it incumbent upon them to display this faculty among their other carefully acquired 'accomplishments'; many more saw the novel as a wonderful opportunity of fulfilling their womanly functions as moral arbiters and guardians of society's standards by producing 'conduct books' in a narrative guise; and some, doubtless, saw writing as a thrifty way of filling up their increased leisure in a developing society.

These were, of course, not the only reasons for which women in the nineteenth century wrote novels. George Henry Lewes stated his belief that women novelists wrote to fill an emotional void. His point of view is supported by these poignant remarks, in a letter of 1849, by the bereaved and isolated Charlotte Brontë:

> Lonely as I am – how should I be if Providence had never given me courage to adopt a career – perseverance to plead through two long, weary years with publishers till they admitted me? How should I be with youth past – sisters lost – a resident in a moorland parish where there is not a single educated family? In that case I should have no work at all: the raven, weary of surveying the deluge and without an ark to return to would be my type. As it is, something like a hope and motive sustains me still . . . I wish every woman in England had also a hope and motive: Alas there are many old maids who have neither. (*The Brontës: Their Lives, Friendships and Correspondence*, ed. Wise and Symington, III, 6)

What this says, however, is not that it is necessarily novel-writing which fills the void, but work. Writing was the only respectable way into the world of work for any woman above the rank of laundress or milliner. But equally remarkable is the condescension implied in the question; Lewes does not trouble to ask why *men* write novels, though they have emotions (and voids) too.

Try as they might to live up to and propagate the values of the masculine society in which they lived, these women never really shook off their status as curiosities who had to be watched over, accounted for, explained away. Far from being able to establish a truly female tradition of novel-writing in the nineteenth century, these women were lucky to be able to publish at all. It was doubtless their awareness of this fact which kept them so notably loyal to that sex which had given them their chance in making them the boss-boys of the women's sector.

We cannot reproach them for not being what it was impossible for them to be. We must simply guard against mistaking them for anything other than what they were. Their invaluable contribution to the history of women's writing is that for the first time in the nineteenth century women proved that they could write novels like men. This in itself set an inalienable precedent. It was left to twentieth-century women writers to show that they could write like women.

CHAPTER 4

The feminine novel

The advent of female literature promises woman's view of life, woman's experience: in other words, a new element. Make what distinctions you please in the social world, it still remains true that men and women have different organisations, consequently different experiences . . . but hitherto . . . the literature of women has fallen short of its functions owing to a very natural and very explicable weakness – it has been too much a literature of imitation. To write as men write is the aim and besetting sin of women; to write as women is the real task they have to perform.

George Henry Lewes, 'The Lady Novelists' (1852)

No more books. Books all led to the same thing. They were like talking about things. All the things in books were unfulfilled duty. No more interest in men. They shut off the inside world. Women who had anything whatever to do with men were not themselves. They were in a noisy confusion, playing a part all the time.

The heroine's New Year resolutions in Dorothy Richardson's
Interim, 1919 (1938 edn, p. 321)

The idea of the woman writer which the nineteenth century pursued with such vigour received a radical redefinition in the early decades of the twentieth. These years brought the first attempt to establish women's writing on its own terms. Many women continued to produce, by the ream, fiction in the old Trollopian mode, as they still do; the 'three-decker' novel offering a thumping 'good read' has not perished, but forms the enduring staple of novel-writing even now. However, in the twenties and thirties the most admired and influential of women writers were seen, and in certain cases saw themselves, as expressing through their work the feminine consciousness, in such a way as to bring out clearly its difference from the male.

Foremost among these in her time was Dorothy Richardson. Her

massive *oeuvre*, *Pilgrimage*, a fluid novel in twelve separate volumes*
written between 1915 and 1938, shows in its title as well as in
themes and structure the interiorisation of the novel which was to
be its characteristic development in the twentieth century. It shares
with other works of its own age the experience of the spiritual
voyage, the search for identity and meaning which was still being
conducted, and in very similar metaphors, half a century
later – consider Doris Lessing's *Briefing for a Descent into Hell* (1971).

What makes Dorothy Richardson unique is her deliberate
attempt to challenge the supremacy of the 'masculine' novel of
externally observed and authoritative reality by focusing totally on
the feminine point of view. Her method consisted of recording the
developing consciousness of her heroine in overwhelmingly minute
detail over years of her life. The reader is systematically denied the
usual fictive signposts and guidelines; factual information about the
heroine is released spasmodically and piecemeal in order to ensure
that we never settle into the cosy sense of 'really knowing' the
character. Males are only significant in so far as they impinge on
the heroine's awareness; there is no effort to present the man's side
of events.

Another distinctive feature of Dorothy Richardson's writing is
the consistent presence of anti-masculine feeling and comment.
Partly this proceeds from the author's insistence that her heroine is
more important than anyone around her. But there is also an
actively hostile response to the masculine principle in general. This
emerges as an important consideration for women writers of the
early twentieth century. They tended on the whole carefully to
avoid any overtly feminist stance, displaying for instance little
interest in suffrage, that cataclysmic struggle which remained
unresolved even in 1918, with the restriction of female suffrage to
women over thirty. Like George Eliot earlier, they lent moral
rather than practical support to the emancipation movement where
they lent anything at all, and it was left to a male writer, Howard
Spring, many years later, to attempt to fictionalise the suffragette
campaigns in *Fame Is the Spur* (1940). The major women on the
literary scene held aloof, and viewed events without much
enthusiasm: Virginia Woolf wrote of her most openly feminist

*The twelve volumes of Dorothy Richardson's *Pilgrimage* are: *Pointed
Roofs* (1915), *Backwater* (1916), *Honeycomb* (1917), *The Tunnel* (1918),
Interim (1919), *Deadlock* (1921), *Revolving Lights* (1923), *The Trap*
(1925), *Oberland* (1927), *Dawn's Left Hand* (1931), *Clear Horizon*
(1935), and *Dimple Hill* (1938).

book, *Three Guineas* (1938), that it might have more practical value
than any of her novels, but that she herself could regard it no
higher than as a 'good piece of donkey-work', and could not feel for
it the emotion that she felt for her novels (*A Writer's Diary*, 1953,
p. 288).

But even though there was little strong political consciousness of
the structures of male domination, there was a growing resentful
awareness of the ramifications of social oppression among women
at this time. Typical in this respect is Vita Sackville-West's *All
Passion Spent* (1931). A novel without any outstanding literary
merit, this book nevertheless touches a central nerve of contemporary thought. Its theme is that of the unfulfilling marriage, but as
the novel makes clear, an empty marriage means a totally wasted
life for a woman who is supposed to find her whole life's work
within it. The heroine, Lady Slane, has married under the subtle
pressures of the man's apparent devotion and her mother's wish to
have a daughter well married; the novel begins with the husband's
death and traces the heroine's past career through her remi-
niscences in old age. One by one she becomes awakened to
different truths about her history and situation whose cumulative
power finally enables her to begin, however belatedly, to live as
herself.

An initial difficulty which has to be overcome is the assumption
of the heroine's grown children that as she has depended wholly on
their father during his lifetime she will now be incapable of self-
government. She realises that she has achieved nothing but their
contempt as the price of a lifetime's subordination of herself to her
husband and family: 'Mother had no will of her own. . . . It was
assumed that she had not enough brain to be self-assertive. "Thank
goodness," Herbert sometimes remarked, "Mother is not one of
those clever women".' Looking back it seems to her as if all her
life's relationships have been poisoned by the urgent requirement
of society that a woman should accomplish her destiny through
and within the constraining limits of a man. First she comes to see
her own mother's role in the marriage as deeply suspect:

> . . . these weeks before the wedding were dedicated wholly to the
> rites of a mysterious feminism. . . . Matriarchy ruled. Men might
> have dwindled into insignificance on the planet. Even Henry
> himself did not count for much. (Yet he was there, terribly there,
> in the background; and thus, she thought, might a Theban
> mother have tired her daughter before sending her off to the
> Minotaur.) (p. 158)

Later she extends her anger and bitterness to the whole of her sex:

> Oh, what a pother, she thought, women make about marriage!
> And yet who can blame them, she added, when one recollects
> that marriage – and its consequences – is the only thing that
> women have to make a pother about in the whole of their lives?
> Although the excitement be vicarious, it will do just as well. Is it
> not for this function that they have been formed, dressed,
> bedizened, educated – if so one-sided an affair may be called
> education – safeguarded, kept in the dark, hinted at, segregated,
> repressed, all that at a given moment they may be delivered, or
> may deliver their daughters over, to Minister to a Man? (p. 159)

The heroine has made sporadic attempts to break out of the
mould. She is not the entirely passive victim that the recurrent use
of the sacrificial metaphor might suggest. In her youth she
experienced, as the author herself did, subdued sexual fantasies,
narcissistic and implicitly lesbian, romantic extravaganzas of
'escape and disguise; a changed name, a travestied sex, and
freedom in some foreign city' (see Nigel Nicholson's fascinating
account of his mother's emotional life, *Portrait of a Marriage* 1973).
In her maturity she takes up painting, but is defeated in this by her
husband's inability to regard her art as anything but a pastime. She
is forced to the conclusion that 'he had decoyed her into holding
him dearer than her own ambition'.

As the novel gathers momentum we are led to feel that it is men
who are the genuine enemies of women's freedom; other women are
merely agents of the male-dominated social process. The utterly
conventional good and successful husband Henry is arraigned for
his 'Jovian detachment and superiority', for his smug self-
importance, and for 'entering into the general conspiracy to
defraud her of her chosen life'. Sackville-West is at pains to avoid
any suggestion that this is merely an expression of female paranoia,
by creating another male character whose major function is to
remind the heroine of all she might have been and done; he tells
her at the close, in almost Ibsenish terminology, 'Your children
your husband, your splendour, were nothing but obstacles that
kept you from yourself. They were what you chose to substitute for
your real vocation. . . . When you chose that life you sinned against
the light. . . . ' He clinches the accusation against the husband: 'He
merely killed you, that's all. Men do kill women' (p. 221).

This is the strongest note sounded in the course of the novel, and
the advice comes too late for the heroine to profit from it. Nor does

the novelist have any intention of allowing her heroine to develop
into a St Joan of S.W.1. Feminist protest is consistently sounded
only to be immediately muted; each passage of complaint is
followed by something which undermines it, as the writer pulls
back from the insight which produced it:

> Yet she was no feminist. She was too wise a woman to indulge in
> such luxuries as an imagined martyrdom. The rift between
> herself and life was not the rift between man and woman, but the
> rift between the worker and the dreamer. That she was a
> woman, and Henry a man, was really a matter of chance. She
> would go no further than to acknowledge that the fact of her
> being a woman made the situation a degree more difficult.
> (p. 164)

The heroine's inability to complete the analysis of her situation has
meant that she has never known how to change it. One by one she
closes up the doors of her soul and merges into the life framed for
her by her parents, husband, and children, following one another
in grim succession. The writer shows clearly how this sort of
woman is always somebody else's property and responsibility, and
never her own: 'She remembered acquiescing in the assumption
that she should project herself into the lives of her children.' Such
relationships are not necessarily based on love. Freed at last by the
death of Henry, she is able to escape the final course of the typical
destiny, dependence upon children. She owns to herself at last the
dislike she feels for her offspring, and shrugs them off like old
shoes. But this is the full extent of her revolt. Lady Slane does not
progress beyond the reaction characteristic of the well-bred young
girl, to want the victory without the fight, the change without the
unrest. She wants to be free without shaking off the oppressor, she
wants her own way without having to contradict someone else's.
This is made explicit in an important central section, in which Vita
Sackville-West returns again to the 'woman question':

> Was there, after all, some foundation for the prevalent belief that
> woman should minister to man? Had the generations been right,
> the personal struggle wrong? Was there something beautiful,
> something active, something creative even, in her apparent
> submission to Henry? . . . Was this not also an achievement of
> the sort peculiarly suited to women? of the sort, indeed, which
> women alone could compass; a privilege, a prerogative, not to be
> despised? All the woman in her answered, yes! All the artist in
> her countered, no!

And then again, were not women in their new Protestant spirit defrauding the world of some poor remnant of enchantment, some illusion, foolish perhaps, but lovely? This time the woman and artist in her alike answered, yes. (pp. 175–6)

So much for the feminist revolution: women must stay as they are, 'foolish perhaps, but lovely'. As this suggests, there is some sympathy for the heroine, but the novel's orientation is undoubtedly male-identified. The feminist theme is used, exploited even, to trick out what is basically an inferior romance, masquerading as a serious piece of fiction. The writer lets herself off most of the challenges of the subject. There is no attempt, for instance, to consider the difficulties of ordinary women; Lady Slane's life is only adjudged wasted because she had an artistic talent, and the implication is that marriage is a perfectly suitable repository for the ungifted female. Again, the 'free' Lady Slane does nothing more outrageous than take a flat away from her children. She is too old and frail to recapture anything except a little winter sun. There is no pain in her story; it is all tastefully softened into old age and the message is lost in a geriatric twilight.

There were, however, other ways than this of making a mark as a woman writer in the thirties. One woman above all seemed to her contemporaries to be the writer who discerned 'the peculiar nature of typically feminine modes of thought and apprehension, and their peculiar value as the complement of masculine modes' (Joan Bennett, *Virginia Woolf, Her Art as a Novelist*, 1945, pp. 76–7). Virginia Woolf has long been regarded as epitomising the spirit of 'Bloomsbury', and the literary temper of the period. There is a sense in which she must also be regarded as the archetypal 'woman writer' as well. Looking back on the great myth-making decades of the twenties and thirties, whose effects we are still struggling to identify, let alone free ourselves from, it seems in retrospect as if the quintessentially male writer of the Lawrence/Hemingway type was evolving by contrast with the essential woman writer. Both then and now Virginia Woolf both created and fitted into the received impression of the woman writer which has been little affected through the years by the achievements of robuster geniuses like George Eliot. Moody, intuitive, alert to detail, and constantly suffering and expressing her feminine sensibility, she has come to hold a position in some quarters of literary history which would have filled her with disdain. It is almost as if, in those prepotent years, novelist and novel were apprehended as one reality; the novelist male or female at this time seems to have been more than usually subject to the common fallacy of the confusion between writer and work. Novel equals self in the general awareness of both Lawrence and Woolf – male and female self, that is.

Virginia Woolf was herself keenly alive to the difficulties of writing as a woman in her time:

> . . . I found, directly I put pen to paper, you cannot review even a novel without having a mind of your own, without expressing what you take to be the truth about human relations, morality, sex. And all these questions, according to the Angel of the House, cannot be dealt with freely and openly by women; they must charm, they must conciliate, they must – to put it bluntly – tell lies. [This is] a real experience; it was an experience that was bound to befall all women writers at that time. Killing the Angel in the house was part of the occupation of a woman writer. (*The Death of the Moth*, p. 151)

This diagnosis of the operation in literature and criticism, as well as in society at large, of sex-based beliefs and expectations, has proved unerringly accurate. Virginia Woolf was herself, perhaps more than any other woman writer, haunted by criticial conscious-ness of her sex. David Daiches's sense of her as a woman writer is nowhere modified by his knowledge of the disdain with which his subject regarded the idea: he wrote in *Virginia Woolf* (1945, p. 145), 'there can be little question that she was the greatest woman novelist of her time, though she herself would have objected to the separation of her sex implied in such a judgment'; and like other critics of her work he keeps her sex firmly before the reader by referring to her as 'Mrs Woolf' throughout. By other critics she is supposed to illustrate through her female characters 'essential womanliness'; this again must surely be critical projection of an acquaintance with her own nature and characteristics?

She was, in her life, limited largely to one social sphere, and to a very small range of moral and intellectual types. This resulted, among other things, in the fact that she never tried to treat any other than women of her own kind in any depth. Women of action in general and feminists in particular are shown to be comic (though she was not out of sympathy with the movement, treating it favourably in *A Room of One's Own* as well as in *Three Guineas*). In addition Virginia Woolf positively hated 'common' women, lapsing into her most banal and unoriginal 'character-sketch' type of writing in dealing with Mrs Haines in *Between the Acts* (1941), for example. Even her admirers sometimes feel as if the light of her imaginative comprehension only plays upon the educated and sensitive, the social, moral, and aesthetic elite; are we really to accept that only in the females of this caste is 'essential womanliness' to be found?

Virginia's famous 'sensitivity' has at times dogged her like a bad name, especially after the emergence of what Mary Ellmann dubbed the 'warty-lad novelists' of the 1960s and after. But it is more complex than an everyday manifestation of a female mode of feeling. Her superfine awareness of every grain in the texture of living, her presentation of her characters as raw to life and experience, spring in part from her own defensive paranoia: 'I am alone in a hostile world. The human face is hideous. This is to my liking' (*The Waves*, 1931, p. 113). Although aware of the pitfalls confronting characters whom she makes react like this, Virginia Woolf nonetheless asks us to empathise with them. Many readers have been repelled by what seems to be the very clearly defined class-consciousness of her main subjects; attitudes like Neville's 'I cannot read in the presence of horse-dealers and plumbers' (p. 51) appear to exemplify that mixture of intellectual and social snobbishness which its detractors see as the essence of 'Bloomsbury'.

But a closer look at the whole passage makes it plain that Neville's disgust with his travelling companions is not really that, as lower orders, 'they will make it impossible for me always to read Catullus in a third-class railway carriage'. It springs from his desperate conviction that 'we are all pellets'. Neville is much harder on himself than on others. Contemplating his own future he concludes: 'It would be better to breed horses and live in one of those red villas than to run in and out of the skulls of Sophocles and Euripides like a maggot, with a high-minded wife, one of those University women.' A feminist critic might observe the routine belittling of intelligent women, even, as here, by an intelligent woman, but would also have to concede that the men do not come off so well, either; there is an unmistakable trace of antipathy to the masculine principle in Virginia Woolf's 'sensitivity'.

In part this is a legacy of Cranford conventions – men have big boots and loud voices. But there is always in Virginia Woolf the slight shudder of aesthetic disdain felt towards male characters who are physically or mentally unattractive (think of the wretched Tansley in *To the Lighthouse* [1927], and compare this treatment with the kindness always shown by Jane Austen towards plain men and women – even the rebarbative Mr Collins in *Pride and Prejudice* gets off remarkably lightly). Virginia Woolf's fiction similarly inhabits a world of minute social and personal gradations, but as the writer is without Jane Austen's fine sense of character and circumstance and the variety of flexible techniques by which she proves to the reader that her judgments are accurate, the tendency is for Virginia Woolf's writing to appear to be the expression of the pervasive elitism of her own personal life, projected untreated on to the page. She was herself alive to the limitations of her own talent and method:

> I think I have got at a more direct method of summarising relations; and then the poems (in metre) ran off the prose lyric vein, which, as I agree with Roger, I overdo. That was, by the way, the best criticism I've had for a long time; that I poetise my inanimate scenes, stress my personality; don't let the meaning emerge from the matière. (*A Writer's Diary*, p. 311)

Another element of Virginia Woolf's anti-masculine feeling arises not so much from sensitivity as from fear. The judgment which rejects with distaste the man who is short, ignorant, or graceless, is in fact deriving its axis from an intimidatingly high standard of masculine superiority. So the reader is baldly informed that Mr Ramsay in *To the Lighthouse* is 'the greatest metaphysician of the time', when the height of his performance in that line is represented by the reflection that 'the very stone one kicks with one's boot will outlast Shakespeare', or by the empty rhetoric of 'Does the progress of civilisation depend upon great men?' There are occasions on which he is touched by authorial irony; now and then his position in the novel is undercut as his self-assessment is shown to be overrated and his behaviour as a consequence absurd:

> He shivered, he quivered. All his vanity, all his satisfaction in his own splendour, riding fell as a thunderbolt, fierce as a hawk at the head of his men through the valley of death, had been shattered, destroyed. Stormed at by shot and shell, boldly we rode and well, flashed through the valley of death, volleyed and thundered – straight into Lily Briscoe and William Bankes. He quivered; he shivered. (p. 52)

But this is not characteristic of the presentation of Ramsay as a whole. He is a threatening figure of power and drive; his ego-needs dominate the novel, and his progress forms its structure, though many critics assume that the book is 'about' his wife. Although like most successful men he lives almost entirely apart from his wife and family, his personality operating among them is a major influence upon their lives. They dread, with reason, the irruption of his presence; we are mainly introduced to him in the early section of the novel through the apprehension of his wife and son. And as the echo of 'The Charge of the Light Brigade' in his thoughts above makes clear, he is subliminally compelled by ideas of war, strife, and suffering. He is driven to express his aggression at times, regardless of the effect on Mrs Ramsay:

> To pursue truth with such astonishing lack of consideration for other people's feelings, to rend the veils of civilisation so wantonly, so brutally, was to her so horrible an outrage of human decency that, without replying, dazed and blinded, she bent her head as if to let the pelt of jagged hail, the drench of dirty water, bespatter her unrebuked. There was nothing to be said. (p. 54)

Readers unfamiliar with the world of Woolf, but reared on William Burroughs's *Wild Boys* (1972), J. G. Ballard's *Crash* (1973), or D. M. Thomas's *The White Hotel* (1981), may be surprised to learn that the husband's offence is to have said 'Damn you' – also that within seconds of Mr Ramsay's retraction of the curse, his wife has subsided once more into her ill-founded but compulsive attitude of reverential submission: 'She was not good enough to tie his shoe strings, she felt.'

Nor is it only in his authority role that Mr Ramsay is frightening. He plays an important part in the sexual structure of the novel. Sexual themes are, characteristically, treated very allusively indeed in Virginia Woolf, approached (when at all) via the metaphor, under cover of the symbol. The strong sexual undercurrent to much of her writing has not so far been fully investigated; but note the very precise sexual symbolism of Mr Ramsay's 'blade', as well as his general association with war and weapons. Linked with his father's sexual tensions is the small son James, who is growing by degrees into more and more of Mrs Ramsay's langourous, almost erotic tenderness – the boy's fascination with the dangerous flashing scissors (given Virginia's love of and familiarity with classical Greek) surely represents an allusion to the castration myth of Cronos and Uranus? Other characters too are woven into the sexual scheme of the novel; any post-Freudian will recognise the significance of Cam's alternating hostility and love, while Mrs Ramsay's very special relationships with men, followed by her sudden swift death, recalls the ancient dance of *eros* and *thanatos*. Consider, too, the elegiac treatment of the loss of Minta's 'jewel', her maiden state; there is a genuine mourning and sense of bereavement here. But Mr Ramsay it is who despite his complete lack of obvious sexuality conveys the novel's main sexual charge, representing as he does the masculine principle of vengeful authority.

The kind of sensitivity to the implications and abrasions of personal relationships also strongly marked the work of another female writer of this period; indeed, it is the predominant characteristic of women's writing in the early decades of the twentieth century. Katherine Mansfield was so ill for so much of her mature productive phase that it is unfair to suggest that her delicacy arose simply from 'nerves'. Nevertheless, the feeling expressed here pervaded her fiction as her life:

> Yesterday was simply hellish for me. My work went very well, but all the same, I suffered abominably. I felt so alien and far away, and everybody cheated me, everybody was ugly and beyond words cruel. (*Katherine Mansfield's Letters to John Middleton Murry, 1913–1922*, 1951, p. 38)

Again and again this note recurs; 'Everybody is too big – too crude – too ugly' (pp. 200–1). This exaggerated sensibility is only part of Katherine Mansfield's disturbed personality. Throughout her life she was unsure of her sexual and personal identity. At times she accepted her dependence on Middleton Murry for her writing; at others she became aggressive and dominating, pure 'masculine' ego. Beneath it all, however, lurked the motherless child – 'Talk to ME. I'm lonely, I haven't ONE single soul' (*Letters*, p. 597). As a person she alternated constantly between female and male, adult and child. But as a writer she almost invariably subordinates men to women and children in her stories. Does she then 'play the man' with her brainchildren as she claims to have had to do with Middleton Murry?

Both Virginia Woolf and Katherine Mansfield pose the question of the nature of the creative process in women writers. Virginia Woolf's admirers may point enthusiastically to her mastery of the new technique of impersonal subjectivism, her destruction of the hegemony of exterior reality, and will feel that her method of multi-personal representation does in fact achieve the synthesis which is its aim. But detractors will continue to insist that she merely 'poetises' her *own* self, and has no power to grasp the felt existence of another individual. This is expressed by D. S. Savage: ' . . . she lacked the first requirements of a good novelist: the ability to create living, credible characters whose life is projected into an interesting and significant narrative pattern' (*The Withered Branch*, 1950, p. 71). In much the same way Katherine Mansfield habitually went inward rather than out in her search for material, summing up her two motives for writing as 'joy – real joy' and '*a cry against corruption*' (*Letters*, p. 149). She was aware of the need to lend credibility to the characters surrounding the central figure who carries the main weight of the fiction's thematic burden, writing to Sylvia Lind:

> I find my great difficulty in writing is to learn to submit. Not that one ought to be without resistance – of course I don't mean that. But when I am writing of 'another' I want so to lose myself in the soul of the other that I am not . . . ' (Ruth Elvish Mantz, *The Critical Bibliography of Katherine Mansfield*, 1931, p. 193)

But it is interesting that she expresses her approach to the craft of writing in intensely emotional terms, almost as an act of love; and interesting too that she instinctively uses the 'female' metaphor of submission to describe what has traditionally been regarded as the 'masculine' act of shaping and constructing. There can be little doubt that the work of Dorothy Richardson, Virginia Woolf, and Katherine Mansfield has contributed substantially to the impression that women's writing consists in the main of the heightened subjective, with a heavy reliance upon the minutiae of living: 'Do you, too, feel an infinite delight and value in *detail* – not for the sake of detail but for the life in the life of it?' (Mantz, p. 183).

Virginia Woolf and these other writers of the period undoubtedly succeeded in developing what was regarded as a distinctively feminine style. But as the history of the century has shown, the 'feminine novel' was fated to enjoy a relatively brief life-span. A number of elements combined to create a reaction against the novels themselves, and against the women who wrote them. The form proved to be of limited validity, a highly specialised mechanism capable of operation by very few, and cut off from the main flow of the evolution of the novel. Mary McCarthy makes this point:

> Even when it is most serious, the novel's characteristic tone is one of gossip and tittle-tattle . . . if the breath of scandal has not touched it, the book is not a novel. That is the trouble with the art-novel (most of Virginia Woolf, for instance); it does not stoop to gossip. (*On the Contrary*, pp. 264–5)

Even in her own time there were those who objected to Virginia Woolf's purpose and techniques; D. S. Savage led the pack who felt that 'her method was one of retraction rather than extension – a narrowing of focus to take in only that which readily lent itself to appropriation by her extraordinarily limited vision' (p. 79). Those critics who judge as Savage did by the standards of the old 'well-made' Victorian novel, as solid, safe, and comfortable as a four-poster bed, will inevitably be out of sympathy with Virginia Woolf's efforts to evolve the new novel mode which she tentatively christened an 'elegy'. But even later commentators and sympathetic fellow-travellers like Rosamond Lehmann observe that 'blinds sway, brooms tap, chairs creak too frequently'. Leon Edel 'noted the extent to which some of the male members of [his] Princeton seminar had actually resented being manoeuvred by Dorothy Richardson into the mind of an adolescent girl' (1955, p. 71). And as late as the 1960s Norman Mailer was still orchestrating the sneers of the philistines and chauvinists against what he called the 'lady-book'.

The novels of Virginia Woolf have survived throughout this century, and her reputation is as secure now as it was in her lifetime. Katherine Mansfield too is assured of a faithful if smaller following. But the once-massive reputation of Dorothy Richardson faded so rapidly that a modern reassessment of her work had to be subtitled 'Unknown Genius'. Similarly women like Elizabeth Bowen, Rosamond Lehmann, and Rebeccca West had to suffer in the second halves of their lives the steady erosion of the fame which they had spent their early years building up. The emergence of the British all-woman publishing house Virago in the 1970s did much to reverse this trend. But the women writers rescued by Virago from oblivion had to be reintroduced to the reading public as new authors, so far had they sunk from view. Subsequently new feminist imprints of major publishing houses like Pandora Press continued the work of reclamation of women writers by publishing both the texts of their novels, and critical works of revaluation. In the course of this general trend of the consolidation of key women writers, many new resonances came to light; Kate Fulbrook's *Katherine Mansfield* (1986), for example, looked at the feminist grounding of her work in a fresh and interesting way.

But only Virginia Woolf really succeeded in the attempt to make women's writing 'a psychological sentence of the feminine gender', in her own description of the work of Dorothy Richardson. It is important to realise that for Virginia Woolf 'feminine' did not exclude feminist. As Dale Spender comments (1986, p. 143):

> She associated the injustice of the suppression of women's meanings with social injustice on a grand scale and she insisted that it was imperative – for the sake of society and the survival of the species – that women's *different* meanings should be reinstated in literary (and other cultural) traditions. Part of Virginia Woolf's argument was based on the premise that *one* world view – the view of men who exercised power – was simply not

enough to provide full understanding about the way the world worked. It was too limited. Too much was left out. It was the very perspective of those who did *not* exercise power, over whom power was exercised, and who were defined as alien, other, and unworthy of recognition, that was needed for a full view of the world, she insisted. It was her fundamentally simple assertion that women could see much that men – because of their position – could not; that women could see in men precisely what men could not see in themselves; it was this that led her to argue that the meanings forged by women and represented in their writing, should be included in the cultural heritage. Only then would it provide a fair and reliable basis for making sense of the world.

But, for Virginia Woolf, 'feminist' did not mean *free*. Women still living under the tyranny of the 'Angel of the House' stereotype of womanhood, she bluntly asserts, had to '*tell lies*'. It had to be left to succeeding generations of women writers to begin on the task of telling the truth, the whole truth, and nothing but the truth of women.

CHAPTER 5

The battle lines

Men have had every advantage of women in telling their own story. Education has been theirs in so much higher a degree: the pen has been in their hands.

Jane Austen, Persuasion (1818), ch. XXIII

Literature cannot be the business of a woman's life, and it ought not to be. The more she is engaged in her proper duties, the less leisure will she have for it, even as . . . recreation.

Robert Southey, Poet Laureate, writing to
Charlotte Brontë (1837)

Since the novel has been and is a prime area for acts of definition and self-definition, both personal and social, it has never, of course, been employed by women only. Male writers too have sought to exploit its resources, taking it not only as an arena for their own endeavours, but as a territory which consciously or unconsciously they need to keep re-staking and defending for men only. So the constant denial and derogation of writing by women continues apparently unchecked. In *The Craft of the Novel* (1975, pp. 16–17), Colin Wilson lays down his prescription for the true novelist, betraying his emotional antecedents and allegiances as he does so:

> No writer should underestimate the importance of his trade . . . He has so much inside him that he wants to get out that he dreams of an autobiographical novel the size of *War and Peace* . . . He begins to understand what Hemingway meant when he said that writing looks easy, but is actually the hardest work in the world.

Within this framework it is hardly surprising that this 'examination of novels and novelists', which includes such great male names as Jeffery Farnol, Thurber, Simenon, and Tolkien, can only muster Jane Austen, Daphne du Maurier, and Sigrid Undset, author of

Kristin Lavransdatter (1920–2), to represent women writers. Nor is Wilson's anti-feminism a random and isolated phenomenon. In recent books on the novel like John Orr's *Tragic Realism and Modern Society: Studies in the Sociology of the Novel* (1977), and Frank Kermode's *Essays on Fiction 1971–82* (1983), virtually no acknowledgment is made of women writers, while in Martin Seymour Smith's *Fifty European Novels: A Reader's Guide* (1980), which purports to 'outline the development of the novel since Rabelais', only *one* female name is to be found!

This palpable hostility to women's work and achievement within the novel has to be set within the context of a long history of anti-feminism in the English Literary Tradition, on both sides of the Atlantic. The diarist Aubrey may have believed that "tis not consistent with an harmonical soul to be a woman-hater', but a great deal of the characterisation of women recalls Lord Chesterfield's remark to his son that women are 'only children of larger growth'. At its worst the attitude of some male authors can only be explained on the grounds that they must have been bitten by a woman in their infancy. Fictional representation of anti-feminism has been a staple of literature from its origins, often by men not known to be personally unsympathetic to women. It was an old tale that Chaucer gave his pilgrims through the mouth of the Wife of Bath, and Shakespeare similarly rekindled an assortment of ancient grudges in the words of Posthumus:

> For there's no mention
> That tends to vice in man but I affirm
> It is the woman's part; be it lying, note it
> The woman's; flattering, hers; deceiving, hers;
> Lust and rank thoughts, hers, hers; revenges, hers;
> Ambitions, covetings, changes of pride, disdain,
> Nice longings, slanders, mutability,
> All faults that man may name, nay, that Hell knows,
> Why hers, in part, or all; but rather, all;
> For even to vice
> They are not constant, but are changing still
> One vice but of a minute old for one
> Not half so old as that. I'll write against them,
> Detest them, curse them.
>
> *(Cymbeline, II. v. 20–33)*

Posthumus abandoned his purpose upon the reconciliation with Imogen, whose imagined faithlessness provoked this outburst. But his cause is not forgotten in Katharine Rogers's study of anti-feminism in literature, *The Troublesome Helpmate: A History of Misogyny in Literature* (1966). It is interesting how many books *by* women writers *on* women writers have used, half ironically and half apologetically, the derogatory comments of anti-feminists upon their sex – *Frail Vessels, Their Proper Sphere, The Singular Anomaly*, and *The Troublesome Helpmate* are all labels which would be best left unresurrected, even in irony. Only Virago, the new feminist publishing house of the 1970s, seems to have successfully re-colonised an anti-feminist meaning, and recaptured it for strong, positive use. For as Katharine Rogers demonstrates, not all anti-feminism springs from the sort of grotesque hostility expressed by Posthumus, which Shakespeare presents firmly as a temporary breakdown, an obscene derangement like the sexual jealousy of Othello and Leontes. There is an implicit and inescapable anti-feminism in any insistence upon the difference between the sexes.

For Captain Harville, in *Persuasion* (ch. XXIII) is by no means the only man to believe sincerely on behalf of his sex that there exists 'a true analogy between our bodily frames and our mental; and that as [men's] bodies are the strongest, so are our feelings; capable of bearing most rough usage, and riding out the heaviest weather'. As this shows, anti-feminist attitudes do not always develop simplistically through mockery or belittlement, nor is any deliberate disparagement of women necessarily intended by the author. On the contrary, the young soldier's love for Lyubov in Solzhenitsyn's *The Love-Girl and the Innocent* (1969) is an expression of spiritual aspiration and a proof that he has retained his humanity and is not yet dwindled into pure ravening ego like the rest of the camp inmates. But even in this context there is something deforming to the female in the male transformation of her into a complementary and, typically, a non-competitive figure. The soldier does not intend the offer of his love to be taken in this way, but the 'love-girl' senses it as based on an imperfect acceptance of her nature, and is correspondingly uneasy.

Another kind of anti-feminism, and one more deeply ingrained in the British novel tradition, occurs when male authors require their female characters to suppress independence of mind, and freedom of body or soul, on pain of being presented otherwise as freaks. Dickens in particular stiffens his narratives with monitory cases of out-of-hand females. Consider the terrible trio in *Bleak House* (1853); Mrs Snagsby, the neurotic henpecker, held up as an example of wives who pay too much attention to their husband; Mrs Jellyby and Mrs Pardiggle, glutinous images of self-involved wives who pay too little. It is axiomatic in Dickens that women who concern themselves with anything other than home and family must be failures as mothers. So he presents the pathetic troupes of grotesquely neglected little Jellybys and 'unnaturally constrained' young Pardiggles. Females, to Dickens, must be pretty and pleasant or they are not females, and every one of his books contains some expression of this prejudice like his reflection upon the brother's widow in chapter IV of *Martin Chuzzlewit* (1844), who, 'being almost supernaturally disagreeable, and having a dreary face, and a bony figure, and a masculine voice, was, in right of these qualities, what is commonly called a strong-minded woman'.

Yet it is ironic to contemplate the vigour with which Dickens mocks the efforts of women who do conform to the contemporary social requirements. The daughters of the strong-minded woman affect the fashionable small waist, with the result, Dickens comments mirthfully, that 'sharp lacing was expressed in their very noses'. And what are the odious sharp-nosed Merry and Cherry but gross parodies of type of female behaviour which Dickens elsewhere, without much shift of emphasis, invites the reader to admire?

Perhaps the most interesting case here, though, is Esther Summerson. Her irritating oscillation between little girl and little old woman, indeed her entire existence in the diminutive which culminates in her being set up, without her knowledge or consent, in a miniature version of Bleak House at the end of the novel, was even in her own time attacked by the critics, and today's reader will predictably recoil from her earnest morality, her coy ways, and her whole Pollyanna ethos. But does she deserve her creator's revenge, the blinding and disfigurement which are inflicted on her and only partially revoked, when her sight is restored almost in order that she may see and appreciate the blasting of her face?

Twentieth-century anti-feminism has taken a new turn. C. B. Cox, in *The Free Spirit* (1963) drew attention to the growing importance of the cult of bullhood in the contemporary novel (later stigmatised as 'the New Virility School of Literature' by Shulamith Firestone in *The Dialectic of Sex*, 1971), and commented on the fictional use of women characters to restore the flagging bulls' faith in life and in themselves. But when women are exploited, abused and downgraded by the macho way of life and standard of values, what restores *their* faith? The classic masculine attitude is expressed by Captain MacWhirr in Conrad's *Typhoon* (1903, ch. V): 'Facing it – always facing it – that's the way to get through. You are a young sailor. Face it. That's enough for any man.' The assumption here that strength and endurance are inherently masculine, and required only by males because of the nature of their different lives and work, colonises this territory for men only and leaves women out in the cold.

During the 1960s, 1970s and 1980s the ideal of heroic male self-fulfilment was steadily eroded by the attacks of the women's movement, a wider spread of psychological knowledge, and a mounting uncertainty about the needs and entitlements of the white Anglo-Saxon Protestant male. The modern hero has more often been found dodging it than facing it – be it work, conformity, the draft, or the girl next door. But one at least of the most celebrated twentieth-century men writers spent a great deal of time and energy in his life 'facing it', even when that meant contriving it. Where danger, the enemy, the man's life with the sun at your back and the gun in your hand, did not exist, Ernest Hemingway continuously and quite literally went hunting for them. Where they could not be found, he made them up. Hemingway's numerous admirers and imitators have blinded themselves to the dangerous absurdity of much of Hemingway's fiction. The MacWhirr stance, 'facing it – always facing it', relevant in both style and matter to a genuinely extreme situation, becomes ridiculous when the occasion is sought, created, manufactured even as in Hemingway. The he-man Hem-hero appears too clearly as the fictional projection of the wished self. Poor Hem! and with what a slight shift of focus does big man turn into little boy. The famous preference for 'primitive' over Anglo-Saxon women, the weakness for little pussy girls, furry and feline, the conviction that mothers are failures, that if women are not subjugated they can only be destructive, and that the truly virile man does without them, chooses trout-fishing instead, all suggest a temperament marked by fear and inability to cope rather than the macho role-model of his adherents' apprehension. What else is the reader to make of the short story 'Now I lay me . . . ' in *Men Without Women* (1927), *The Sun Also Rises* (1926), or *Across the River and into the Trees* (1950)? The darkest suspicions of the state of Hemingway's psyche will only be confirmed by the publication in 1986 of his last, abandoned novel, *The Garden of Eden*. Here, in some extraordinary scenes of cross-dressing and sexual confusion, Hemingway confronted (but never published) a more complex reality than he is generally credited with.

But in the authorised version of the myth the stress is always on the heroic compulsion, and Hemingway was not writing for anyone likely to be reading Freud between the lines. Indeed, in his rejection of the twentieth century, in his search for a purer, cleaner time of heroes, Hemingway was trying to discover some escape from ideas so disruptive of a man's peace of mind as Freud's. And in the Hemingway world, where value lies in action, and the

highest form of reflection is response, where the shaping activity of
the intellect is deliberately suspended as an expression of weakness,
the feminine values will have little place. There is no time for cooperation, love, tenderness, for the exercise of the gentler emotions,
when the chips are down, the numbers up, and the clichés
whistling like hailstones about the ears. What is interesting about
Hemingway's attitude is that he has precious little time for women
anyway. At best they provide a restful interlude, and the
opportunity for what another great hero, Lord Montgomery,
termed 'horizontal refreshment'.

For like Lawrence, Hemingway basically apprehended women as
functions or stages in a man's life, rather than as autonomous
individuals living their own. He too felt convinced that at the
difficult and demanding moments of life a man has to go it alone;
women simply are not capable of keeping up, or even of following.
The total androcentricity of Hemingway's thought is well illustrated
in *The Snows of Kilimanjaro* (1938): here the dying big-game hunter
and writer drinks deep of the spring of terminal philosophy and
comes up with 'Love is a dunghill . . . and I'm the cock that gets
on to it to crow.' The best of his conclusions about his wife, who
lovingly tends him, is coldly self-involved: 'Why should he blame
this woman because she kept him well?' Why, indeed? But this is
the kindest impulse that he feels for her, and she is shown not only
as ineffectual but as too stupid to perceive that her husband is in
fact dying.

But simple density is not the only reproach Hemingway offers to
womankind. He had in fact a far greater fear than of being
misunderstood. Through his nightmares stalked a totally ruthless
and destructive female, and much of his writing may be construed
as an effort to exorcise her. It is indicative of this feeling that
women appeared high on Hemingway's personal list of the writer's
'enemies of promise', above drink, money, ambition, and other
evils. (See Mark Schorer, *The World We Imagine*, 1969, p. 377.)
Occasionally this trait is associated with aristocratic women (again
as in Lawrence) like Lady Brett Ashley in *The Sun Also Rises*. More
usually it is just plain female.

A classic picture of the female predator is the wife of the
eponymous hero of *The Short Happy Life of Francis Macomber* (1938).
This woman can only tolerate her husband while he is the moral
equivalent of the proverbial seven-stone weakling. When he 'grows
up', in Hemingway terms, finding his misplaced manhood by
killing a buffalo, she shoots him down. With complete disregard for
consistency of characterisation, Hemingway then pushes on to
make the wife pay for it. He cannot leave the memory of

Macomber without having the other member of the safari, the
white hunter Wilson, punish the destructive wife. But what can we
think of a fearsome predatory bitch, more deadly than the animals
of the jungle, who after the kill capitulates instantly before Wilson's
reproof and collapses into feebly drivelling, 'Oh, please stop
it. . . . Please, please stop it'? Here, as elsewhere, the need to shore
up the threatened masculine ego and restore the *status quo* overrode
aesthetic and artistic considerations. Always, always, the drive to
creat some emotional consolation for his psychic injuries dulled
Hemingway's better judgment. Here he bluffs it out through the
mouth of Harry Morgan, the dog-eared warrior-god of *To Have and
Have Not* (1937):

> The hell with my arm. You lose an arm you lose an arm. There's
> worse things than lose an arm. You've got two arms and you've
> got two of something else. And a man's still a man with one arm
> or with one of those. (p. 98)

But these thoughts cannot keep out the cold. Among Harry's
regrets in life is his failure to have a son, as he finds his three
daughters 'not much'. His wife comforts him with one of the old
wives' favourite ego-boosters: 'That's because you're such a man.
That way it always comes out girls.' The portentous solemnity of
this primitive misogynistic nonsense would raise a smile but for its
insistent pathos. If ever a man unwittingly stripped his sleeve and
showed his scars, it was Hemingway. The pomposity, the
absurdity, only highlight the waste and pity of it all.

The tides of time have flowed fast in the last thirty or forty years;
too fast for Hemingway, who was at the last abandoned and
washed up in both senses of the term, a great beached whale
contemplating with bitter distaste the antics of the minnows who
were to survive him. But his legacy of anti-feminism remains.
Subsequent efforts to handle the themes of male and female have
been dogged by the compendium of attitudes to which he made
such a distinctive contribution; and the more free of hampering
conventions twentieth-century characters become, the more freely
they display their creators' deeply cultured notions of male and
female and their associated prejudices and resentments.

This is not to say that novelists should not undertake this task.
Sexual definition, the struggle to discover the key themes and the
terms to discuss them in, is rightly the eternal preoccupation of all
writers. Like birth, sex difference is simultaneously commonplace
and esoteric, an unconsidered fact of everyday life and its most
powerful mystery. Each society, each generation and individual,

has to find a working relationship to this area of human experience, which, by continually shifting its bounds, is constantly redefining the terms of discussion.

It is not necessary to resort to anthropology and sociology to show that 'man' and 'woman' have different meanings in different cultures; they do so between different people. For sex definition is both a cultural and a personal activity. These are not necessarily distinct – what is called a well-integrated personality may simply be one in which exterior and interior definitions correspond. Individual effort often pulls against the contemporary cultural flow; Oscar Wilde is one of society's many cautionary examples here. As his life shows, sex definition cannot be only a personal preoccupation. It is not as if the creative spirit can come to terms with its own sexuality and leave it at that. Sex defines itself as much by exclusion as by any other process – male or female is not only what the 'I' of any fiction is, but also what it is not. It varies too much with different people, at different times.

No artist can therefore avoid encountering sex difference as a theme. Each must work out its place in relation to the other ideas and observations which he or she wishes to convey. And as a theme, sex definition is so vast that it could hardly be overlooked. That wide expanse of human awareness and behaviour which is loosely signified by the term 'sex' can indeed become a catch-all for every other impulse or activity. Iris Murdoch's hero of *The Black Prince* (1973) protests against the subsumption of all other activities into this category which so commonly occurs:

It is customary in this age to attribute a comprehensive and quite unanalysed causality to the 'sexual urges'. These obscure forces, sometimes thought of as particular historical springs, sometimes as more general and universal destinies, are credited with the power to make of us, delinquents, neurotics, lunatics, fanatics, martyrs, heroes, saints, or, more exceptionally, integrated fathers, fulfilled mothers, placid human animals, and the like. Vary the mixture, and there's nothing 'sex' cannot be said to explain . . . (p. 112)

Needless to say, Bradley Pearson's protest, like his creator's conviction that we should resist classification and try instead to confront the startling singularity of every being and event, is more noted than acted upon. 'Sex' has been the conditioning force of most art, supplying attitude and theme, fusing subject and object. Relationships between male and female, to take just one of its territories, constitute their own wide universe and secret world;

they also provide a microcosm of the larger (real?) world outside – both these functions are well grasped by the Genesis novelist in his study of Western civilisation's first married couple, Adam and Eve. 'Sex' is a living social issue – so much so that a quasi-barometrical indication of any society's values will be given by its assumptions of what is appropriate sexual behaviur, the status of its women, and so on.

The degenerative tendency of language, perhaps of human nature, ensures that 'sex' today is all too frequently understood as 'copulation'. Is it too late to reclaim the word from this tabloid-newspaper usage? The term ought rather to stand for any aspect of behaviour which is suggested or shaped by the state of being male or female. On this standard the world of Cranford, 'in possession of the Amazons' yet always needing the help of a 'tame man about the house', is as full of sex activity as *Tropic of Cancer*; fuller perhaps, as showing a more developed sense of sex in its relation to every region of human activity, and not merely the horizontal.

The process of sex definition has had a special relevance to the history of the struggle for social control of meaning through the agency of the novel. In the two hundred or so years since its decisive origination as a modern form, the novel has come to be the most popular and influential of all fictional modes, with the inevitable exception of television. Poetry and drama rapidly became and remain minority interests in comparison. From its birth the novel has shown its capacity for functioning as an agent of examination and prescription in the realms both of the immediate journalistic survey (Defoe) and of the extended metaphysical essay (Richardson). In this century at least, and probably earlier, to go no further back than Dickens, the novel has been the primary agent of the moral imagination of society. Whatever is occurring even peripherally in individual or cultural consciousness at large, will be examined, debated, and regulated through the novel.

Historically too the novel has been particularly well equipped to execute and transmit definitions of sex. Nineteenth-century readers turned to the novel as a listener to a tale, in the pupil relationship to the omniscient narrator. Among much that they came to expect from the novelist was instruction concerning the operation and interaction of character. Sex, as the first known positive character (Shakespeare's Old Shepherd in *The Winter's Tale* approaches his fostering with the basic question, 'A boy or a child, I wonder?') inevitably forms a major division of the material confronting the novelist. On occasion it has constituted a gulf requiring all the resources of inspiration and technique to bridge; and can it truly be said that Dickens, for instance, with all his tremendous imaginative energy, all his reserves of satire and sentiment, of love, bluster, and despair, ever got across to the side signposted 'female'?

In the twentieth century, readers have been required to make a different effort. They have had to submit to being drawn into the mind of the novelist and taken on that interior voyage which has made up so much of modern fiction. Contemporary stress upon the importance of the individual psyche throws each writer back upon the decisive origins of human uniqueness. Sex awareness is the first essential factor of humanity, and it is throughout life the primary imperative of being, feeling, knowing. Leon Edel, in *The Psychological Novel 1900–1950* (1955, p. ix), has referred to this 'inward-turning to convey the flow of mental experience' as the single most characteristic aspect of the twentieth-century novel. Certainly modern readers have been educated to see the confrontation of loneliness rather than the establishment of community as the business of the novel today; and as the psyche casts about in search of its own self, it must encounter, somewhere in the process, that principal constituent of selfhood which is sex.

Non-literary factors have also been at work to ensure the prominence of the theme of sex differentiation in the modern novel. Freud's notions of sexual biology have spilled over to colour our thinking about the distinctive characteristics of the sexes, and of women in particular. His linking of psychological with physiological features to produce an overall view of female nature as weak and unable, has undergone a fierce onslaught by feminist critics in books like Betty Friedan's *The Feminine Mystique* (1963), Kate Millett's *Sexual Politics* (1969), Germaine Greer's *The Female Eunuch* (1970), and Juliet Mitchell's *Psychoanalysis and Feminism* (1975).

But how far has Freud's formula genuinely been discredited or abandoned? Consider his summary of the chief characteristics of the female: passivity; a fragile ego with an undeveloped sense of self; a feeble superego resulting in an under-operative conscience; the renunciation of active aims and ambitions; an incapacity for abstract thought; a retreat into inward action and fantasy. Examine pornography and pulp romance and you will find this exemplified throughout.

Nor is it only at the subliterary level of fiction that the characterisation of women in these terms is carried on. Much serious work has been directed towards exposing the ironic results of such statements as this:

I believe that all reforming action in law and education would break down in front of the fact that, long before the age at which a man can earn a position in society Nature has determined woman's destiny through beauty, charm and sweetness. Law and custom have much to give women that has been withheld from them, but the position of women will surely be what it is: in youth an adored darling, in mature years a loved wife. (Ernest Jones, *Sigmund Freud, Life and Work* (1953, I, 192)

The traumas of Chloe in Fay Weldon's *Female Friends* (1974), of Miss Aroon in Molly Keane's *Good Behaviour* (1981), and of most of the heroines of writers as different as Jean Rhys, Doris Lessing, and Alice Walker, are located in the simultaneous establishment and betrayal of the unreal expectations here expressed. The big, plain, or graceless female hopelessly fails this chocolate-box test of the 'beauty, charm, and sweetness' of womanhood; the deserted or divorced woman measures the extent of her loss by the magnitude of this overstrained statement of her need for protection.

This picture of Freud as a simple-minded sentimentalist does less than justice to the contradictions of his position, and his constant effort to strive for truth through his work. These tensions are indicated in his reproachful self-instructions – 'The loved one is not to become a toy doll, but a good comrade . . . I have been trying to smash her frankness . . . ' – and in the equally genuine-sounding note of bafflement in this remark: 'The great question that has never been answered and which I have not yet been able to answer, despite my thirty years of research into the feminine soul, is "What does a woman want?"' (Ernest Jones, I, 122–3, and II, 468). But note the dangerously generalising assumption that there exists to be discovered a truth which will sum up and explain 'a woman', all women. Despite Freud's sincerity there is an inevitable contraction and belittlement in this unconscious reduction of the entire sex to one type. Inevitably too, like all great thinkers, Freud is recalled and transmitted via a simplified outline of his teaching rather than for his full theoretical philosophy with all its qualifications. The search for the answer to Freud's 'great question' goes on unabated. It is one of the staples of twentieth-century fiction.

Another historical factor which has brought sex definition to the fore as a preoccupation of the modern period is the breakdown of the nineteenth-century consensus. In an age when so much is slipping so fast, when previously accepted forms of masculine authority like those of the church, the law, the school-masters, and of course the paterfamilias himself, are being questioned and repudiated along with outdated concepts like 'the head of the family' and 'the breadwinner', traditional sex roles are assailed but sex itself remains a constant of existence. For the uncertain it becomes the only certainty.

This is in part the explanation of the importance given to the theme by writers as diverse as D. H. Lawrence and Ernest Hemingway. The failure of the bank of common assumptions means that the novelist cannot begin the dialogue on the basis of shared truths already agreed. But some community of belief is required for the successful transmission of art; consequently the modern novelist has to discover or create his or her own people. Up to a point this has to be a missionary activity; the prophet who has found truth takes it to those in darkness; and this may account for if not excuse the messianic strain in Lawrence which is something of a trial even to his admirers. But these writers' assertion of masculinity in terms of supremacy not only over women, but over all other animals, difficulties, and setbacks, must be seen against the background of their period. Those men who had survived the holocaust of the First World War were under a variety of pressures to examine and exert themselves, but at the same time found that various previously accepted modes of masculine behaviour – father, husband, soldier, lover – were never again to mean what they had meant before. Small wonder then that *cojones*, in Hemingway's evocative term, seemed to emerge as the ultimate standard; here, at least, was something a man could hold on to.

D. H. Lawrence has been the key figure in the twentieth-century novel's attempts at sex definition. He himself drew attention to the primacy of this theme in his thinking:

> The great relationship, for humanity, will always be the relation between man and woman. The relation between man and man, woman and woman, parent and child, will always be subsidiary.
>
> And the relation between man and woman will change for ever, and will be the new central clue to human life. ('Morality and the Novel', *Calendar of Modern Letters*, December 1925)

This intense conviction never left him. It is not the least of the tributes to his powers that he was able to create a similar conviction in the minds of so many others. In trying to describe what he saw and felt, in seeking to render scrupulously what to him was literal truth, Lawrence articulated one of the most potent myths of our time, that of the fundamental and irreconcilable opposition of male and female. It is unjust to attribute all the excesses of the cult of advanced bullhood to Lawrence. It is at least arguable that his contribution was to posit the primitive loneliness

of the soul as wandering in the void between male and female. But
so often in Lawrence's fiction, with only a slight shift of perspective
the void becomes a minefield dividing the sexes, a state of
hostilities is assumed though not always declared, and the
participants are required to stand and defend their ground.
Inevitably the positions adopted in such a war situation are
extreme; loyalties become polarised and competition destroys cooperation:

> His eyes grew round, he did not know where he was. How could
> she, his own wife, say such a thing? But she sat there, small and
> foreign and separate. It dawned on him she did not consider
> herself his wife, except in so far as they agreed. She did not feel
> she had married him. At any rate, she was willing to allow he
> might want another woman. A gap, a space opened before him.
> (*The Rainbow*, 1915, ch. III)

Generations of the uncertain have turned to Lawrence for his
handling of moments like this. He seems to offer unique glimpses
into the heart of the matter, rare flashes of perception of the
genuine state of relationships betweeen female and male. Many of
his readers have found reassurance if not certainty in Lawrence's
treatment of the man's role in sex-relations. It has been widely
taken as offering a new form of authority and power to replace the
older social and political means by which man declared and
supported his supremacy.

Lawrence himself never says anything as simple as this. But his
work typically suffers distortions in transmission. All his subtleties,
refinements, qualifications are lost as a handful of phrases, ideas,
scenes are culled and popularised – not for nothing has he been
called a 'seminal' writer. And Lawrence himself clouded his
utterance not only by his liking for pseudo-gnomic and would-be
reverberant obscurities, but also by his reliance upon some quite
ineffably drivelling notions of human behaviour and needs (see
Frank Kermode's *Lawrence*, 1973, for an unduly uncritical account
of some hysterical and dangerous theories which in a lesser man
would have been plainly recognised as lunatic).

Most of Lawrence's follies have perished now, and lie in an
obscurity from which it wrongs him to rescue them. But some of
his damaging doubts and ambivalences have proved enormously
influential, particularly his rooted anti-feminism, originally exposed
by Kate Millett as long ago as 1969, but still a raw and
irreconcilable element even of his best fiction. What are we to make
for instance, of Lawrence's habit of launching overt attacks upon

his female characters, with the implied suggestion that they contain a truth about women's nature in general? Or the repeated assertion that his ideal of the 'freedom in love' of 'two pure beings' is spoiled by the female instinct to turn love into 'a worship of perfect possession':

> But it seemed to him, woman was always so horrible and clutching, she had such a lust for possession, a greed of self-importance in love. She wanted to have, to own, to control, to be dominant. Everything must be referred back to her, to Woman, the Great Mother of everything out of whom proceeded everything and to whom everything must finally be rendered up. (*Women in Love*, 1921, ch. XVI)

Then there is the constant use in the novels of women characters merely as agents in the growth and career of a man, rather than as individuals in their own right; for they have no individual right, in that sense, in Lawrence's eyes. Birkin makes this point via a grossly unflattering comparison:

> 'And woman is the same as horses: two wills act in opposition inside her. With one will, she wants to subject herself utterly. With the other, she wants to bolt, and pitch her rider to perdition.'
> 'Then I'm a bolter,' said Ursula, with a burst of laughter.
> 'It's a dangerous thing to domesticate even horses, let alone women,' said Birkin. 'The dominant principle has some rare antagonists.'
> 'Good thing too,' said Ursula.
> 'Quite,' said Gerald with a faint smile. 'There's more fun.'
> (*Women in Love*, ch. XII)

The woman here is seen only and entirely in the context of her 'rider'. There is in this sequence, which follows the episode of Gerald's torturing the mare, a sadism which is not even latent. With such attitudes, these men turn love into an insulting denial of their partner's womanhood and real self. Birkin makes his conditions clear to Ursula in these terms:

> I don't *want* to see you. I've seen plenty of women, I'm sick and weary of seeing them. I want a woman I don't see . . . I want to find you, where you don't know your own existence, the you that your common self denies utterly. But I don't want your good looks, and I don't want your womanly feelings, and I don't want

your thoughts nor opinions nor your ideas – they are all bagatelles to me.

When Ursula protests at this, Birkin dismisses her complaints as 'meretricious persiflage'. So although he refines his offer as 'an equilibrium, a pure balance of two single beings: – as the stars balance each other' we see that the question of her equality in the relationship is absurd.

This is later reinforced by Lawrence when he shows us Birkin's tomcat demonstrating his superiority over a female cat by cuffing her. Ursula's disapproval draws on her the contempt of master and beast. Again, as in the scene with Gerald, her feminism is made to appear petulant and ridiculous, exercised as it is in defence of animals. So many of Lawrence's studies of women are subtly reductive in this way, trivialising their actions and concerns. And so much is conveyed, too, by the deployment of the un-acknowledged generalisation. For despite the very marked surface dissimilarities between his female characters, which have given him the largely undeserved reputation of being expert in the mysteries of woman's nature, all Lawrence's women suffer from the same complaint in differing degrees: 'will', the 'darkness in the blood', and dreams of dominance.

Lawrence's personal conduct has also had a measurable effect upon the establishing of twentieth-century ideas of sexuality. He approached the whole business in a crusading spirit, and the knight-errant is to be seen through the numerous dramas of his less-than-private life. Much of his energies were devoted to the continuous effort to live his own philosophy and to get others to do so too. His attempts to influence the personal relationships of those he encountered according to his own theories can be seen in his fictional revenges on those who failed to accept his direction; Compton Mackenzie considered a writ over *The Man Who Loved Islands* and Katherine Mansfield and Middleton Murry found it almost inconceivable when they learned that they had served as models for Gudrun and Gerald in *Women in Love*. There are several other such examples.

Yet all this, paradoxically, has enhanced rather than diminished Lawrence's reputation as a great contemporary seer and prophet. He has been interpreted by many as a man who spoke and wrote from a far wider sexual experience than they would ever have, and who, at whatever cost to others or to himself, like Ibsen's Brand, practised what he preached. In the same way as Freud, Lawrence has been remembered and transmitted in terms of a readily digestible version of his ideas rather than through the dark maze of his complex world picture. And so, by a process which lies midway between the intensification natural to art and the simplification inherent in popularisation, the formula, the Lawrentian formula, has evolved. Sex relations constitute a struggle for mastery, which the man must win, for the psychic health of the woman as much as for his own. Women, dark and dangerous, need 'phallic hunting out'; they need a man, but, through innate inferiority and the envy that it produces, will almost invariably damage and fail him.

Whatever a distant posterity pronounces upon Lawrence, when the dust that he raised in his lifetime finally settles, there can be little point in denying him his place in contemporary literary history. It is fair to say that he was the first novelist to achieve a specifically and exclusively sexual focus in his presentation of female character; he began the intense interest in women's sexual emotions and needs which has burgeoned in our time into a little subspecies of the novel of its own. Bernard Bergonzi, in *The Situation of the Novel* (1970, ch. I), pointed with some reservations to the fragmentation of the modern novel into 'genres' particularly those concerning 'a very sensitive, rather neurotic girl . . . having sexual difficulties – conventional, or lesbian, or both'. The appearance and continued popularity of this type of 'woman's novel' may without too much difficulty be laid at Lawrence's door. As with Freud, we see again how easily the shocking and hard-won definitions of one generation become the models and stereotypes of the next.

Of course the recognition and discussion of women's sexual needs which we owe to Freud and Lawrence in chief, was a tremendous liberation for both sexes from the manifold and deforming constrictions of the nineteenth century. But it has, with a deep irony, become a new tyranny. It sometimes seems as if women cannot be studied in fiction now except in terms of their sexual emotions, often interpreted unflatteringly; the unacknowledged urges, the will to harm, the masochistic search for the man who will dominate. Even so chic a trifle as Muriel Spark's *The Driver's Seat* (1970) conforms to this outline in every particular. Strip away the modish accessories with which Muriel Spark delights to equip her characters – the pine-lined flat, the intercontinental flights, the luxury hotels and hired cars – and this novel, which has been hailed as a stylish allegory, is seen as yet another picture of a dim and deadly female with a massive neurosis due to shortage of sex, who flies to Italy, home of Latin lovers, determined to do and die.

As this suggests, the effects of the Lawrentian formula have been just as potent upon women writers as upon men. It is not simply a myth operative upon adolescent males, and mercifully outgrown in maturity, like acne. It has defined for men and women of all ages what seemed to be a commanding and imaginative version of sex relations. Women have studied themselves in Lawrence's terms, accepting his basic notions as authority – a parallel might be sought with the position in psychology which the Freudian view of women held for so long, with women psychoanalysts like Helene Deutsch enthusiastically endorsing the anti-feminism work of their male colleagues. Even allowing for some distinguished exceptions, it is still alarmingly axiomatic even in serious fiction that love is 'woman's whole existence' and that human relationships are the *real* work of a woman's life. Twentieth-century literature shows no more sign of rejecting the Lawrentian formula than the Freudian; indeed, psychology and literature have combined to offer a doctrine which is now become dogma.

Lawrence's repeated stress on the secret and primitive nature of sex difference has perhaps been his most important single legacy. Both men and women writers since have been straining every nerve to capture the difference and set it down. Sexual definition has become something between a fine art and a neurosis in the novel of the second half of the twentieth century. Ironically, in a world which many feel offers more prospect of equality and justice to each individual than at any historical moment previously, male and female are in fact (and in fiction) emotionally drawing apart. Sexual definition has come to mean for many writers a convulsive effort of separation, of division.

To this we owe that tension between the sexes which must accompany any heightened awareness of these differences. Clearly this is not the discovery of the modern period alone. *Lysistrata* turns as closely on the theme as *The Way of the World* does. The ancient world amply illustrates too that fear of women which expresses itself as anti-feminism, or through various propitiatory devices – Medusa, Clytemnestra, the Erinnyes who hounded the taboo-breaker to a terrible death, all were aspects of the female, just as much as Penelope or poor Iphigenia, the eternal victim.

All cultures will afford many such examples of the tradition of hostility if not downright antipathy between the sexes. But the modern emphasis upon sex differentiation has put a new edge on the old blade. Fresh insights into sex difference increase polarisation of attitudes. Female emancipation may not have freed all women from their historic servitude to traditional concepts, but it has helped to awaken their consciousness of it; even one of the more privileged of her sex could write with the latent bitterness which always marked her comments on the subject: 'Women have served all these centuries as looking-glasses possessing the magic and delicious power of reflecting the figure of man at twice its natural size' (Virginia Woolf, *A Room of One's Own*, 1929, p. 53).

What is interesting, however, is the new determination with which male writers of the second half of the twentieth century have seized upon the novel as the arena for the exercise of acts of self-definition which produce if not a full cry to battle stations, at least a 'red alert' with regard to women, women writers, and in fact anything to do with the female sex. Side by side with what the media called 'Women's Lib', the growing educational, economic, social, and sexual emancipation of women, has come a rising tide of a new kind of anti-feminism, all the bitterer for displaying a frank, brutal, and no-holds-barred aggression.

Historically the new anti-feminism of the 1960s derived from the 'angry young man' cult of the 1950s. The prototype in the drama of the time was John Osborne's Jimmy Porter. The hero of *Billy Liar* by Keith Waterhouse and Willis Hall was another, more whimsical example. Simultaneously the novelists were evolving their own version, and taking his origins from another Jim, Kingsley Amis's *Lucky Jim*, this tiresome fellow made his way through the pages of John Wain, Stan Barstow, Alan Sillitoe, and many others. In these fictions it was axiomatic that any female, no matter how good or bad, existed primarily as a landmark on the hero's road to self-definition, and should never be allowed to get ideas above this station. The bad ones, like Lucky Jim's Margaret, a man must nerve himself to leave behind as quickly as possible; the good ones are the prize at the end of the road. Joe, in John Braine's *Room at the Top* (1957) 'learns', as 'a truth', that the ownership of the attractive girl is 'simply a question of money, of the price of the diamond ring on her left hand'.

The characterisation of Joe, in all its crudity, plainly exhibits the trap of this fictional type, which Mary McCarthy categorised as the lineal descendant of the Hemingway hero and dubbed 'the pitiless phoney-detector'. Where he is the custodian of all standards and values, and at the same time displays such a woeful impoverishment of principle, feeling, and even vocabulary as Joe does, then he cannot escape the apparently unrelated pitfalls of being both a boor and a prig. But it is pitching it too high to consider the novel in this way. From its first pages the discerning reader will sum it up for what it is, a painfully earnest trip through the 'Ah Bisto!' land of young man's fancy. There is a diagrammatic simplicity in the presentation of the two goddesses of adolescent male fantasy, Mother-Earth Alice (the one with the big breasts) and Sweet Sue (the one with the rich daddy). The man/Caliban who wakes from such a dream might understandably cry to dream again. But what does a woman dream meanwhile?

Among the targets of the women's movement as it gathered momentum in the late sixties and early seventies was the claim that women should no longer be regarded as points of development in men's growth and fulfilment, but as fully sentient and responsible adult beings in their own right. One of its successes has been a concerted attack on the domination of the disparaging generalisation – 'Women adore to be noticed'; 'Lawrence strove to put woman back in her rightful place'; 'Women have no character at all'. These categorising and reductive statements may be picked out by the handful from the fiction of almost any time and place. They have been important, probably invaluable masculine weapons in the sex war between male and female.

Through the long history of world literature the men have attacked while the women have numbered their losses and counted their dead. Until recently there were only a few ineffective guerrilla skirmishes from female territory, and no organised onslaught on the firmly defended stronghold of masculine superiority. But the tide was due to turn. Amis's *Lucky Jim* was luckier than he knew in being born before his right to existence was challenged. Within a very few years women were organising, writing, rewriting, dismantling the structures of dominance and the masculine pretensions on which they were built. Only when men were challenged was the sex war acknowledged. But it was not abandoned; on the contrary, it simply moved into a more vigorous and vicious phase.

This point is made with excruciating precision by Philip Roth in his brilliant *Portnoy's Complaint* (1967). Whatever the precise nature of Portnoy's complex condition, among his drives is certainly the need continually to test his concept of manhood along with other misleading and inadequate notions of behaviour which he has inherited from his culture. His heroically unflagging attempts to define himself through the pursuit of 'pussy' are both symptom and illness; the cure will fail because the cause continues to flourish. Portnoy's confusion, we are told, is rooted in his mother's determination to turn him into the type of male most acceptable to a Jewish mother. The constant urging to be a good Jewish boy produces a bad Jewish boy, perpetually fixated in the 'badness' of boyhood, pathologically unable to grow up. His suffering is produced by his awareness of his situation, and by the tension between his drive to be a man and his dissatisfaction with traditional methods of demonstrating manhood, the meaningless rites of masturbation and copulation.

Portnoy's feelings of desperation escalate into frenzy. He is impelled into reckless and savage acts of sexual aggression, which do not relieve but restore and renew the tensions of his failure. Here he decides to give venereal disease to a kibbutz girl whom he has met on holiday in Israel, because she has refused, not surprisingly, to take seriously his offers of love and marriage.

'Oh, I am going to fuck you, Jew girl,' I whispered evilly . . . 'you have got a lesson to learn, Naomi,' and pressed, pressed hard, to teach my lesson: O you virtuous Jewess, the tables are turned, *tsatskeleh! You* on the defensive now, Naomi – explaining your vaginal discharge to the entire kibbutz. Wait'll they get a whiff of this! . . . Then perhaps you'll come to have the proper awe for us fallen psychoneurotic Jewish men! Socialism exists, but so do spirochetes, my love! So here's your introduction, dear, to the slimier side of things. Down, down with those patriotic khaki shorts, spread your chops, blood of my blood, unlock your fortressy thighs, open wide that messianic Jewish hole! Make ready, Naomi, I am about to poison your organs of reproduction! I am about to change the future of the race!

But of course I couldn't. Licked her earholes, sucked at her unwashed neck, sank my teeth into the coiled braids of hair . . . and then, even as resistance may actually have begun to recede under my assault, I rolled off her and came to rest, defeated, against the wall – on my back. 'It's no good,' I said 'I can't get a hard-on in, this place.' ('In Exile')

Only physical failure, not moral scruple, prevents this rape. Portnoy simply cannot feel for women other than as lust objects. They do not have the reality of humanity in his eyes. With unselfconscious directness he sets out his idea of sex: 'What I'm saying, Doctor, is that I don't seem to stick my dick up these girls, as much as I stick it up their backgrounds – as though through fucking I will discover America. *Conquer* America – maybe that's more like it.' He also uses incidental women, in his travels through 'the cunt in country-'tis-of-thee', to pay off scores inflicted by men of their social class, though through no fault of theirs, on his own family. He sums up his affair with a girl from a good background in these words: Sarah Abbot Maulsby 'was just something nice a son once did for his dad. A little vengeance on Mr Lindabury for all those nights and Sundays Jack Portnoy spent collecting down in the coloured district. A little bonus extracted from Boston and Northeastern, for all those years of service, and exploitation.' Note the chop-logic which compensates for one form of exploitation with another; and notice the betrayal of the ignorant, trusting Sarah, too. What price any love, affection, respect for the individual when each encounter is a cold grinding of the axe of resentment and rage?

Portnoy is of course a comic novel, often side-splittingly funny in its fertility of wit and invention. Many have argued that to analyse it in this way is to take it too seriously. Norman Mailer has similarly complained that women critics of Henry Miller fail to see that Miller is 'only' being humorous, that he does not intend his sexual scenarios with their use and abuse of women to be taken too earnestly. Mailer in his turn has consistently failed to perceive that this is precisely what women object to – that the joke is, quite literally in some cases, on them. Feminist critics have expended a good deal of energy in establishing that male humour has various functions, but none of them is intended to please or benefit women. As a bonding device, assisting male solidarity, it excludes women. As a smoke-screen, set up to dissipate an aura of good humour, it distracts and deceives women. Finally, as a form of assault, a teasing attack, it serves to consign women to that time-dishonoured region, their place. In any event it is used to avoid, to impede, or to deride the possibility of free equal relationships between men and women. That is how it is used in Mailer, Miller, and Roth. And that is what women now feel that they don't have to grin and bear any longer.

Henry Miller is long passé, his faded dreams superseded by works that make his trailblazing efforts seem tame. But where one ageing comedian quits the stage, there is always another with a great sense of humour waiting in the wings. The obsession with tough masculinity, with sexual aggression and physical prowess as a means of defining manhood, is nowhere more clearly expressed than in Anthony Burgess's *A Clockwork Orange* (1962). This novel, although puffed as one big laugh, 'horror farce', is clearly nothing so light-hearted. It was and is, for all its humour, to those who could see it, prophetic, a sermon on the dangers of the cult of brutalism in modern England.

The hero, Alex, is first presented to the reader as an expert practitioner in the art of 'sheer wantonness and vandalwork', not to mention grievous bodily harm and sexual assault. Physically he is fully mature, indeed accomplished enough to take on two of his 'droogs' armed with knife and chain, and defeat them. So implicitly do we accept these manifestations of adult manhood that it comes as a shock when Burgess reveals half way through the novel that Alex is only fifteen. Yet if fifteen seems not to be his physical age, it is even more discrepant with his emotional age. His is not the

painful stirring consciousness of adolescence, but the total clarity
and overwhelming ego of the child. He exerts his male power in a
moral void, a man in all but the one controlling factor, the
maturity of adulthood which enjoins a sense of responsibility for
others.

The novel also brings out the latent violence and hostility to
women which is implicit in the cult of bullhood. This passage links
the act of destruction with that of sex as temporary outlets for
Alex's brutality and aggression. The negative drive of his purpose,
rape and mayhem, is startlingly contrasted with the vital creativity
of the prose, his own special language, in which he relates it:

'All right, Dim,' I said. 'Now for the other veshch, Bog help us
all.' So he did the strong-man on the devotchka, who was still
creech creech creeching away in very horrorshow four-in-a-bar,
locking her roockers from the back, while I ripped away at this
and that and the other, the others going haw haw haw still, and
real good horrorshow groodies they were that then exhibited
their pink glazzies, O my brothers, while I untrussed and got
ready for the plunge. Plunging, I could slooshy cries of agony
and this bleeding writer veck that Georgie and Pete held on to
nearly got loose howling bezoomny with the filthiest of slovos
that I already knew and others he was making up. Then after me
it was right old Dim should have his turn, which he did in a
beastly snorty howly sort of a way with his Peebee Shelley
maskie taking no notice, while I held on to her. Then there was a
changeover, Dim and me grabbing on to the slobbering writer
veck who was past struggling really, only just coming out with
slack sort of slovos like he was in the land in a milk-plus bar, and
Pete and Georgie had theirs. Then there was like quiet and we
were full of like hate, so smashed what was left to be
smashed – typewriter, lamp, chairs – and Dim, it was typical of
old Dim, watered the fire out and was going to dung on the
carpet, there being plenty of paper, but I said no. 'Out out out
out' I howled. The writer veck and his zheena were not really
there, bloody and torn and making noises. But they'd live.

So we got into the waiting auto and I left it to Georgie to take
the wheel, me feeling that malenky bit shagged, and we went
back to town, running over odd squealing things on the way.
(ch. 2)

'Odd squealing things' – Alex's view of his suffering human
victims is pathologically distanced. In other recent portraits of
men's hatred of women, the obsessive detail of the scrutiny serves

to fuel the violence of the attack. In Martin Amis's *The Rachel Papers* (1973, p. 11), one of the male characters explains the function of marriage:

> It's not something you do, it's something you get done. The over-twenties, I grant you, must see it largely as a matter of obligation too: but to the partner, not to oneself, like us. Take a look at the scaly witches round your local shopping centre, many of them with children. Grim enough with their clothes on. Imagine them naked! Snatches that yo-yo between their knees, breasts so flaccid you could tie them in a knot. One would have to be literally galvanised on Spanish fly even to consider it.

For this character, *noblesse oblige*. But the Amis man does not always go gentle into the good night of his social and sexual destiny:

> 'These fucking slags!' he yelled, head thrown back. 'All they can bloody do is gorge down great fucking fry-ups and squirt ponce all over themselves.' He flicked on a tap and rolled up his sleeves, tone getting jerky with righteous sarcasm. '*You* work all bloody day, and they're wiggling their bums in fucking *dress* shops and spending pounds in Sleazy fucking Wheezy's or whatever the fucker's name is. You're up the shop while they're on their arses doing their eyes.'
> His voice rose half an octave. 'Juskers they wear the tits doesn't mean – ' He cut out on a long, shuddering moan of rage and frustration. (p. 65)

This theme, described as 'the true awfulness and strangeness' of women in the blurb for Kingsley Amis's *Stanley and the Women* (1984), also exercises the imagination of Amis *père*. His hero, if we can stretch a point, spends his days in the grip of an infantile mammary fixation, unable to think of anything else about any and every woman he meets. Even as a female psychiatrist is trying to talk to him about his son's schizophrenic breakdown, he remarks, 'suddenly I noticed that her breasts were a size or two bigger than the rest of her'. But the pose of relentless visual priapism is a cover for a darker concern: Stanley and a doctor friend share a common male 'joke', 'the one about the fellow who was afraid to go to bed with girls because his mother had told him there were teeth down there'. And however dimly, both men are aware of the hatred men feel for women:

Cliff was looking thoughtful. 'According to some bloke on the telly the other night,' he said, 'twenty-five per cent of violent crime in England and Wales is husbands assaulting wives. Amazing figure that, don't you think? You'd expect it to be more like eighty per cent. Just goes to show what an easy-going lot English husbands are, only one in four of them bashing his wife.'

'The root of all the trouble,' I said, 'is we want to fuck them, the pretty ones, women I mean. Just try and imagine it happening to you, everyone wanting to fuck you wherever you go. And of course being ready to pay for you if your father's stopped doing that. You'd have to be pretty tough to stand up to it, wouldn't you? In fact women only want one thing, for men to want to fuck them. If they do, it means they can fuck them up. Am I drunk? What I was trying to say, if you want to fuck a woman she can fuck you up. And if you don't want to she fucks you up anyway for not wanting to . . . they used to feel they needed something in the way of provocation . . . but now they seem to feel they can get on with the job of fucking you up any time they feel like it. That's what Women's Lib is for.' (pp. 253–4)

The mixture of violent aggression and paranoid fear here is some indication of the confusion being experienced, a confusion only compounded by the degraded interplay of meaning between 'fuck' and 'fuck up'. But there is no hesitation in Stanley's mind about what women, and 'Women's Lib', are for – they're there to get on with the job of fucking up men. In this new, post-feminist stage of society, the MacWhirr stance ('facing it – always facing it') no longer avails. 'It', in the shape of stronger, freer women trying to get on with the job of living their own lives, is proving rather too much. The boys don't like it. But they aren't yet ready to let go without a fight.

Or so they would have us believe. In view of the length of the tradition of anti-feminist hostility in literature and society, it's more than possible that they are not so much threatening as ritualistically repeating gestures of domination and defiance, sabre-rattling, spear-shaking, while all the time devoutly hoping the beast will quietly return to its lair. Male writers of this persuasion need to understand that they must abandon their embattled ways of thinking and, after all these ages, finally come out of the laager and join the human race.

CHAPTER 6

Moral themes

You know what fiction is. It will keep bursting over into real life,
and vice versa.

> Fay Weldon, *The Shrapnel Academy* (1986)

Literature is entitled to be dangerous.

> Margaret Mahy, New Zealand author (1986)

Among the most exciting of the developments in the contemporary
novel has been the way in which women writers have been
extending their range, pushing forward into new areas of human
experience, reported with a new and confident claim for attention.
It has often been said, and as usually believed, that women's
writing is by its nature limited, interior, domestic. Women did not
handle the 'big' themes of war, politics, madness, and crime, the
argument ran; they concentrated instead on the literary equivalent
of flower arranging or *petit point*. The very nature of their sheltered
lives debarred them from the epic arena. Erica Jong has reported
her disconcerting discovery that writing 'was a masculine noun':

> The visiting author went on and on about how women *couldn't
> possibly* be authors. Their experience was too limited . . . They
> didn't know blood and guts and fucking whores and puking in
> the streets . . . ('The Artist As Housewife', 1973)

There may have been some truth in this historically, when
women were severely restricted in their movements and never
allowed to go to war or to seek their fortune like their brothers. Yet
whatever access women have had to war, for example, they have
made the most of, and one of the most famous war novels of all
time came from a woman's pen.

Margaret Mitchell's *Gone with the Wind* (1936) proves on close
inspection to be skilful in its use of the backdrop of hostilities. The
ebb and flow of the fighting is exploited to add tension and interest

to the actions and emotional entanglements of the principals. The same is true of Iris Murdoch's account of the Irish troubles, *The Red and the Green* (1965). It is significant in this context that the 'war novel' of Elizabeth Bowen which was most highly praised when it appeared, and which some critics regard as her masterpiece, *The Heat of the Day* (1949), deals in fact with the lives and actions of a group of people who did not go to the war, but stayed at home: it is the *impact* of the war, not its action nor external structure, that provides the focus of the novel and the real story.

When war is on a woman writer's agenda, the emphasis tends to fall on the personal rather than the general implications of the situation. Susan Hill's *Strange Meeting* (1971) tells the story of two of the generation of 'doomed youth' who come together in the forcing-house of the First World War. Susan Hill goes to great pains to avoid any homosexual or even strongly emotional colouring in her handling of the developing love between two young officers at the front. This, taken with the fact that the hero is a classic of the type that E. M. Forster made his own, the unawakened heart, makes for a certain coldness, a lack of engagement about the whole thing, despite some vigorous trench details, of smells, wounds, and rats. But nowhere does the writer flinch from the realities of the war situation that she has created.

The convulsions of society in one of its periodic outbursts of uncontrolled violence may require all the skills of a Tolstoy to render. But it is remarkable that relatively little interest was shown by women writers of the past in the political operations of society in that state of controlled violence which we call peacetime. Many readers would agree with Stendhal's *The Charterhouse of Parma* (1839) that 'politics in a work of literature are like a pistol shot in the middle of a concert, something loud and vulgar and yet a thing to which it is not possible to refuse one's attention.' But this cannot explain the almost total absence of anything that might remotely be described as overtly political in novels written by women.

Winifred Holtby's *South Riding* (1936) is one of the few works of women's fiction which does concern itself with this area of experience. It deals at length with the machinery of local government, without attempting to make humorous capital out of its shortcomings. Winifred Holtby presents the councillors in session, and in private life, drawing on the experiences of her own mother as an alderman and mayor. The novel gives a lively picture of the inter-party tensions and parochial bickering of local government, yet also succeeds in conveying the fact that these decisions are no less difficult or important because they concern local rather than national issues.

Nor is this the limit of Winifred Holtby's interest in politics. On the wider front there is an insistent feminist note sounded throughout. This is expressed through the character of the emancipated young headmistress, Miss Burton, many of whose arguments, especially about the education of girls, remain depressingly relevant today. There is, too, an early association of the cause of women with that of other oppressed groups, principally that of blacks, in a way reminiscent of the origins of the modern women's movement in America. Here is Sarah Burton defending her point of view against a traditionally-minded male:

> You know the story of the difference between the North and South Americans and their attitude towards the negroes? The Southerner says: 'You're a slave, God bless you'; the Northerner: 'You're a free man, damn you!' I remember how a man I used to know in South Africa said he loved the natives. He was an Afrikaans farmer who believed in flogging blacks for breaches of the Masters and Servants Act . . . I hate this feudal love in which there's no give and take. 'I love the ladies.' 'I love my labourers.' Love needs the stiffening of respect, the give and take of equality. (Book 2, ch. 4)

In her time, Winifred Holtby stood alone. Most women, it seems would rather write *Grand Hotel*, *The Daughter of Time*, or *The Murder of Roger Ackroyd*, or even nothing, than write anything which could stand comparison with some of the political novels for which America or Germany is famous. The theme is present, as is so much else, in Carson McCullers's *The Heart Is a Lonely Hunter* (1943), and handled with characteristic use of resonant allusion and luminous detail. In the McCullers universe, politics provide yet another arena in which human ideals and aspirations are pitifully measured against human weakness and wickedness. The black doctor, Copeland, one of the main characters, embodies a series of paradoxes – he is a healer, yet dying of tuberculosis; he is intensely proud yet forced to endure the routine contempt of every white man; he is a committed father, yet estranged from his children.

Copeland's politics naturally fit in with this pattern of longing and disappointment. His passionate vision of socialism yet denies the true (and the social) nature of his own race; his christening his son Karl Marx signifies his idea, but shows too how he unknowingly undermines it by his determination to westernise his people at all costs, even at the price of their ethnic identity. The destruction of his hopes is indicated with poetic economy and poignance of effect by the fact that his son is never called anything but 'Buddy', itself an ironic comment upon the inability of human beings to entertain anything but the outward show, the shallow clichés of friendship and brotherhood.

Parallel with Copeland stands the itinerant labourer, Jake. He has no history, and is 'one of the people' in that he simply emerges from the slow swell of humanity into the foreground of the narrative. He has no cash, no capital, no house, no land. He works for his livelihood, and believes in his work and his fellow-workers. But the failure of his brand of socialism is revealed through his failure to mobilise, or even to get on with, his fellows. Just before Jake disappears from the story, hitting the road out of town like so many characters in American fiction, he is repeatedly brought into contact with a mad evangelist, a ludicrous and unregarded prophet of primitive Christianity. In this crushing association Carson McCullers ironically illustrates how Jake appars to the millions who have no time or use for his 'message'.

The final effect of the novel is not so melancholy as this summary might suggest. Copeland, Jake, and the other characters all revolve around one man, Singer. Singer, who is gifted with great grace, sweetness, and fidelity, and handicapped by being congenitally mute, stands for the richness of human love, and also the mystery of limitation and incomprehension which lies at its heart. He loves and is loved, as do the other characters in their own ways. But none understands him, nor he them, nor do these varied impulses of love manage to coincide or even coexist. The habit of the imperfect lover to adopt only those aspects of the beloved with which he can identify is expressed by the fact that Copeland believes Singer to be Jewish, while Jake, who is constantly linked with the Irish, claims Singer as Irish too. In this way Singer offers, however unconsciously, to each what he can take, and after his death his legacy is one of goodness. As his love for his friend Antanopoulos began the novel, so Carson McCullers draws to a close by showing how the thoughts of another character, at Singer's funeral, bring him to a vision of love between individual people set against 'the endless fluid passage of humanity through endless time'. So human beings must walk, is the conclusion, somewhere 'between irony and faith', with no reliance upon political theories or structures but guided by the dictates of what Carson McCullers elsewhere called 'the mortgaged heart'.

On these grounds, Carson McCullers is to be seen as the most political of novelists, male or female. For as Roland Barthes insisted in *Mythologies* (1972):

One must naturally understand *political* in its deeper meaning, as describing the whole of human relationships in their real social structure, in their power of making the world.

Nadine Gordimer was interpreting the term in this sense when she declared that 'politics is character – in South Africa'. Through Mekring, the pig-iron dealer and central character of *The Conservationist* (1974), she explores 'the conglomeration of circumstances and inherited attitudes that make up the inner personality', shown here in and through Mekring's relations to blacks. Although his behaviour is no worse than that of any other affluent South African, Mekring is eventually arraigned for the reader's censure of his limitations of awareness and false consciousness of the true situation.

In *The Burger's Daughter* (1979), Nadine Gordimer returned to this topic, one of the most critical questions of the twentieth century: 'Who shall inherit South Africa? How shall it be governed?' This novel, described by Robert Boyers in *Atrocity and Amnesia: The Political Novel since 1945* (1985) as 'one of the best political novels of our period', covers a number of different areas in its discussion of ways of relating to the public world. On one level of generation conflict, it takes as its starting point Rosa Burger's resistance to everything that her dead father stood for. From here it moves through to an examination of family bonds, and the way they inform and lead outward to public, political actions. Nadine Gordimer's conclusion is austere, but not hopeless – Rosa must join the struggle, even though its outcome is unforeseeable.

A political struggle of a very different kind is the story behind Marge Piercy's *Vida* (1980). Before the novel opens Vida has been a prominent political activist until targeted by the FBI as a dangerous revolutionary. Now a vulnerable, driven fugitive, Vida moves through the fragmented political underground of America struggling to keep her faith, her emotions, herself intact in a series of extreme situations. Yet this is not a negative or depressing account. On the contrary, the vitality of the portrayal of this woman revolutionary stamps her as a genuine female survivor, and harmonises all her drives in one resistance to all forms of life-denying domination:

> The hell with him. On impulse she dashed into the dining room, grabbed a photo and wrote a note to her roommates in purple marking pen on the back of it, then stuck it near the door where they'd see it. A little vandalism for the Vassarette she hoped would give him syphilis. 'No, Mopsy, stay! Stay, girl.' Maybe

he'd like a job with *New Day* too. Off to greener pastures.

'We aren't his brothers and sisters any more, we aren't his comrades, we're his fucking material,' she said as she burst from the elevator and raced across the lobby, waving to Julio, their friend who tipped them to surveillance, and then into the street. She felt like Wonder Woman streaking through the city. Fast, fast she went down the block, too fast for any man to give her trouble. Running lightly in her sneakers. Into the subway, she vaulted over the turnstile and bolted into a train. That was Movement style, perfectly executed. Show the people they can do it too. An example to other women.

Tomorrow she'd tear that dress up and make a rag of it. Tomorrow she'd be on the streets; they'd bring the city to a halt. They'd show the government what it meant to shoot down kids and try to terrorize the Movement. Then the day after that, The Little Red Wagon would roll. Leigh didn't matter. She had wanted to break security to talk their action over with him, she had wanted to break the faith of their group for the sake of telling Leigh what she was about, but he had stopped her. She would show him. He didn't have enough respect for her. He didn't know how serious she was. So much the worse for him. He'd see. (p. 220)

Set against works of this kind, the absence of novels by women writers which take us onto the battlefield, or down in a submarine, pales into insignificance. What women writers do and have always done is to handle moral rather than self-confessedly epic themes – and then not infrequently raise them to an epic level through the dimensions of the treatment. Of all contemporary women novelists, one who has been most wholeheartedly concerned with moral themes is Iris Murdoch. As her philosophical writings make clear, she is interested in exploring and asserting 'the sovereignty of good', in the title phrase of her essay on the subject. She is aware that it is hardly an engrossing contemporary preoccupation; as she drily observes, 'It is significant that the idea of goodness and of virtue has been largely superseded in Western moral philosophy by the idea of rightness, supported perhaps by some conception of sincerity.' She is not seeking simply to reverse this trend by a plain statement of her beliefs and an attack upon those who do not conform to them as 'trimmers, time-servers, toadies, compromisers, comfort-lovers, any of the varieties of coward', in Mary McCarthy's style. Iris Murdoch's method, and the magnitude of her task, is nearer to that outlined by Dostoevsky in his preliminary comments upon *The Idiot* (1886):

The idea of the novel is my old favourite idea, but so difficult that I for long did not dare to attempt it; and if I have attempted it now it is certainly because I found myself in a desperate situation. The principal conception of the novel is to depict the positively good man. There is nothing in the world more difficult, particularly nowadays. Of all writers (not merely our own, but European writers too), those who have attempted to depict the positively good have always missed the mark. For it is an infinite task. The good is an ideal, and both our ideal and that of civilised Europe is still far from having been worked out. In the whole world there is only one positively good man, Christ. . . . Of the good types of Christian literature, the most perfect is Don Quixote. But he is good only because at the same time he is ridiculous. The Pickwick of Dickens (an infinitely weaker conception than Don Quixote, but still immense) is also ridiculous and succeeds in virtue of this. A feeling of compassion is produced for the much ridiculed good man who does not know his own worth, and thus perhaps sympathy is evoked in the reader. This rousing of compassion is the secret of humour. (E. H. Carr, *Dostoevsky 1821–1881*, 1931, 1962 edn. pp. 159–60)

If Dostoevsky's theory that compassion and humour are near kin provides any bearing upon Iris Murdoch's work, then it is one that is sorely needed; her methods and materials have often dazzled and befuddled her readers. First, there is her interest in a variety of forms: her tendency to parody the romantic or the Gothic, for example, illustrates her fascination with the use and management of these classic fictional genres. Consider *The Nice and the Good* (1968), which begins with a shot in Whitehall and an uncharacteristic flutter in the corridors of power. Any fan of the detective novel will feel at home with sequences like these:

He moved round the desk on the side away from Radeechy's face and leaning over the chair saw a round hole in the back of the head, a little to the right of the slight depression at the base of the skull. The hole was quite large, a dark orifice with blackened edges. A little blood, not much, had run down inside the collar. (pp. 8–9)

Similarly readers of *The Unicorn* (1969) will not query Hannah's refusal or inability to leave the remote dwelling where she is some kind of prisoner; it is a convention of Gothic fiction that the princess is and must be in the tower, and she is not usually asked whether she wants to be there or not.

Another diverting and distracting feature of this writer is her rich allusiveness, which springs from her inexhaustible interest in word and symbol. The basis of communication may be language but everyone means and understands by every word and expression something different from everyone else; and a communication failure inevitably involves a reduction of personality in the people concerned. Thus David Levkin, the Russian Jew who cannot even get his name pronounced properly in England, expresses his feelings: 'Nothing means anything to me outside Russia. Your language is dry, dry in my mouth. Here I am a non-man' (*The Italian Girl*, 1964, p. 189). It is possible that what has been regarded as one of Iris Murdoch's artistic defects, the occasional lapse into what A. S. Byatt calls her 'sloppy style', her woman's novel style, should be interpreted in this light. When she makes a character cry out such extraordinary lines as 'Coward and fool! . . . You have made your own future!' (*The Sandcastle*, 1957, p. 312), she surely cannot be unaware of the tone here. It is arguable that she is parodying a common human weakness, the tendency to try to elevate life's moments of crisis into full melodrama, by resorting to this attitudinising phraseology. Language, which should further communication, commonly retards it by providing human beings with a vehicle which they use mainly for the transport of their own feelings.

Again, Iris Murdoch's well-known fondness for the doubling, if not trebling, of themes and motifs (a truly Shakespearian prolixity here) is a quality which has frequently caused her readers to confuse wood and trees. To mention her predilection for magic, witchcraft, symbolic names, impenetrable sibling relationships, letters, weather, play-acting, bells, roses, dogs, foreigners, concentration camps, and cancer, is to recall not one book but her entire opus, which sometimes seems to be composed of a series of intricate variations upon a handful of themes. When certain effects recur, as the ritual breast-showing does, for instance, in *The Flight from the Enchanter* and *The Italian Girl*, they take on a mythic quality which is quite mesmerising; and to read a new Iris Murdoch in the light of all that she has written before, has been compared to the feeling of the acolyte as another layer of the *arcana* is revealed. These preoccupations, and their accompanying paradoxes, are summed up in *The Sea, the Sea* (1978, p. 471):

White magic is black magic. A less than perfect meddling in the spiritual world can breed monsters for other people, and demons used for good can hang around and make mischief afterwards.

There can be little doubt that Iris Murdoch quite deliberately sets out to create little puzzles and intellectual teasers for her readers. She expects, for example, that they will be sufficiently well informed to know the Latin meaning of the name of Felix (fortunate, happy) in *An Unofficial Rose* (1962). But is this an ironic reflection upon his bad fortune in having his life broken apart by his beloved Ann and her cruel, killing other half, her daughter Miranda, or does it subtly indicate his luck in *escaping* from them, like the adulterous husband Randall (randy?)? Iris Murdoch encourages us through her own complex system of cross-referencing to supply our own links from literature, history and life; thus, in *Under the Net* (1954), the 'Fall of Rome' is surely an ironic allusion to the failure of an idea of democracy, as well as a gentle gibe at the Hollywood epic idea. Mischa Fox's name in *The Flight from the Enchanter* may plausibly be accounted a vernacular evocation of Jonson's Volpone, but is also intended to summon up the animal for us, to bring out Mischa's feral attributes.

Often the significances of Iris Murdoch's work proliferate even more fully and suggestively. In *The Time of the Angels* Elizabeth is presented as a Lady of Shalott figure (the web image is operative in this context), while otherwise she is a white form opposing the black Madonna of the black servant Pattie in the structure of the novel. Pattie's door-keeping function also makes her a kind of Cerberus, so that by extension the Rectory which she guards so devotedly is Hell. Along this line the dreadful Muriel is an angel of death (this links with her destructiveness as a false writer, committed to the death of truth); and Marcus's entry through the black coal hole makes him inescapably demonic, while the coal hole's other use as a 'back passage' serves as a comic metaphor for his repressed homosexuality.

It has to be said that Iris Murdoch's handling of her chosen themes is not infallible. Although her stress on the uniqueness of every individual forms the philosophic basis of all her work, she is not exempt from lapses of judgment and presentation. She has recorded her respect for Shakespeare's enormously varied yet faithful and considerate character-drawing. This is a harsh self-comparison, yet on any level it is hard to feel anything but embarrassed by the portrait of Mrs Carberry, the daily woman in *An Accidental Man* (1971), additionally handicapped as she is by the possession of a retarded son. This gruesome twosome recalls Oscar Wilde's remark about the death of Little Nell, that one would have to have a heart of stone to read it without laughing. The comicality here derives from an unaccustomed failure of tone and technique which is highlighted by the success of another portrait of a working woman, Pattie in *The Time of the Angels*. This character – servant, housekeeper, lover, black Madonna to the mad, terrible Carel in the deserted Rectory – is a classic study of the psychology of service, the emotional mechanism which ensures that the coals will still be brought in even though the house is (literally) about to come down. The warmth and immediacy with which Pattie is drawn, the compassionate but complete demonstration of her inadequacy, her devotion, and her misery, make this an entirely vivid and convincing character-study. At the same time, they lift it to something more. Pattie, in all her rarity, eventually comes to stand for all those who have known what it is to perform hard and humiliating work without either spiritual or financial recompense; and who, whatever their efforts 'downstairs', have usually figured in the collective consciousness of 'upstairs' as no more than 'trouble with the servants'.

The rich and allusive nature of Iris Murdoch's writing is only suggested, never exhausted, by these games of association. But this concentration upon the White Witch of Oxford can obscure the sly social satirist at work. Much criticism has been devoted to bringing out the purely imaginative elements of Iris Murdoch's writing, the magic, the myth, the religions primitive and modern, the old dark gods of convention and the new dark gods of neurosis. At times it seems as if the reader has to be permanently at full stretch of the interpretative capacity in order not to miss a moment of the philosophy, metaphysics, and enchantment that she hands out. What is equally important is the vein of naturalism, typically observed and recorded straight from life in minute social detail. Later ages may even come to regard her in the way that we now look at Dickens, as a historian and reporter of his epoch as much as an inspired teller of tall tales.

Earlier in her career, some of the social observation is not as sharp as it later becomes. In *The Sandcastle* (1957), for instance, it is never made plain how Mor, the minor public-school master and close friend of the Churchillian Demoyte, can expect simply to pick up a safe Labour parliamentary seat, even granted that his friend Tim is Chairman of the Constituency Labour Party, and that these are the palmy days of the 1950s before Socialism became modish. There is, too, always the threat of the flicker of patrician disdain, if not the sneer at least the raised eyebrow, at the sauce bottles on the sideboard, the overcareful vowels, the flushed face and the fat thigh bulging unattractively over the stocking top. Over the years there has been an increasing command over this type of material. Iris Murdoch has clearly given some thought to polishing up this aspect of her considerable repertoire of effects: a notable triumph in this genre is *An Accidental Man* (1971), which, with its large cast of juveniles and socialites, its comment upon the student problem, the state of the economy, and the Vietnam War, is among the most comprehensive of her social satires. When Austin, the central character, muses comfortably, 'What was so relaxing about Mitzi was that he did not care a fuck what Mitzi thought,' his use of the obscenity in an unchallenging and totally casual context places the character very precisely. This and other closely observed touches locate the novel so exactly that it conveys the very flavour of the year in which it was written.

Yet even at its most pointed Iris Murdoch's satire is not marked by the contemptuous detachment, or the virulent desire to 'flap the bug with gilded wings' which we associate with classical satirists. Hers is more nearly the blend of laughter and love which Dostoevsky so acutely isolated as the mark of the true novelist. If one thread emerges more than any other from the dense fabric of her fictions, it is this: the importance of love, the scarcity of it, and the desperate difficulty, if not impossibility, of living up to its rigorous demands. Most of the characters have to settle for far less than full happiness: they have to take what they can get and console themselves with that; they have to agree with the summary of *An Accidental Man* that 'love, even fake love, even dream love, was something after all'.

'Fake love, dream love'; Iris Murdoch is especially interested in the people living in frameworks socially sanctioned as the vehicle of love, which may in reality either disguise its absence or deny its very existence. Love is conventionally understood as expressed in and through marriage. But to Iris Murdoch, 'a married couple is a dangerous machine'. *The Bell, An Unofficial Rose, Bruno's Dream, The Black Prince, Nuns and Soldiers*, and others of her novels give us marriages in states of decay or dissolution. More painful perhaps are the marriages in which both partners are still very much alive and kicking. Iris Murdoch is adept at exposing the power of the institution as a terrible mechanism *sui generis*, and the day-to-day misery of living in an unequal partnership:

> He suffered deeply from the discovery that his wife was the stronger. He told himself that her strength sprang only from obstinate and merciless unreason; but to think this did not save him either from suffering coercion or from feeling resentment. He could not now make his knowledge of her into love, he could not even make it into indifference. In the heart of him he was deeply compelled. He was forced. And he was continually offended. (*The Sandcastle*, pp. 10–11)

Given the individual's irrational egotistic drive, any structured relationship, not only marriage, can be an engine of unforeseen danger and destruction. Love, understood as the selfless concern for another's welfare above our own, is more frequently expressed in Iris Murdoch's fiction through unhallowed relationships than through those society is familiar with; it is as if the extra trials involved in keeping up a feeling which cuts across the barricades of class, age, or sex, will themselves define and continually test the genuineness of it.

A classic illustration is to be found in the homosexual marriage between Simon and Axel in *A Fairly Honourable Defeat* (1970). Theirs is a very conventional and discreet union; Axel especially has a fastidious horror of the seedy underworld of London lavatories and young soldiers. Their day-to-day living is also solidly constructed as an echo of a heterosexual marriage – Axel is strong and silent, good at taking decisions and winning bread; Simon is dependent, fearful, extravagant, and convinced he's 'not good enough' for Axel, but nevertheless a lovely cook and a sweet person.

Yet although they move in a circle of worldly and tolerant people and are not forced into ignominious antics to conceal their love, they are still under constant pressure from the hostility or incomprehension of others, and from the doubts and fears within themselves that their 'marriage' can survive. It is a reversal of all the reader's carefully created expectations when the relationship between these two men proves supple and strong enough to withstand the assaults on it of private malice and public ignorance. It is also highly ironic that at the end of this novel, a story very much about marriage in modern times, the central conventional marriage has foundered and the sun goes down upon two un-marriages, one a partnership between a pair of homosexuals, the other between two sisters.

Iris Murdoch does not exclude the possibility of the expression of sexual feeling in relationships like these. But in the main she is concerned to establish that there is no such thing as an intrinsic connection between love and sex. Indeed, she tries hard to undermine in her work the contemporary confusion of the two. This conviction, that these are *not* the same, nor even necessarily kin, is a vital principle of her fiction (it is also a central theme of her husband John Bayley's book *The Characters of Love*). See how many times Iris Murdoch casts an eye of the sort that is commonly described as unerring over the laboured contortions of the human frame caught in the act of (may we meaningfully say?) love:

A projection upon one body is laboriously inserted into a hole in another . . . a pitiful awkward ugly inefficient piece of fleshy mechanism. . . . It's supposed to be something to do with love, at least that's the legend, but love is just a comforting myth and even if it wasn't it couldn't possibly have any connection with sex. We don't mix up love with eating do we? Or with farting or hiccuping or blowing one's nose? Or with breathing? Or with the circulation of the blood or the operation of the liver? Then why connect it with our curious impulse to shove parts of ourselves inside other people, or with our in some ways equally curious impulse to thrust our damp evil-smelling mouths and decaying teeth up against other such unsavoury gluey orifices in other bodies? Answer me that, dear lady. (*A Fairly Honourable Defeat* ch. 5)

This emphasis upon the absurdity of sexual behaviour originates partly in Iris Murdoch's belief that it should be a private, personal activity, yet it so rarely is. A married couple may or may not be a dangerous machine; but whatever else it is, it is a bicycle made for two, and the knowledge or observation of a third party invariably allows the ridiculous to creep in. Thus Isobel in *The Italian Girl* comically expresses a puritan disdain of a couple's sex activity which she can only see as fatuous, ignoring the animal playfulness and vitality it implies: 'I've heard them whining and barking at each other.' This reaction is juxtaposed with her husband's more admiring response to variations on the theme: 'I read in a paper about a man who couldn't make love to his wife unless he had her all tied up in brown paper like a parcel' (*The Italian Girl*). Partly, too, sex may be absurd because the body itself is so. There is at times in the minds of Iris Murdoch's characters a whiff of Augustinian despair and disgust at the exigencies of the flesh, even a sense of *soma sema*, the body as the tomb. Here Mitzi, a gross Amazon and one of those grotesques of Iris Murdoch who are intensely real to themselves if to no one else, muses upon the men in her life:

The sky was producing rain again. Austin said, 'I'll go and pee if you don't mind'. He went through the studio and out into the ragged garden. Mitzi followed and watched him. He went over by the wall with his back to her. As the sky slowly darkened he looked like Mr Secombe-Hughes, standing there sturdily with his feet apart. The smell of male urine was wafted on the damp air. I hate men, she thought. I just hate men. I hate them. (*An Accidental Man*, p. 29)

In the Iris Murdoch universe the wonder is that love can exist at all, menaced as it is on every side. All are frail; and even relatively trivial things like the weather, emotional upsets, or alcohol, can dislocate human responses and distract attention from others and from the business of loving in hand. Iris Murdoch made a philosophical statement of this point in an earlier essay (*Yale Review*, vol. 49, Winter 1960): 'I take the general consciousness today to be ridden either by convention or by neurosis'; these are 'the enemies of understanding, one might say the enemies of love'. She afterwards amplified this in *The Sovereignty of Good* (1970, p. 91) in a way that throws considerable light upon her own concept and process of character development:

> The difficulty is to keep the attention fixed upon the real situation and to prevent it from returning surreptitiously to the self with consolations of self-pity, resentment, fantasy, and despair. The refusal to attend may even induce a fictitious sense of freedom: I may as well toss a coin . . . it is a *task* to come to see the world as it is.

So in various ways individuals lose touch and fail. Iris Murdoch sums it up, 'In the moral life the enemy is the fat relentless ego' (*The Sovereignty of Good*, p. 52). Loving is the most basic moral activity of life, and the task which Iris Murdoch enjoins upon her characters and by implication upon her readers too, that of maintaining 'respect for the real', is probably the most immediate form of loving that most people are required to undertake. But human failure and its attempts at compensation for it frequently mean that love, far from restoring and recreating, becomes a form of assault; and few writers have given more attention than Iris Murdoch to its power of destruction. Love as rape, love as enslavement, love the prerogative and stock-in-trade of the manipulator, the entangler, the false prophet – these few phrases delineate the outlines of the Murdoch landscape and conjure up that race of character-types she has made her own. All her readers must have their favourite example of the species – Palmer in *A Severed Head*, Matthew in *An Accidental Man*, Mischa in *The Flight from the Enchanter*, Julius in *A Fairly Honourable Defeat*, Arnold in *The Black Prince*. Each of these, in his respective narrative framework, is an active enemy of truth and love; each joins with all the other inert forces and impediments to understanding and fidelity in the attempt to render lifeless a relationship in his vicinity. This activity, in Iris Murdoch's fiction as in real life, commonly goes unreprehended and even undetected. It is a primal outrage, because a moral one.

The majority of people today, in the West at least, do not go to war. They need not even know that it occurs elsewhere unless they choose to. They do not engage much in politics, even at a local level; they do not commit thievery and murder; they do not, obviously at least, go mad. But they do have to live out and work through personal lives in which the boss, the wife, the first husband, the teenage offspring, the elderly relative, trouble their peace and demand some response, if not solution. If Iris Murdoch offered only a description and analysis of these life situations, that would be something. But she gives us too a moral frame, a series of standards by which to judge not only the characters in her novels but the characters of life itself. In an era when the moral stance has increasingly been abandoned in favour of the psychological analysis, Iris Murdoch's fusion of the two makes hers a distinctive voice.

Other women writers too have not flinched from grappling with the epic theme of the individual's growth into life and love. Of particular interest have been the strenuous and successful attempts by women writers to develop a female *Bildungsroman*, as a long-overdue and necessary counterweight to the long tradition of Portraits of the Artist as a Young Male. One poignant and highly effective study was that of Carson McCullers in *The Member of the Wedding* (1947). Hers are among the most successful efforts in fiction to represent the experiences and emotional development of girlhood. She knows what most of us have succeeded in suppressing, that a child's growth does not occur in a steady progression, but in wild and usually painful spurts, where a previous formula of life, sense of personal solidity or satisfaction with the way things are abruptly becomes inadequate, and a bewildering new idea of reality replaces the previous and itself imperfectly assimilated version.

Frankie's story, in *The Member of the Wedding*, is that of a young girl, but its breadth of understanding is such as to make it applicable to any young person. Notice how wryly Carson McCullers catches in Frankie the close correspondence of comedy and pathos in the behaviour of the human young. Frankie is tormented with a fear of smelling which causes her to advertise her personal fastidiousness to all the world – 'Boy!' she said. 'I bet I use more perfume than anybody in this town.' Her other fears, of exclusion from the select gang of older ones, of growing too tall, of sexual experience, of being 'found out' by the police, of her own aimlessness, are ruefully recognisable as the commonplace tortures of adolescence, but given here with a total freshness and precision, and carrying an unassailable conviction.

The success of Carson McCullers's portrayal of this child derives from the fact that she does not see her as a child. Her primary theme, and one which she consistently pursued throughout her work, was the still sad music of humanity and the loneliness that that entails. Her aim was to give us the development of a consciousness, not a snapshot of a young girl. But it is also her strength that the more she concentrates upon the individual, the parochial even, the more we find her treatments opening up as fables and assuming the status of timeless, placeless narratives whose only location is somewhere within the eternal swell of human experience.

This claim, that the experience of a young girl may stand as a paradigm for that of the whole human race every bit as much as a boy's can, is made again by implication in Angela Carter's tender account of a young girl's 'coming-out':

> When we first heard her sing, in my room at the Hotel de l'Europe, it sounded as if the song sang itself, as if the song had nothing to do with Mignon, and she was only a kind of fleshy phonograph, made to transmit music of which she had no consciousness. That was before she became a woman. Now she seized hold of the song in the supple lassoo of her voice and mated it with her new-found soul, so that the song was utterly transformed and yet its essence did not change, in the same way a familiar face changes yet stays the same when it is freshly visited by love. (*Nights at the Circus*, 1984, p. 247)

'Her new-found soul' – how much have women readers needed the reassurance of women writers through fictional representations of girlhood that they too can grow up to possess one! In Grace Nichols's *Whole of a Morning Sky* (1986), the eleven-year-old Gem moves with her family from the country in Guyana to Georgetown, where she loses her safe and familiar surroundings for the more complex and threatening world of the city. Yet despite the difficulties they encounter, the city 'has something holy about it' for the family. To Gem's mother, 'this was a blessed country, a firm, fertile green country, a piece of paradise'. Through the child's eyes the reader sees the adult world afresh, both in its public and political aspects, and in its most personal moments: 'And to think before we married, the man was acting so nice,' says one woman to her. 'But you know what old people say. You never know where the house leaking till you live in it.'

Grace Nichols's clear, lyrical, and unforced portrayal of her young heroine is only one of a number of novels on this theme that

women writers have been producing in recent years. Caribbean or
American, the young black girl's rite of passage has now
established itself as a genre in its own right, through books like
Maya Angelou's *I Know Why the Caged Bird Sings* (1969), Alice
Walker's *The Color Purple* (1983), Ntozake Shange's *Betsey Brown*
(1985), and Jamaica Kincaid's *Annie John* (1986). In these varied
and valuable books, women writers addressed their readers with a
degree of conviction that lent an irrefutable authority to what they
had to say:

> If growing up is painful for a Southern Black girl, being aware of
> her displacement is the rust on the razor that threatens her
> throat.

Maya Angelou's comment aptly sums up the situation of Betsey
Brown, in Ntozake Shange's book of that name. Here Betsey, her
mind on the school elocution competition she is desperate to win,
falls foul of the older girls and boys at her school, and the dreaded
principal himself:

> 'Get a move on, rhiney heifer! Whatchu think this is, you' desk?
> I got traffic to move heah!'
>   Betsey thought she was gonna cry or faint. She wanted Liliana
> and Mavis to like her, but here she'd made them mad . . .
> 'Rhiney heifer,' that's all she needed, a new nickname . . .
>   Liliana and Mavis were long gone by the time Betsey gathered
> her thoughts, her books, her crush on the basketball player,
> Eugene Boyd. He was like another poem to her. She didn't know
> him but she 'read' him the way you read poems . . .
>   Not only were the floors of the Clark School shining like the
> halls of Tara, but Betsey's brow was weeping with sweat, as
> were her panties and underarms. She imagined she shone like an
> out-of-place star in midday. She felt hot. And there was
> Mr. Wichiten with the razor strap at the head of the hallway,
> justa swinging and smiling . . .
>   Soon as she's passt Mr. Wichiten – Praise Be to the Lord –
> dumb Butchy Jones came rubbing himself up behind her. Betsey
> dropped her books again, but this time she screamed: 'You nasty
> lil niggah, keep yo' hands off me.' And here came Mr. Wichiten,
> strap justa swinging, Mr. Wichiten justa smiling . . .
>   'Mr. Wichiten, Sir, Butchy did, uh . . . I can't explain what he
> did exactly, Sir, but it wasn't nice and I got scared. I said bad
> words to make him go away cause that's all he could
> understand, Sir.'

Mr. Wichiten looked about slowly for the shadow of a creature Elizabeth Brown was calling Butchy and saw nothin. He knew she was probably telling the truth, but with negro children, no matter what ilk, there's always that shady side. (pp. 35–6)

Through the mouth of Betsey, who knows it is 'very important to say "Sir" to the likes of Mr Wichitzen', Ntozake Shange speaks as one who knows; as one also who has to speak for large numbers of black women who have previously been silent. This is not to say that black women writers have not previously existed. They did not simply begin to write for the first time in the 1970s in the wake of the women's movement; there had been continuous literary activity among black women ever since Phillis Wheatley in the eighteenth century. Most of this work, however, had remained locked up in attics, diaries, trunks, and the authentic voice of the black woman exploring her experience and sharing it with her society at large was something long overdue on both sides of the Atlantic.

This is not to be taken as a denial of previous efforts by white women writers to come to terms with the issue of racial difference and the ways in which it affected women's lives. As part of a more general concern with moral and political themes, they have widely sought definitions of the alternative modes in which people may live decently together, and this concern has not always been expressed in family and parochial terms. Doris Lessing, in her first novel, *The Grass Is Singing* (1950), made an early attempt to confront the post-imperial legacy of racial hatred. She tells the story of Mary, a woman married to a poor white South African farmer; given the weak foundation of the relationship between them and the tensions produced by the difficulties of working the farm, the tragic conclusion is inevitable. They have married on the strength of unreal and delusive visions of each other; both are ordinary mortals, as their names, Mary and Dick, signify, yet each sees and expects an illusory glamour in the other. Through Mary, Doris Lessing attacks the burden that is placed upon women by the social expectation that they must marry, or be accounted failures. Mary's weaknesses are fully detailed, but she is also presented as a victim of her culture and society: 'All women become conscious, sooner or later, of that impalpable, but steel-strong pressure to get married.' Mary marries to fulfil a social obligation, not through an overwhelming desire to spend the rest of her life with Dick.

This novel is not only Mary's story. Its unsung hero is 'the native', brought into prominence first through Mary's inability to deal with those whose situation is ironically analogous with hers. This affinity is partly suggested through the language difficulty –

Mary's reluctance to learn 'kitchen kaffir' in order to be able to speak with the natives symbolises her awkwardness of communications with all people, and her inability to make the effort to meet them in conversation. In addition her relations with the natives are warped, from the start, by her regarding them with the distorting perspective of the white view, here sardonically outlined by Lessing (pp. 92–3):

> Whenever two or three farmers are gathered together, it is decreed that they should discuss nothing but the shortcomings and deficiencies of their natives. They talk about the labourers with a persistent irritation sounding in their voices: individual natives they might like, but as a genus, they loathe them. They loathe them to the point of neurosis. They never cease complaining about their unhappy lot, having to deal with natives who are so exasperatingly indifferent to the welfare of the white man, working only to please themselves. They had no idea of the dignity of labour, no idea of improving themselves by hard work.

Mary feels herself to be cheated and downtrodden by this life. But when, through her husband's illness, she takes over the running of the farm and the management of the natives, she discovers within herself the attitudes of the oppressor in the heart of the oppressed. She lashes a native across the face with a *sjambok*, a climactic moment which is rendered with an almost disgusting vividness: 'A thick weal pushed up along the dark skin of the cheek as she looked, and from it a drop of bright blood gathered and trickled down and off his chin, and splashed to his chest.' This infliction of the wound establishes an unbreakable bond between them – she always recognises this native by his scar, in defiance of the natural law which dictates that one black looks like another to a white woman. This man, symbolically named Moses, assumes greater and greater importance in Mary's life. As she goes mad and 'rotten', her mental horizon narrows until all her being is concentrated upon this one man who comes to be both her life and death to her.

Like all ambitious first works, *The Grass Is Singing* is not without its stereotyped moments, even in those areas where it passes over relatively untrodden ground – the life and behaviour of 'the native', for instance. Moses is 'a great hulk of a man', possessed of 'some dark attraction'. Mary feels 'helplessly in his power', and he asserts a Lawrentian masculine authority over her. He develops an 'easy, confident, bullying insolence', and she is subdued by his 'conscious power', 'the superior sexual potency of the native'. Doris Lessing presents him increasingly through his physical presence, and he impinges on Mary's weakening mind more and more as a force than as a person. She moves him in and out of the action, rarely allowing him to say anything – wisely, perhaps, when one of his few permitted conversational sallies is, 'Did Jesus think it right that people should kill each other?' Eventually, however, Moses is successfully brought through not as a human individual but as part of the nightmare in which Mary is swallowed up.

Something similar is achieved through the use of the desert in this novel. Initially it is a real, physical landscape, on and in which Mary has to live. But subtly and gradually, as her hopes fail like a doomed springtime crop, the desert becomes a symbolic landscape as well, its aridity internalised, its vast wastes an external reproach commensurate with her own inner devastation. This fearful symbol continued to haunt Doris Lessing's imagination, even years after leaving her native South Africa for the cold and damp of London. The breakdown of Anna, heroine of *The Golden Notebook*, is conveyed through this image; her fantasy fear of personal and literary sterility finds its worst and most crippling expression in her dreams of the desert, parched and cracked. The desert in the South African stories exerts this kind of power over those who live in it, even those who think to master it by growing rich from it. Much of her early work is concerned with attacking the dryness of the colony way of life, with its petty pretensions, its restrictions, and its overheated response to the pervasive irrational dread of 'the kaffir'.

Despite its sometimes plodding realism, the doggedly accurate re-creation of the very grain of life in the bush, Doris Lessing's African fiction attains at its best an impressive fidelity towards the themes that it raises. Doris Lessing is, however, writing of the black men and women of the South African bush and farm, and her focus is specifically on their relationships with the white 'bosses'. She rarely gives us black characters on their own, quite away from whites, and as a result we see little of their own way of life. Her black man is perpetually a 'kaffir', presented as he exists to white South African eyes, an inferior version of humanity because first moulded, and then judged and rejected, by an alien and hostile white culture.

A different method is to be observed in Carson McCullers's treatment of the black inhabitants of southern America. It has frequently been noted that the blacks in Carson McCullers's fiction are not a separate group but an essential constituent of her total view of life. She was remarkable for her ability to show these characters as they are to and with each other, and not only in their relations with whites, however sympathetically that may be done. McCullers never underrated the special quality of being black in the South; she renders it in its own authentic speech in such a way as to capture the blackness, but not *only* the blackness, of the southern American negro life. It is signficant that McCullers ascribes Dr Copeland's failure in *The Heart Is a Lonely Hunter* to his refusal to recognise the real cultural needs of his race, and she never stresses the special qualities of being black at the expense of their right to a share in the characteristic business of being human.

The business of being human means, for Carson McCullers, an inescapable involvement with the rhythms of love and death, shown constantly in alteration and alternation, sometimes even expressed as each other. It is this ability to represent archetypal human passions in their continuous everyday motion which gives Carson McCullers's work its mythic power. In the life of the blacks the flux and reflux of emotion and event is given an added urgency by the uncertainty of their jobs, their houses, the whole framework of their lives. No one knows where or when the blow will fall. Carson McCullers patterns out her stark view of their prospects in the very structure of her novels, which usually contain a series of escalating disasters for the black characters, or, at the very best, no improvement in prospects, however vital or sanguine each individual may be.

One brief example will illustrate this. Who could forget the wonderful Berenice in *The Member of the Wedding* (1947), seen first in her pride with her oddly assorted male companions 'T.T.', and her 'lavender coloured' foster-brother Honey? Bernice has little and expects less, content to live with what her fate has allotted her. Yet within a few weeks her life is blown apart by the imprisonment of Honey, the agonising death of her six-year-old charge, John Henry, and the removal of the white family she works for to a new home where she will not be wanted. The sole course of action open to her is marriage to T.T., who although 'a proper man' and well-off, lacks the one quality that Bernice looks for in a man – 'he don't make me shiver none'.

This theme, of the sadness, desperation and frequent failure of black women's lives, has been engrossing and ongoing. Novels by black women portray their heroines as struggling against complex difficulties and disadvantages: as Shirley Chisholm expresses it in *Unbought and Unbossed* (1970, p. xii), 'of my two "handicaps", being female put many more obstacles in my path than being black.' The problems they encounter do not only stem from the racist hostility of outsiders. As Alice Walker explained, their own men, forced to address all white men as 'Mister', humiliated in street, shop and plantation, inevitably humiliated in turn those closest under their own hands:

> 'Just remember you ain't white,' he said, even while hating with all his heart the women he wanted and did not want his wife to imitate. He liked to sling the perfection of white women at her because color was something she could not change and as his own colored skin annoyed him he meant for hers to humble her. (*The Third Life of Grange Copeland*, 1970, p. 58)

This agonising dilemma of the black girl who has internalised all the aesthetic values of the white beauty is poignantly dramatised both in Maya Angelou's *I Know Why the Caged Cird Sings* (1969), and in Toni Morrison's *The Bluest Eye* (1972), where the young heroines pine in vain for pale skin and blue eyes. No wonder, according to Toni Morrison, if the young black girl was

> . . . edged into life by the back door. Becoming. Everybody in the world was in a position to give them orders. White women said, 'Do this.' White children said, 'Give me that.' White men said, 'Come here.' Black men said 'Lay down.' The only people they need not take orders from were black children and each other. (*Sula*, 1974, p. 108)

Yet for all this, extraordinarily enough, the women find the strength and spirit to fight back against their multiple oppression. Some draw their courage from the simplest and most profound assertion of their human right of existence:

> You say I'm a woman and colored. Ain't that the same as being a man? . . . You think I don't know what your life is like just because I ain't living it? I know what every colored woman in this country is doing . . . Dying. Just like me. But the difference is, they dying like a stump. Me, I'm going down like one of those redwoods. I sure do live in this world. My lonely is mine. (*Sula*, pp. 142–3)

Others 'gradually ascended the emotional ladder [from disappointment] to haughty indignation, and finally to that state of stubbornness where the mind is locked like the jaws of an enraged bulldog', in Maya Angelou's phrase. And through her much-abused heroine Celie in *The Color Purple*, Alice Walker celebrates the power of love at its regenerative work of healing pain and restoring the joy of life:

. . . It sort of like you know what, she say, grinning and rubbing high upon my thigh.

Shug! I say.

Oh, she say. God love all them feelings. That's some of the best stuff God did. And when you know God loves 'em you enjoys 'em a lot more. You can just relax, go with everything, and praise God by liking what you like.

God don't think it dirty? I ast.

Naw, she say. God made it. Listen, God love everything you love . . . I think it pisses God off if you walk by the color purple in a field somewhere and don't notice it.

What it do when it pissed off? I ast.

Oh, it make something else. People think pleasing God is all God cares about. But any fool living in the world can see it always trying to please us back. (p. 167)

As this shows, black women writers do not allow their characters to sink under their tribulations. Their vivid humour and appetite for life are brilliantly illustrated through the frank exuberance of Rita Mae Brown's *Rubyfruit Jungle* (1973), with its luscious, lyrical allusion to the female genitalia in the very title. Dancing, singing, quarrelling, loving, and just living, these characters throng off the pages and crowd the reader's mind with their colour, vitality, and bustle. There can be no going back to the thin gruel that has passed for 'fine writing' in these islands, in the absence of more satisfying fare.

CHAPTER 7

The sex war

She felt her outlines waver; she felt herself trapped forever in the reflection in Walser's eyes. For one moment, just one moment, Fevvers suffered the worst crisis of her life:

'Am I fact? Or am I fiction? Am I what I know I am? or am I what he thinks I am?'

Angela Carter, *Nights at the Circus* (1984)

To emancipate woman is to refuse to confine her to the relations she bears to man.

Simone de Beauvoir, *The Second Sex* (1952)

'Free women,' said Anna wryly. 'They still define us in terms of relationships with men, even the best of them.'

'Well, *we* do, don't we?' said Molly, rather tart. 'Well, it's awfully hard not to,' she amended hastily.

Doris Lessing, *The Golden Notebook* (1962)

No matter how hard women work on their relations to society and to its major thematic preoccupations, sooner or later they necessarily return to the question of that between the sexes. The theme of what can only be called the sex war has received attention from many of this century's most individual, distinguished, and distinctive women writers. It is, of course, hardly new. In *Mary*, her novel of 1788, Mary Wollstonecraft wrote movingly of the situation of a woman forced into marriage, who finds it so intolerable that she clear-sightedly welcomes death in preference:

The time too quickly elapsed, and she gave him her hand – the struggle was almost more than she could endure. She tried to appear calm; time mellowed her grief, and mitigated her torments; but when her husband would take her hand, or mention anything like love, she would instantly feel a sickness, a faintness at her heart, and wish involuntarily, that the earth

111

would open up and swallow her . . . Her delicate state of health
did not promise long life. In moments of solitary sadness a gleam
of joy would dart across her mind – She thought that she was
hastening to that world *where there is neither marrying*, nor giving in
marriage. (pp. 67–8)

Notice that there is nothing specifically objectionable about the
individual male here – it is the *institution* of marriage, and all the
unbearable social pressures to conform to it, that literally kill Mary
in heart, mind and body. Over a hundred years later in 1899 Kate
Chopin tried to tell the story of *The Awakening*, an account of a
young wife who cannot accept that 'it is a holy privilege [for
women] to efface themselves as individuals' within the service of
wifehood. She also resists the loss of her individuality consequent
upon being swallowed up by motherhood, declaring, 'I would give
my life for my children, but I would not give myself.' *The Awakening*
proved too much for the contemporary American readership.
Greeted with a barrage of scorn, derision and shock on all sides, it
was overwhelmed with hostility and sank into an obscurity from
which it was not rescued until the 1960s.

A British woman writer of the same epoch enjoyed considerably
more success with her attacks upon male institutions and the
masculine mode of society, largely because her ironic tone and
oblique method avoided laying any direct blame at the door of the
men. Indeed, throughout her work, Ivy Compton-Burnett
deliberately blurs the elaborate and carefully erected distinctions
between the sexes, as a further means of attacking the whole social
structure of sex distinction with its implicit hierarchy of superior
and inferior.

It is the continued implication of Ivy Compton-Burnett's writing
that each sex is capable of almost all aspects of the behaviour of the
other. Sexual stereotypes therefore are usually the first, last and
intermediate resort of the scoundrel, susceptible as they are to
unimaginable permutations and manipulations, and hence are to
be regarded mainly as battle stations in the sex war, rather than as
relating to any kind of 'reality'. The struggles for dominance for
which her novels are famous are invariably sexual in nature. Her
potent females are those whose drives have been perverted into
masculine forms in a world where female drive as such is not
sanctioned, or at the least has not yet found a socially acceptable
form. Happy marriages, simple contented liaisons, are unknown in
the Compton-Burnett universe, so stark, so unblinking, so Swiftian
even, is her assessment of the gaping discrepancy between form
and content in human relationships. Those who believe that they

love, or are loved, are almost invariably exposed as being hideously deceived and self-deceived. This devastating cynicism makes Ivy Compton-Burnett one of the most radical of writers on the theme of sex situations in society, although, relishing the irony, she enjoyed a reputation as a Jane Austenish old thing writing quaintly and wittily of the days of yesteryear. Her method of undermining received notions of behaviour, and of illustrating the embattled nature of sexual relations, is to show the machinery of sexual convention in its full traditional motion, and then to startle us with the logical and usually appalling outcome.

A typical example of this method is Sophia Stace in *Brothers and Sisters* (1950). This female tyrant, who later comes to occupy every nook and cranny of the novel she inhabits, is in the beginning slipped almost surreptitiously into our view as an unremarkable model of conventional daughterhood. The author's first concern is with the father who has shaped Sophia's ideas and manners:

> Andrew Stace was accustomed to say, that no man had ever despised him, and no man had ever broken him in. The omission of woman from his statement was due to his omission of her from his conception of executive life. (p.1)

It is precisely this that the book sets out to rectify. We are shown how Sophia is educated in the techniques of tyranny and bullying by the daily behaviour of her father; we see, too, how the fact that she is female gives her an early grounding in devious methods of obtaining the results which her father achieves by head-on collision – 'she took the method of gaining his esteem, of suppression of her character, and assumption of a sprightliness not her own' (pp. 5–6). Later in her life, trembling like so many of Ivy Compton-Burnett's characters on the edge of a terrible paranoia, Sophia is to exact from her own family every penny of the tribute she has been forced to pay to her father's blind egotism. Her whole life is directed towards undermining her father's decision to leave the family house to his adopted son rather than to her:

> Moreton Edge is not for a woman. The girl will have what will keep her in comfort if she doesn't marry, and make her husband respect her if she does. What more does a woman want? What more can she do with for herself or her family? What is the use of making a woman not a woman? I have never seen it work. (p. 8)

The revelation that Christian is Andrew's illegitimate as well as adopted son does little to mitigate the offence from Sophia's point of view; nor does it disturb her conviction that she was right to marry the man who proves to be her half-brother, so overwhelming is the compulsion to outwit man the enemy by holding on to Moreton Edge.

Even when Ivy Compton-Burnett's male characters appear to praise, understand, or defend women, they usually do so from motives of self-seeking. Duncan Edgeworth, the almost sadistically insensitive and pompous father of *A House and Its Head* (1935) poses the radical moral question, 'Why should a woman's youth be spotless, any more than a man's?' But this unexpected upsurge of feminism has to be taken in the overall context of his repeatedly expressed contempt for 'old maids' and 'brats'. Eventually it emerges that he is only taking this attitude to exculpate himself from past peccadilloes and to get his favourite daughter, Sybil, out of a scrape. This girl's name, with its echo of Disraeli's 'Two Nations', the rich and the poor, in his novel *Sybil* (1845), inevitably awakens an acute sense of the cruelty of social divisions along with its more obvious foreboding implications of witchcraft, evil, and supernatural capacity.

All this later takes on a grim relevance as she reveals herself to be accomplished in lying, scheming, and eventually child murder. It is entirely in keeping with the hidden recesses of Duncan's nature that she is his preferred child. Further, his treatment of his first wife in her last illness, his refusal to allow the dying woman to remain in bed and so miss the family breakfast, his failure to acknowledge even that she is ill until she has slipped beyond his grasp, all evoke with bitter poignancy the thousand nameless cruelties of traditional masculine government.

Nowhere does Ivy Compton-Burnett hold out any hope of change or improvement in men's attitudes or women's consequent situations. The bland bullying Miles Mowbray (note the parody of long-standing English autocracy through the use of the family name of the Dukes of Norfolk) speaks for many generations, kinds, and degrees of men in the following:

> Of course women are not equal to men. They are not so strong or intelligent. That is, they have their own kind of intelligence. And the more important kind, of course. But they are not the same. Naturally they are different. Yes, you may laugh, Ellen. I know you think you are cleverer than I am. And you may be, for all I can say. Of course you are. We all recognise it. And if there is anyone who does so, it is your husband. (*A Father and His Fate*, p. 11)

The ultimate accolade, the masculine seal of approval. There are times when Ivy Compton-Burnett almost convinces her reader that the race of men deserve every drop of the shrivelling caustic irony she pours on them. With her insistent savage irony, her scorn of convention, this ultraconventional writer who observed so scrupulously most of the country-house traditions of English fiction, was arguably one of the most political of writers on the twentieth-century scene. Her radicalism is expressed through a series of attacks upon figures of authority and accepted social structures: her general feeling was that no person or institution can stand up to scrutiny. The theme of equality was central to her work and her acute sense of the lives of the underprivileged was expressed through her pitiless censure of the egomaniacal self-absorption of the well-to-do.

This is not to say that Ivy Compton-Burnett ever really understood or cared warmly for the servants in her fiction, or for those in real life for that matter. This is exemplified by one of her memories of her girlhood:

I remember a thing happening that couldn't possibly happen now. The manservant used to roar out the hymns in a very loud voice, and the cook – that particular cook we had then was a woman my mother was afraid of, my mother was a woman who feared neither God nor man, but she did fear that cook – and that cook liked singing. She was a Plymouth brother, and she was always singing hymns, and one of her temperance hymns was 'I'll drink his water bright'. Well, she used to like these weekly prayers, you see, and she used to love singing, but the manservant drowned her voice and my mother said, 'Harvey, try to keep your voice back a little, you drown the women's voices.' 'Very good 'um', he said. And my mother said, 'Harvey, don't say very good 'um. I'm always telling you to say, "Yes, very good 'um".' I always remember that scene. (Kay Dick, *Ivy and Stevie*, pp. 4–5)

There is an unmistakable tone of pleased amusement at the antics of the lower primates in the human zoo here. But Ivy Compton-Burnett was even harder on those who regarded themselves as the higher of the species. She consistently suggested that if those who have had every advantage of wealth and position do not behave in a civilised way, how much less should be expected of those who have little, yet live in daily contact with those who have too much. Her servants have a further importance too as metaphors for the enduring human situation. All are by the nature

of society imprisoned in some hierarchical structure, 'superior' to
some and 'inferior' to others. It is how the individual defines
'superior' and 'inferior' which defines them.

Ivy Compton-Burnett illustrates this point through her presentation of various social groups which have traditionally commanded
respect. Foremost among those to feel the lash are the purveyors of
Christianity. Many critics have remarked on the incidence of
creepy clergymen in her work. Notice the malicious suggestiveness
of the naming of Oscar Jekyll, the vicar without faith in *A House and
Its Head* (1935). The pompous and untrustworthy Edward in
Brothers and Sisters (1950) is another suggestion that those whom the
faithful look to for guidance are themselves stumbling in the dark.
They are inevitably hypocrites, because in the nature of their work
they are pretending to know the way. Ivy spares neither the
deceiver nor the deceived; neither corrupt shepherd nor faithful
sheep merit anything but the lash. Like Mary McCarthy, Ivy
Compton-Burnett unflinchingly explored the idea that 'religion is
for peasants', and suggests that anyone who promulgates it is
serving themselves under cover of the fiction of serving God. Such
a one is the spurious, sickly-sweet Beatrice Fellows in *A House and
Its Head*, who makes a life's work out of going round her 'fellows'
with her 'simple little messages of Christianity', whether people
want them or not.

This disregard of the true need of others in favour of a scheme of
belief preferred by the giver, links the clergy with another
prominent social group in the Compton-Burnett universe, as the
title of her 1925 novel indicates: *Pastors and Masters*. The teachers in
this novel are assessed in terms of the two wings of their profession:
they are seen as creators, and hence are compared with writers;
they are also considered as spiritual mentors, and, in this role, they
are compared with vicars (there are two writers and two vicars in
the novel). The central character, mockingly called Herrick after
the playful Cavalier poet, is both a writer, and, as the owner of the
school, a teacher too; he insists on reading the lesson every
morning in assembly, to reinforce his religious and pastoral
function. But his claims in all these departments are shown to be
hollow, and his intellectual hypocrisy is exposed when he attempts
to plagiarise another man's work.

Hollowness is in fact the general failing of these educators. Every
character in the novel engaged in the care of the young is shown to
be a shoddy fake imposing upon the credulity of the ignorant. Here
Ivy Compton-Burnett demonstrates the meanness, intellectual
poverty, and reflex sarcasm of the inadequate teacher:

Well, this is a nice thing! A nice thing this schoolmastering! Up
at seven and in a room with a black fire. . . . I should have
thought it might have occurred to one out of forty boys to poke
it. . . . (p. 7)

Another dreadful example is presented in the person of Richard
Bumpus, an Oxford Fellow, and another plagiarist (dare we
suspect Ivy of indecent punning intent in the naming of this
homosexual?). Finally it is worth observing that none of Ivy
Compton-Burnett's teachers has more than an imperfect or half-
realised relationship with anyone of either sex; teachers are, she
suggests, incomplete human beings.

But school, as one of her characters reflects in *The Mighty and
Their Fall*, 'cannot have the fine edge of family life'. It is in and
through the family that Ivy Compton-Burnett sees the socialisation
of the individual being accomplished, at whatever private cost. Ivy
Compton-Burnett's nineteenth-century settings are deceptive here –
it is the mythic substructure of the fiction which is the important
element, linking Greek tragedy with Victorian Surrey to demonstrate the author's profound sense that the modern family has lost
none of its primitive power to damage and deform.

Ivy herself always asserted that what she called 'the important
things', such as 'human nature', do not change. Social and
personal forces act upon individuals now as they did in the '1885'
which is her perennial timescape. She felt too that her work had
the permanent relevance of any achieved work of art. She told Kay
Dick in conversation, 'I haven't written any rubbish,' and further
claimed to be 'quite perfect morally'. As this suggests, she saw her
work as both relevant and important, and herself as concerned
with the most serious aspects of human life, good and evil. She
insisted that 'people have a way of not coming out well in a
temptation. They generally behave quite as ill as they can.' Against
this 'you must recognise certain moral laws. Otherwise you
couldn't have any human life, any literature or anything.' These
statements, terse as they are, fully indicate the range and scope of
her vision of life.

This sense of sexual and political as symbiotic in contemporary
society is one that Ivy Compton-Burnett has shared with several
other important women writers of the twentieth century. A rather
more light-hearted study of the process is to be found in Iris
Murdoch's Annette, the younger of the heroines of *The Flight from
the Enchanter* (1956). Of all Iris Murdoch's novels this is the most
explicit 'about' the sex war, and interest has mainly centred on the
lurid tale of Rosa and her twin Draculae, the Polish brothers, not

to mention the dotty ancient suffragettes and the complementary
male machinations of Mischa Fox and Calvin Blick. But the part
played by Annette is a substantial contribution to the theme of
woman's imprisonment in conventional roles. In a novel where the
other women characters are successively essaying politics, work,
mothering, man-trapping, and self-beautification in their search for
fulfilled womanhood, and where in addition they all stand
measured against the long shadow of Rosa Luxemburg, Annette is
the perpetual girl-child.

She is first introduced to us in connection with her expensive
finishing school, which draws attention to her unfinished childhood,
her little-girl name, her habit of running and skipping, and her
juvenile vocabulary ('beastly', 'horrid'). Even her systematic
acquisition of clothes and jewels is not the mark of a mature
female, but a pathetic reminder of her unvalued and unsatisfactory
childhood, and an attempt to stabilise her environment at a
pleasant level. Despite a gush of sentimental pity for 'the poor
Minotaur' when she encounters his story, Annette is blind to the
real implications of this dark and ancient tale, as she is also to the
feelings of those around her. Not only is she in the grip of the
narcissism of adolescence; the fish and mermaid imagery with
which she is associated conveys her cold, half-developed intersex
quality. This is reinforced by the fact that she is half of yet another
of Iris Murdoch's terrible twins, and as a result, through her close
love for and dependence on her brother, only half a person.

But Annette is also a nubile young woman and it is in her efforts
to define herself in this respect that she runs into trouble. There is
about her a strong suggestion of the capricious princess of folklore
and fairy tale: for her the 'essence of freedom' lies in the notion that
people are ceaselessly toiling for her benefit. When Annette is
surprised at the dressmaker's by the novel's central character and
source of power, Mischa Fox, Nina the dressmaker removes the
half-made dress from her, leaving her in her underwear before him
as if she were a child or a dummy. It is not made clear whether
Nina is trying to neutralise Annette's sexuality out of jealousy, or if
she wishes to protect the younger woman from this latter-day
Volpone. Either way, Annette is not to be deterred from spreading
her wings. She counters Nina's move by making a bold but
essentially schoolgirl pass at Mischa – 'Will you take me in your
car to my next appointment?'?– the last phrase, like the sea-green
brocade dress for which she is being fitted, an attempt to imitate
what she takes to be the aura of the sophisticated worldly woman.
Later, in a more down-to-earth sexual situation with Rainborough,
she wavers between the adolescent warily scenting out the

possibility of adult irony, and the female entirely at ease with the trite conventions of womanhood: '"I don't know," said Annette, "I'm not much good at anything." She smiled in a helpless feminine way.'

As the situation develops along traditional lines, Annette's poise increases. Rainborough's laboured and inexpert grope brings out her superficial expertise, and she is quite in command, even ironic at his expense – 'I'm afraid I can't recall your Christian name,' she says as he attempts to insert his hand into her blouse. What she values, however, as Iris Murdoch makes quite clear, is the conventional structure of what is evidently for her a highly conventional occasion. She submits, 'doll-like', with the traditional token opposition – 'John, please!' – as he exposes her breasts.

But she is not yet woman enough to take any responsibility for the mutuality of the experience. What enrages her, and provokes her to curtail sharply his further advances, is his pompous insistence that she is 'making this scene' as much as he is. Unable to tolerate this crude breaking of the convention, Annette unexpectedly reverts to type, becomes 'a powerful fish' in his grasp, cold, sinewy, all eyes. But this upsurge of her mermaid self exhausts her, and when an unexpected visitor arrives to disturb the amorous proceedings, she submits, doll-like again, to Rainborough's panic, and is thrust unresistingly into the china cupboard (surely an echo of the famous 'china' scene in *The Country Wife* here?). Passive, submissive, she remains there throughout the long colloquy between Rainborough and his visitor, and even then, recovered half-naked and half-dead from the cupboard, weeping and crushed, she still feels the age-old female compulsion to exonerate the male and shoulder the blame: 'It wasn't your fault, John.' But John, not surprisingly, has gone off the boil, and feels nothing for Annette so strongly as an intense weariness and desire to be rid of her.

None of Iris Murdoch's riddling morals is easily drawn from the gorgeously lush and fleshy symbolism of her imaginative landscape. But this seems to be one of her plainer lessons for ladies, that the careful cultivation of the appropriate role mannerisms is nothing but a waste of time. Men are not really attracted or moved by what has been so effortfully acquired and produced. Annette is linked in this with the well-groomed 'Harpies' of Rainborough's Civil Service section. As long abundant hair always serves in Iris Murdoch's work as a symbol of natural vitality, the 'Harpies' are sharply caricatured through their artificial and unnaturally set hairdos adopted in compliance with prevailing beauty conventions.

Yet there is no easy escape from the tyranny of the convention that marriage and a respectable life within the existing social structures are a woman's only and true destiny. Beverley Gasner cast a cold eye over the process in *Girls' Rules* (1969, p. 6):

> Don't be sorry for mousy girls. Marina instructed herself, meanly; they all turn into rats eventually. Marriage does the job, the man, children, eighteen of monogrammed everything. The mouse puts on muscle; now she can put other people in their places. For example, she can say to her zero mouse-mate, Let's not have the Yoo-hoos this time; she's such a pill. And the male loser says happily, Sure, leave 'em out, who needs 'em because he, too, must have some old scores to settle, or why did he marry a mouse in the first place?

Gasner's heroine, Marina, is not presented as a habitually unkind or dismissive girl. But she is rendered negative and destructive by the gulf that she perceives between her personal standards and society's expectations. She is too critical to make the sort of marriage which she sees her friends all around settling down to – marriage which simply intensifies in its participants their worst and most anti-social characteristics, so that 'mice' inevitably become 'rats'. The reader is readily brought to sympathise with her contempt for the vacuous ostentation of suburban marriage ('monogrammed everything'), and to feel that Marina rightly disdains both the socialite hostess and the identikit guests the Yoo-hoos (Yahoos?).

Yet the passage is acute with jealousy and the longing for what is censured. It seems desirable to be able to 'put other people in their places'; it assumes a place of your own from which to operate the social mechanisms of condescension. For Marina's education and her bachelor graduate life in New York have not freed her from even the most basic dictates of a restrictive social structure, whose workings she glimpses as she suffers from, but whose decrees form a series of inescapable absolutes for her. All her thinking is debased by assumptions of competition and acquisition. She automatically reduces any less lively female to the sub-human level of 'mouse', and stamps on the temptation to feel pity for this creature on the grounds that she will turn not into a human being like herself, but into a rat, an enemy and super-competitor. Released and empowered, the mouse demonstrates how well it has learned the lessons of aggression and competition; and herself a victim of the same syndrome Marina never questions that this must always happen. Finally she judges the male partner by these values – he is a loser by definition if he is married, and to such a specimen – yet paradoxically even he in his inferiority can convey the sacred status; 'marriage', the infallible social bromide, 'does the job'. This crude phrase is used to indicate both Marina's contempt and her desperation. The only defence she can muster for her beleaguered ego is the petty sartorial revenge: 'Celia ought to know that big high collars and short necks do not belong together': a line direct from the world of women's magazines, those immensely powerful shapers of attitudes and creators of values which in every way reflect and regulate the consumer nightmare which is Marina's existence.

As this suggests, marriage, however much desired, is paradoxically not a prospect that women can view with much enthusiasm. And contrary to popular belief, women do not necessarily 'grow into' or 'settle down' to it:

My mother, in the acuteness of her distress after my father left her, spent her nights for a time with Henry Whitechapel. Or so he told me later, and I have no reason to disbelieve him. There was certainly no point in asking her. Mother would have denied it and believed her denial, whether she had or whether she hadn't. At a time when women's instincts were so much at a variance with the rules of society, such localised amnesias were only to be expected. But was this episode out of character; or was it that her whole life otherwise was out of character? Was my mother, from the age of thirty to the age of seventy, living out a part that did not suit her at all? I believe the latter. (Fay Weldon, *Praxis*, 1978, p. 35)

Interestingly, this sense of not knowing, of groping for bearings, was anticipated, like so much else, by Virginia Woolf: 'the ancient consciousness of women, charged with suffering and sensibility and for so many ages dumb, seems in them to have brimmed and overflowed and uttered a demand for something – they scarcely know what – for something that is perhaps incompatible with the facts of human existence' (*Collected Essays*, 1972, I, 204). For 'the facts of human existence', of course, read women's subordination to men. This issue surfaced with particular vividness in the 1960s, as women writers began to roll around their minds the ideas of the new women's movement filtering over from America. Amongst the earliest and still one of the most profound responses to this deep disturbance of accepted ideas was Doris Lessing's *The Golden Notebook* (1962). With meticulous precision she reported her heroine's questioning of everything she had been brought up to believe, and the conflicts that this provoked:

Willi said, 'Things are different for men and women. They
always have been and they always will be' . . . We had had this
quarrel before; we knew all the phrases either was likely to
use – the weakness of women, the property sense of men, women
in antiquity, etc., etc., etc., *ad nauseam.* (p. 906)

The conflicts, however, are not confined to tensions between men
and women. The heroine, Anna, finds herself also at odds with her
friend Molly, for the long shadow men inevitably cast falls between
them too:

> If I join in now, in a what's-wrong-with-men session, then I
> won't go home, I'll stay for lunch and all afternoon, and Molly
> and I will feel warm and friendly, all barriers gone. And when
> we part, there'll be a sudden resentment, a rancour – because,
> after all, our real loyalties are always to men, and not to
> women . . . I want to be done with it all, finished with the men
> vs. women business, all the complaints and reproaches and the
> betrayals. Besides, it's dishonest. We've chosen to live in a
> certain way, knowing the penalties, or if we didn't we know now,
> so why whine and complain? . . . and besides, if I'm not careful,
> Molly and I will descend into a kind of twin old-maidhood,
> where we sit around saying to each other, 'Do you remember
> that man, what-was-his-name said that insensitive thing, it must
> have been in 1947 . . . (p. 46).

This is precisely the sort of episode which lends a bitter irony to
Anna's efforts to make herself a 'free woman'. Here she is shown as
resisting intimacy with a female friend, while elsewhere she is all
too ready to enter into the most unpromising liaison with a man.
The women are further divided by a false consciousness of each
other's lives: to the comment of another friend, Marion, 'You are
what I want to be – you're free, and you have lovers, and you do as
you like,' Anna replies, 'I'd like to be married. I don't like living
like this.' For to Anna, women can never be free while they are still
prisoners of the old dependency on men:

> . . . it was over a year since Paul had left her, and everything she
> did, said or felt still referred to him. Her life was shaped around
> a man who would not return to her. She must liberate herself.
> This was an intellectual decision unbacked by moral energy. She
> was listless – flat. It was as if Paul had taken with him not only
> her capacity for joy, but also her will. (p. 263)

When the man withdraws his presence, his comfort and companionship, the woman almost ceases to exist; she needs the continual
validation of a male in a society which decrees that she is nothing
on her own. All the problems of Lessing's Anna, psychological,
sexual, social, and professional, originate in this sense of denial.
She suffers a diminishing of her sense of self-esteem which is
particularly expressed through sharp feelings of sexual inadequacy.
In this difficult phase of her life, these increasingly painful
developments force her to turn more and more in on herself.

From the outset a rather taut and wary creature, Anna becomes
progressively more constricted. She suffers terrible anxiety, but
cannot act to relieve it. She is utterly the prisoner of her deep and
humiliating dependency upon men – better a tame homosexual to
share her flat than no man at all – and consequently is led to take
males as lovers irrespective of their reliability or kindness.
Successive failures of love then lead her to internalise what she sees
as inevitable, her rejection by men. Masculine hostility internalised
becomes female masochism, working away in the woman's
imagination to confirm belief in the repugnant nature of women
and women's sexuality:

> I remembered Nelson telling me how sometimes he looked at his
> wife's body and hated it for its femaleness; he hated it because of
> the hair in the armpits and around the crotch. Sometimes, he
> said, he saw his wife as a sort of spider, all clutching arms and
> legs around a hairy central devouring mouth. I sat on my bed
> and I looked at my thin white legs and thin white arms, and at
> my breasts. My wet sticky centre seemed disgusting, and when I
> saw my breasts all I could think of was how they were when they
> were full of milk, and instead of this being pleasurable, it was
> revolting. (p. 254) *Golden Notebook*

Certain critics, with obvious satisfaction in some cases (see
Burgess, ch. 1), read this, and other women's fictions of the 1960s
and after, as a crushing indictment of the new 'free woman'. To
them she appeared ill-equipped to face the troubling wastes of a
solitary existence. The price she paid for her 'freedom' was counted
in loss and desolation. There have, of course, been earlier
delineations of the psycho-neurotic heroine; Fanny in *Mansfield Park*
is a touching study of how it feels to be nervous and sad, and
Gwendolen, in *Daniel Deronda* (1874–6), nursing her 'heart-sores',
faces a life 'without pleasure or hope of pleasure' after her marriage
to Grandcourt.

But recent women's fiction, in its search for the source and location of female identity, in its contingent consideration of female weakness and strength, has made a detailed study of the causes and sources of women's debility and neurosis. To those who prefer their women simpler and straighter, the new woman appears a gloomy soul. To others, she presents a realistic picture of a modern woman caught in the trap between realism and romance, painfully unlearning the lessons of adolescence absorbed just as much from *Jane Eyre* as from Mills and Boon. For dark and fascinating men tend not to appear too often over the typewriter, the shop counter, or the washing machine, and all too soon the female horizon is bounded by Superbore or Superbastard rather than by Superman. Margaret Drabble has described criticism of her concentration on the daily realities of life as depressing, an alliance with what she humorously calls 'the "nose-in-the-washing-machine" school of fiction'. Many of Margaret Drabble's heroines do throw off the domestic trammels in favour of some version of personal freedom, however it may be defined. Occasionally, though, this represents the conventional provision of a happy ending too closely to be convincing. What genuine hope is Rose left with at the end of *The Needle's Eye*, for instance?

Other women have taken a far bleaker view of women's prospects in contemporary society and men's responsibility for their suffering. Writers as different as Jenifer Dawson in *The Ha-Ha* (1961), and Sylvia Plath in *The Bell Jar* (1963) have dealt memorably with the theme of women's alienation and mental distress. Among those who have numbered and inspected the pieces as they drop off the crumbling female ego is Penelope Mortimer. Her heroine of *The Pumpkin Eater* (1962) has little autonomy from the first – a bewildered girlhood is succeeded by a badgered wifehood in which everybody else has more edge and conviction, more drive and purpose, than she has. She is overborne by her father's 'pipe down' when she objects to her three eldest children being sent off to boarding school in the interests of woman-excluding masculine solidarity – 'I'm not going to have you crushing the boy with responsibility from the word go.' The father hopes that the fourth husband, Jake, will succeed with her where he has failed – 'It's time she had a firm hand on her tiller' (note the parody of strong masculine jargon, with its implied innuendo, nudge and wink).

It is the centre of the heroine's problem of living that she can express none of the resentment she feels: 'I burned with anger, but dully.' In a final spasm of submission she consents to a termination of pregnancy followed by a sterilisation, only to be confronted by the unbearable irony of the pregnancy of her husband's mistress,

an irony compounded by her realisation that the girl would have
finished with Jake had his wife's pregnancy continued. The final
submission is to the husband's values and terms of living, which he
defines as 'necessarily defective, vicious, careless, an inevitable
time of activity between two deaths'. After crisis, illness, flight, and
retreat, the heroine reflects, 'I was no longer frightened of him. I
accepted him at last, because he was inevitable.'

The 'inevitability' of women's dependence on men, with all the
misery and denial of autonomy that it entails, was explored again
by Penelope Mortimer in *The Home* (1971). Joyce Carol Oates
similarly analysed a woman's colapse into madness and despair,
complicated in the case of her heroine, Karen, by the lethal
cocktail of religious and sexual guilt:

> Her early days in the hospital, in a locked room, Karen had
> spent in a delirium of prayer and sexual excitement, murmuring
> prayer after prayer until her frenzy turned to thoughts about
> Shar – she would cry aloud at the memory of his body, his
> muscles and sweating back, his clenched teeth, his strong thighs.
> She could talk of nothing else to the nurses, who pretended
> professional disapproval. During the first month – which she
> remembered, now, as strangely dark, sunless, and stifling with
> stale air – Karen had refused to go outside, refused to leave her
> room except when forced (when she would turn sweetly and
> viciously abject), refused to talk coherently to the doctor in the
> hopes that she would decide she was hopelessly insane.
> Somehow she knew about the ward in the other wing and had
> begged to be taken there. 'I'm insane, completely insane,' she
> had screamed at the doctor, 'why don't you believe me? What do
> I have to do? What do I have to do?' Later, allowed to come
> shyly onto the sun porch in the company of an attendant, a girl
> her own age, Karen had pretended fear and excitement and had
> rattled the pages of a newspaper so that everyone looked up at
> her. She had smiled naively at them. In the days that followed,
> dissatisfied with them, angry because they did not stare at her
> continuously, Karen had squirmed to show off her body, had
> talked softly to one of the men – a harried-looking salesman
> about to be released – and had ended by upsetting him so that
> he fled. She had gone to another man, pushing the attendant
> away, and told him she wanted him – she wanted him to make
> love to her. Before she could be persuaded to leave she had cried
> hysterically, 'You don't want me! None of you want me! You
> won't let me make you happy!' (Joyce Carol Oates, *With
> Shuddering Fall*, 1964, pp. 296–7)

Since then women from all over the world have been lifting up their voices to add to the chorus of protest against the social dispensations which are supposed to make women so happy and fulfilled and yet which so often drive them to extremes of anger, madness, and despair. 'A man could never have written this book,' said Ingmar Bergman of Marie Cardinal's *The Words to Say It* (1985), commending its compelling account of a withdrawn and suicidal woman in flight not only from the horrific treatment she is prescribed for a cure, but also from her own former married self, a concept also investigated in Maxine Hong Kingston's *The Woman Warrior* (1975), 'on being Chinese and a woman'. Female *Angst* and alienation from the all-pervading structures of male domination are expressed with no less anguish in the 'advanced' world; Marge Piercy's *Woman on the Edge of Time* (1976) pulsates with the passion of its treatment of madness, mental violence, and no-holds-barred observations on male/female relationships (nowhere more so than when she speaks with the clarity of the insane), while Margaret Atwood bleakly surveys the total wreck of the female in *Surfacing* (pp. 124–5) and *Survival* (p. 212) (both 1972):

> I'd allowed myself to be cut in two. Woman sawn apart in a wooden crate, wearing a bathing suit, smiling, a trick done with mirrors. I read it in a comic book; only with me there had been an accident and I came apart. The other half, the one locked away, was the only one that could live; I was the wrong half, detached, terminal. I was nothing but a head, or, no, something minor like a severed thumb; numb . . .

> They can't be trusted. They'll mistake me for a human being, a naked woman wrapped in a blanket: possibly that's what they've come here for, if it's running around, ownerless, why not take it. They won't be able to tell what I really am. But if they guess my true form, identity, they will shoot me or bludgeon in my skull and hang me by the feet from a tree.

In the 'advanced' world, the battleground of the sex war is now the psyche of the individual woman. Elsewhere it is still all too often her body and almost every other aspect of her life. In the Islamic world, women denied autonomy are at best passive subjects of misfortunes for which they are not responsible, at worst readily victimised by those around them able to exploit their cultured helplessness. In Hanan al-Shaykh's *The Story of Zahra* (1986), the heroine is in a pitiful plight from the outset. As we see her used as a cover by her mother for her own infidelity, seduced by a married man, and willy-nilly married off, we are forced to confront the down-to-earth reality of the female victim. Hanan al-Shaykh refuses to sentimentalise her stark and simple tale with a Hollywood ending. Although Zahra is granted a brief respite and the fugitive promise of happiness, the tragic conclusion has the authentic integrity of a refusal to compromise the indictment of the society's treatment of its women.

Hanan al-Shaykh's portrayal of the powerlessness and bewilderment of the woman who suffers under a traditional patriarchy is poignantly illustrated again in the work of the Egyptian writer Ahdaf Soueif. In *Aisha* (1983) she describes at length the ritual accompanying the wedding of the fifteen-year-old Zeina. First an old woman known as the Mashta comes to prepare the bride, to make her body smooth for her bridegroom. Using special paste she rips off the hair of Zeina's legs and thighs, armpits and arms, and upper lip. Then despite her resistance the Mashta, aided by Zeina's aunt and grandmother, spread the paste on her pubic hair:

> It was fire. I tried to struggle up, but they held me down, and the Mashta went on spreading the paste and tearing it off while I cried and screamed until I was completely clean. Then they heated water and poured it into a large brass tub and I sat in it stark naked while the Mashta rubbed me all over with a rough cloth, trilling her joy-cries all the while.

The next day the girl has recovered a little from this ordeal, helped by a beautiful pink dress with sequins and a veil. But her respite is short-lived. Armed with a gun, her uncle takes her to the bridal chamber, where her aunt and her grandmother are waiting, along with her new husband, the middle finger of his right hand strangely bandaged as if he has injured it. Her aunt tells her to take her knickers off and lie down on the floor:

> 'Come on, girl, your uncles are waiting.'
> 'Tell him to get out,' I said, pointing at the man.
> 'The girl is mad,' said my aunt.
> 'He's your husband,' said my grandmother gently.
> 'I won't undress in front of him.' . . .
> Suddenly the four women surrounded me and pinned me to the floor . . . My aunt was pinching my thighs, trying to get me to open up. . . . My uncle hammered on the door: 'What in hell's going on in there? Curse you all. Shall I come in and shoot the bitch?' . . . My aunt bent down suddenly and bit my upper thigh so hard I jerked it away and they immediately pulled my legs

apart and then *he* stepped forward and squatted between them . . . he forced his bandaged finger into me, working it round and round and in and out as I choked and screamed. Finally he took it out. The bandage was soaked in blood. . . . I heard my uncle fire his gun into the air and my other uncles' guns answering it . . . and the joy-cries filled the air and through the door I could see them unwrapping the bandage from around his finger. My uncle wound it round his head, blood and all, and danced slowly and proudly into the crowd, using his gun like a cane to dance with and calling out 'Our Honour, Our daughter's Honour, Our family's Honour'.

As Angela Carter drily asks in *Nights at the Circus* (1984), 'wherein does a woman's honour reside, old chap? In her vagina or in her spirit?' Throughout her work this virtuoso writer questions masculine pretensions and the codes of a masculine society with a variety of dazzling techniques. In *Nights at the Circus*, the ex-whore Lizzie attacks marriage as 'out of the frying pan into the fire!' demanding, 'What is marriage but prostitution to one man instead of many?' (p. 21). Later the heroine, Fevvers, is given the Authorised Version of the great marriage myth:

'Marriage!' she exclaimed.
'The Prince who rescues the Princess from the dragon's lair is always forced to marry her, whether they've taken a liking to one another or not. That's the custom. And I don't doubt that custom will apply to the trapeze artist that rescues the clown. The name of this custom is a "happy ending!"'
'Marriage,' repeated Fevvers in a murmur of awed distaste.

Marriage is of course only one of the instruments through which the dominant males wage the sex war on unprepared, unarmed females, according to the experience of some women writers. For Carolyn Slaughter and Michele Roberts the Christian ideology has a lot to answer for in keeping women down. In *The Visitation* (1983), the heroine muses resentfully that 'God seems to swoop, with unerring accuracy, on those who don't want him,' so that while 'other girls read D. H. Lawrence, Henry Miller, Norman Mailer, Helen is locked into an uneasy love affair with St Teresa of Avila, Julian of Norwich, Margery Kempe, the string of women mystics down the centuries pursued by God and eventually succumbing'. Slaughter's Emily, by contrast, in *Dreams of the Kalahari* (1981), angrily resists 'booklets about Jesus' offered to her, 'thinking Oh Christ, Oh Him, he's just the world's darling, darling boy . . . boys were the darlings of the world – it made her want to spit!'

Whatever girls are, they are not the darlings of the world. And the girls who, through low social status, shortage of money, race, or any other disadvantage, are on the receiving end of what the world's darlings do to them, are just beginning to make their voices heard:

> They bank on keeping us so damn busy and tired we won't even have the idea [of standing up to them]. And they figure they got us all scared to death we'll lose our jobs or get shuffled to a different machine if we don't keep up the production . . . They don't credit us with enough smarts to see that every time they pull off some trick to up production, they're making more money and we're still in the hole. (Maureen Brady, *Folly*, 1982, p. 8)

Still in a hole – Maureen Brady's heroine speaks for the mass of the great social underclass which is the female sex. And the lower down the dominant white male's scale of values the female comes, the deeper the hole. As Rosa Guy's heroine Faith explains in *Bird at My Window* (1966), 'You know, Wade, to the white world every black girl past the tooth-ring stage is screwed.' Her experience of the social operation of sexist oppression has been harsh indeed:

> Faith had a pretty tough time of it too, as she told him later. The authorities had, from the very first, disregarded the fact that she had been sent as a charity case, and had submitted her to a physical examination usually given to delinquents, to verify their virginity, then had placed her with the delinquent girls, girls hardened from the streets about Harlem and the lower East Side. She spent the entire time there protesting she had never been 'touched.' And she had not. The only sexual experience Faith had ever had was with him, and rubbing their bodies together could never, by any stretch of the imagination, be termed intercourse. That night-long beating with its endless prayers and the terrible experience she had undergone after-wards had made Faith so sensitive and ashamed of her body that to be examined by a man, have her innocence questioned, and to be placed with a group of girls to whom sex was an everyday occurrence, touched her in the tenderest part of her. (p. 35)

It is worth remarking that Rosa Guy's account here is not 'pure fiction'. Both literature and life afford abundant evidence to support the claim of Gerda Lerner, that 'every black woman was,

by definition, a slut according to racist mythology; therefore to
assault her and exploit her sexually was not reprehensible and
carried with it none of the normal communal sanctions against
such behaviour' (*Black Women in White America*, 1972, pp. 163–4).
The virginity test described above was no historical cruelty long
abandoned in civilised modern times; but was routinely employed
within recent history. In this context as described by Rekha Basu
in 'Sexual Imperialisms: The Case of Indian Women in Britain',
Heresies 3:4, no. 12, (1981), it served to restrict immigration by
women, as well as to humiliate those who did attempt it:

> During the 1970's [virginity tests] were routinely performed by
> the UK immigration service on Indian women and other women
> of color seeking to emigrate to Great Britain. It is an outrage
> that women of color should be treated by different standards
> than white female immigrants. The British government should
> decide what is proper sexual behaviour for us.

As this shows, women writers whether of fiction or non-fiction
have at last arrived at the state of awareness where they are no
longer prepared to tolerate what Fay Weldon calls 'the old wisdom'
of male dominance of women, and all the social consequences that
proceeded from it. 'The old wisdom' never seems to have been a
good thing for women – but then, what other options did they
have?

> That was the old wisdom, when girls stayed virgins 'til they
> married, and did not waste their lives in impractical sexual
> hankerings, and admired men, and wanted their babies as proofs
> of love – and indeed, when men gave women babies, and did not
> just have their sperm snatched from out of them. Then indeed
> men did despise the girls who slept with them, who could not
> control their lust. Perhaps Dandy still belonged to the old world:
> believed the old wisdom. Girls like me you slept with, shacked
> up with for a bit, but you certainly did not marry them, let alone
> share your head with them. And when lust faded – men's lust
> does seem more prone to fade than women's – why, that was the
> time to move on, and take some decent, flirty, silly virgin out to
> dinner. She need only, of course, be a spiritual virgin: only a
> madman, these days, would insist on an actual one.
>   He did not take me to see his family, I did not meet his
> friends, he did not take me out in public – only sometimes, with
> Pete and Joe whispering and furious at the next table – to eat
> steak and asparagus downstairs in the hotel restaurant. I

thought he wanted me all for himself; I thought this was a measure of his love, not his lack of it.

He loved me. I know he did. It *was*, at first, a measure of his love. Only later, when Pete and Joe and his political friends had been at him, did it turn into a useful and prudent measure, to keep me thus so confined.

Men do like to have women confined. In a million million little suburban houses, women are still confined, by love, loyalty and lace curtains. It is not so terrible a fate. All fates are terrible. (*The President's Child*, 1982, pp. 102–3)

With 'the old wisdom' finally being called to account comes the chance to challenge Weldon's bleak assessment of female prospects, 'all fates are terrible'. Women writers are now beginning to number and name the oppressions they have suffered. One by one they are being hauled out into the light of day. And the name they most frequently answer to is Man.

CHAPTER 8

Man the enemy

'Men – they're so funny – they simply must have you,' said
Estelle. 'It's all they want – you. It's imperative they make love
to you there and then or, well, they'll die. And then whoops, it's
all over and they're not even sure why you're there, in the bed
beside them, taking up so much room. It's not that they lied to
you in the first place. It's just that they're different. We don't
want the sex all *that* much – although it's perfectly nice – we
want the love afterwards. We make love to win love, and they to
lose it'.

Sally Emerson, *Listeners* (1983), p. 38

A curse from the depths of womanhood,
Is very salt, and bitter, and good.
Elizabeth Barrett Browning, 'A Curse for a Nation',
Complete Works, ed. Charlotte Porter and Helen A. Clarke
(New York, 1900), III, 356

'The man, the male, the important person, the only person who
matters.' This phrase, from 1928, might have been taken straight
from the pages of any of the feminist publications of the 1960s and
1970s. Those who complained of the 'stridency' of that wave of
feminist protest might have reflected upon the length of time
during which women had been stating their case to an overwhelming silence from a deaf world. In all her work Jean Rhys was
to be found making weary but still spirited gestures in the direction
of the opposite sex. But with a subtler and tenderer gift than Ivy
Compton-Burnett's, she constantly directs our attention towards
the casualties in the sex war rather than the mechanisms by which
it has operated. All her work is illuminated by what Ford Madox
Ford, in his preface to her first volume of short stories, *Left Bank*
(1927), called her 'terrific . . . almost lurid! – passion for stating the
case of the underdog'. Ford saw this as part of Jean Rhys's
sympathy with the 'left bank' of life itself, the sinister, the

frightening, the out of order. Most of Jean Rhys's characters live among 'the fools and the defeated', on that shabby fringe of society where the need for money, for release, for some assertion of the self as a necessity to survival, leads to financial and social offences and hence into conflict with the organised sections of the community. These offences are not presented as morally culpable; the money difficulties in 'Vienne', the drunk and disorderly outbursts of the young West Indian girl in 'Let Them Call It Jazz', two key stories in *Left Bank*, are set down without comment as symptoms of moral, social, and personal debility, a cry for help rather than an onslaught on the fabric of society.

But it is not always necessary to outrage the bourgeoisie to find yourself in trouble, as Jean Rhys sees it. Hers is a world where it is an offence to be old, ugly, or stupid, so harsh are the operations of the established and administrative classes. 'From a French Prison', in *Left Bank*, gives us an old man and a boy waiting in a queue of visitors. The prison itself, with its bored, preoccupied guards, serves as a microcosm of a society which is both indifferent and incomprehensible to its members. The old man is confused and apprehensive; he doesn't speak the language (always a significant metaphor for this writer, whose work concentrates on the dispossessed inhabitants of several major European cities, notably Paris and London). He fails to hand in his permit, and is deprived of it in tears and fear, unable to grasp what is happening. Even in this early study of impotence, later to prove a major concern in Jean Rhys's work, the rich use of metaphor and symbol, and the evocative choice of location, are remarkable and distinctive features.

In the main, though, it is women who suffer, Jean Rhys does not indict the social system in vague or general terms. She always highlights its malfunction through some specific insult to one person in particular, almost invariably a female. Typically Jean Rhys sees woman as a creature both frail and robust. She is handicapped in the daily battle by the inferiority of her weapons and by her crippling inner sensitivity. Yet at the same time she is fortified by a determination to survive, and by a compulsion to show no outward sign of 'softness', for she believes that to show softness automatically provokes hardness in others. *Postures* (1928), republished in 1969 as *Quartet* with a regrettable loss of the social and sexual innuendo in the original title, offers the prototype Rhys anti-heroine. Marya Zelli is a bewildered expatriate whose marriage to a foreigner has robbed her of her own sense of nationality without providing a new one. Her reluctant association, through his shady and unsuccessful dealings, with the world of petty crime, precipitates her initiation into the dreary round of money shortage, letters home, appeals to men, subsistence on coffee and croissants. The dingy hotel room and the insolence of the waiters are a continuous bitter mockery of better times.

Below the surface realism of the detail, the vein of expressionism in Jean Rhys's work accounts for much of the reverberation of her writing. The linking of Marya's life with crime is a grim symbol of her 'offence' against society, her inability to fit in with the conventional, the acceptable and safe. The 'punishment', deprivation of cash, food, and a place to live is, with nightmarish circularity, a further continuation of the 'crime'. In the course of things the experience of rejection becomes internalised; in the work of Jean Rhys female self-distrust and despair finds its extremest voice. All her heroines are run down by the lives they lead to the point of serious debility, almost illness. They can only endure each day by nursing themselves through it, like invalids. Here is Sasha, in *Good Morning Midnight* (1939), returning to Paris:

> I have been here five days. I have decided on a place to eat in at midday, a place to eat in at night, a place to have my drink in after dinner. I have arranged my little life.

The stress on the 'realities' of life serves to highlight the narrator's acquaintance with the terrible underworld, the subculture inhabited by those without income, security, function. There is a dreamlike quality to the prose here, with a consistent use of dislocation techniques; the heroine looks into a mirror and sees through it the movement of her past, as in the moment of drowning. In this treatment of the sensations of the excluded, the progress through perplexity to panic, the exhausting emotional oscillation between the frenetic and the torpid, Jean Rhys is often reminiscent of Kafka. Like Kafka's K, the Rhys heroine is broken on the wheel of repeated hopeless attempts to placate the implacable, the impenetrable and inexorable machine of authority. There is, too something Kafkaesque about Jean Rhys's irony, her feeling that the whole of life is just one long unspeakable practical joke. A characteristic moment occurs when one of Marya's complacent acquaintances advises her that she should try to 'retrieve' her damaged fortunes by becoming a '*femme nue*' in a nightclub.

As this 'joke' suggests, the work of Jean Rhys has certain affinities with that of Camus. But for her the Outsider is always female. It is her recurrent, almost obsessive theme, that women are permanent and perpetual victims of masculine society. Not only will they be oppressed by individual male bullies; they are everywhere confronted by institutionalised masculine hostility in the shape of the law, the professions, the police and the bureaucrats of every country. Through the power of her analysis Jean Rhys was one of the few women writers able to make explicit the link between the sex war and the class struggle. To be female is to inhabit, without hope of escape, the lowest class of all in a sexist structure. Men may work, singly or in groups, to improve their own position on the social scale, or to revolutionise the situation which forces them to deal in these terms. Women, denied any such recourse, flit about on the edges of the 'real' world, dependent on men for maintaining even the most unsatisfactory existence within it.

One of her most deeply-felt attacks on the system is couched in the form of a mental monologue by Sasha, who has just been humiliated and dismissed by her employer. Note how the economic factor in female dependence is brought out, as well as the enfeeblement of the victim of such treatment:

Well, let's argue this out, Mr Blank. You, who represent Society, have the right to pay me four hundred francs a month. That's my market value, for I am an inefficient member of Society, slow on the uptake, uncertain, slightly damaged in the fray, there's no denying it. So you have the right to pay me four hundred francs a month, to lodge me in a small, dark room, to clothe me shabbily, to harass me with worry and monotony and unsatisfied longings till you get me to the point when I blush at a look, cry at a word. We can't all be happy, we can't all be rich, we can't all be lucky – and it would all be so much less fun if we were. Isn't that so, Mr Blank? There must be the dark background to show up the bright colours. Some must cry so that others may be able to laugh the more heartily. Sacrifices are necessary. . . . Let's say you have this mystical right to cut my legs off. But the right to ridicule me afterwards because I am a cripple – no, that I think you haven't got. And that's the right you hold most dearly, isn't it? You must be able to despise the people you exploit. But I wish you a lot of trouble, Mr Blank, and just to start off with, your damned shop's going bust. Alleluia! Did I say all this? Of course I didn't. I didn't even think it. (*Good Morning Midnight*, p. 29)

Sasha speaks here for all the exploited, all the underpaid and helpless. But it is Jean Rhys's talent to be able to change the focus from the general to the particular at will. Her portrayal of Sasha also offers some painful images of specifically female despair, like crying in the *lavabo* under the gaze of the attendant, or feeling at best 'saved, rescued, fished-up, half-drowned, out of the deep, dark river, dry clothes, hair shampooed and set'. And few women writers have so skilfully summed up the accelerating needs and anxieties of the ageing woman:

> Now, money, for the night is coming. Money for my hair, money for my teeth, money for shoes that won't deform my feet (It's not easy now to walk around in cheap shoes with very high heels), money for good clothes, money, money. The night is coming.

In Sasha's consciousness, her 'film-mind' as she calls it, males play varying but always hurtful parts. At one stage she is tormented by a whore's dream of an *apache*:

> I am in a little whitewashed room. The sun is hot outside. A man is standing with his back to me ... I am wearing a black dress, very short, and heelless slippers. My legs are bare. I am watching for the expression on the man's face when he turns round. Now he ill-treats me, now he betrays me. He often brings home other women and I have to wait on them, and I don't like that. But as long as he is alive and near me I am not unhappy. If he were to die I should kill myself.

Later she is shaken by a harsh blast of self-disgust and caricatures herself viciously as aged and sexually pretentious: 'What an amusing ten days! Positively packed with thrills. The last performance of What's-her-name And Her Boys or It Was All Due To An Old Fur Coat. Positively the last performance. . . . ' The irony in the last phrase is made clear in the novel's stunning climax in which the man who offers sex offers also death and in full awareness Sasha embraces the two experiences, which have for her always been one.

After the appearance of *Good Morning Midnight* in 1939, Jean Rhys ceased publishing for many years. Her subsequent re-emergence with the stunning *Wide Sargasso Sea* (1966) from this self-imposed silence, outlined in Carole Angier's sensitive biographical portrait, *Jean Rhys* (1985), showed that her major preoccupations had developed, but not changed. Womanhood remained, to her, a nightmare dystopia, since a deep fear and hatred motivate the behaviour of men towards women. Male seeks female as his natural adversary; sex *is* war. In the context of this theme, the wartime setting provides more than a historical backdrop to 'I Spy a

Stranger' (*Penguin Modern Stories 1*, 1969, pp. 53–67); it acts as a continuing image of the relations between the sexes, where polarisation determines opposing roles and makes impossible any sort of civilised or humane living. Male aggression reduces the female by stages to foreigner, enemy, refugee; she may resist, but she cannot win.

The victim in this case is Laura, who because of the fighting in Europe has been forced to give up her life there and return to England to lodge with a married cousin for the duration. Here she arouses the hostility of the cousin's husband, who persecutes her and finally drives her into a geriatric asylum. Laura is thus the victim of male belligerence twice over; she loses home, friends, lover, through the external conflict, and refuge, sanity, freedom through her defeat on the domestic front; and Jean Rhys makes it plain which of the two she considers to be the real war. Such is the nature of this war, Jean Rhys implies, that certain women need do nothing in order to draw male fire. They provoke simply by what they are, Laura never offers any insult to the husband. But she challenges him indirectly by displaying many characteristics which are traditionally if unconsciously felt as offences in a female; she is single, she is 'brainy', and she is old. Because she has lived abroad she is regarded as suspiciously un-English – these two features are united in the abusive village nickname for her, 'the witch of Prague'. Further, she is by temperament reclusive and literary, and her actions and preferences in this respect are subtly used to increase her isolation and to stress its pathos. We see her writing endless letters, keeping a diary, cutting out newspaper reports and sticking them into a scrapbook. As in Doris Lessing's *The Golden Notebook*, where the heroine does the same thing as her breakdown gathers momentum, this activity is seen as an apt evocation of the fragmentation of her life, its final resolution into the sensational and ephemeral.

All this is the work of men, the enemy. At times we seem to be in an inverse Strindbergian landscape, and Jean Rhys insists on her interpretation with a rather rigid contrivance by which none of the male characters is permitted any warmth, gentleness, or even common human decency (this recalls Strindberg's treatment of the female characters in *The Father*, *The Dance of Death*, and *The Stronger*). The husband, Ricky, as his name suggests, is conceived in the diminutive, the perennial schoolboy, emotionally retarded at the stage of truculence towards and inability to cope with the female sex.

Male humour is the first weapon with which Ricky seeks to prove and to place Laura. Jean Rhys's bitter assessment of the

reality of intersex warfare emerges nowhere so clearly as in this
sequence, where Ricky is vulgarly cruel under the mask of geniality
and goodwill. Annoyed by Laura's attempts to obtain news of her
friends in occupied Europe, Ricky decides to 'laugh her out of it'.
He offers as a joke the idea of 'the Gestapo getting her sweetheart'.
Her reaction to this confirms him in his view that 'the old girl's got
no sense of humour at all'. Part of the joke for Ricky lies in the
thought of an 'old girl' having a 'sweetheart', though we are told
that Laura has; this is an important theme in Jean Rhys, the
continuance of love among those whom orthodox society feels are,
or rightly should be, beyond it.

At last verbal persecution gives way to the physical violence
which it has for some time been hiding. Becoming increasingly
paranoid about Laura, Ricky details his wife to tell her that she
must go, simultaneously exposing both his cowardice and his
immaturity in the retreat behind the female. As she is leaving,
Ricky decides to speed the parting guest. Approaching her with
one of his crass jokes – 'It's moving day' – he takes her arm to
hurry her downstairs. At his touch she breaks down, screaming
and swearing. She clings to the bannisters and Ricky attacks her,
hitting and kicking, and drags her downstairs. Beaten, dazed, and
more than half mad, she is whirled away in a taxi. But even in the
grim asylum of his choice Laura is not safe from Ricky's
malice – he announces that she can only stay there as long as her
own money lasts – and the reader is left to speculate upon a future
which Jean Rhys has managed so that it presents not a spark of
hope.

All of the other men in the story are introduced to reinforce the
effect of male brutality. A friend of Ricky's, Fluting (the name
indicates the author's derisive view of his capacities), is used to
illustrate Jean Rhys's concept of that area of the masculine
mentality in which sexual and military matters unite with a
peculiarly indecent flourish. This is principally brought out
through the symbolism of weapons – obscene letters threaten 'A
Gun for the Old Girls', and the old cliché is given a new
significance in the remark of his wife that Ricky has 'got his knife
into Laura'. Fluting is an underwear man. He tells Laura that 'the
Waafs up at the station smelt', and waxes 'sarcastic about their
laundry allowance'. In the general context of this piece, Laura's
vigorous counter-attack – 'Sir, they smell; you stink' – seems not a
victory but a defeat, a descent to Fluting's level. Further, the direct
echo of one of Dr Johnson's most famous remarks highlights
Laura's pathos and frailty by the evocation of the vigorous and
articulate Great Cham of English Literature.

And males band together, Jean Rhys warns. The crisis for Laura comes symbolically at the height of the worst air-raid of the war, when her neglect of her blackout curtain unites against her the forces of law and order in the attentions of the air-raid warden and the police. The police are doubly enemies, of sex and class, as males and as custodians of the male social order. They have 'a good laugh' (male humour again) over Laura's diary-scrapbook, and Ricky gives orders that it must be destroyed. Even the doctor, who might be thought impartial, comes to Laura not in his office of healer but because Ricky sends for him in order to get Laura certified. The doctor refuses this, but out of professional cussedness, not true sympathy. The level of his concern for his patient is shown in the following exchange:

> Pratt asked her if she was willing to go to a sanatorium for a rest and she said 'Why not?' Ricky shouted at her 'You get off to your sanatorium pronto. You ought to have been there long ago.' 'You're being inhuman,' Pratt said. Ricky said, 'Well, will the bloody old fool keep quiet?' Pratt told him he'd guarantee that.

Set against this efficient male bonding, even between men who are antipathetic to each other, like Ricky and Pratt, is the inability of women to offer even the most elementary support for one another. Laura's cousin, Mrs Hudson, cannot help her, though aware of her sufferings. This woman is implicated in Laura's story not only through the narrative connection, but structurally, by Jean Rhys's use of a framing device by which Mrs Hudson relates the events to her sister, Mrs Trant.

A key passage makes clear the interaction of all the women's lives. The diary writing, the only part of Laura that we encounter directly, is used to convey her sense of the reduction of life and the erosion of her personality. She feels 'like a cog in a machine'; she sees herself as 'shamming dead'. But above all she is alienated and finally destroyed by the English man's attitude to women. This piece involves the sisters in Laura's plight, drawing added importance from the fact that Laura's voice is reaching us from the grave of the asylum, and through the mist of the incomprehension of the two women who are reading it together:

> There is something strange about the attitude to women as women. Not the dislike (or fear). That isn't strange of course. But it's all so completely taken for granted, and surely that is strange. It has settled down and become an atmosphere, or, if you like, a climate, and no one questions it, least of all the

women themselves. There is *no* opposition. The effects are
criticized, for some of the effects are hardly advertisements for
the system, the cause is seldom mentioned, and then very
gingerly. The few mild ambiguous protests usually come from
men. Most of the women seem to be carefully trained to revenge
any unhappiness that they feel on each other, or on children – or
on any individual man who happens to be at a disadvantage. In
dealing with men as a whole, a streak of subservience, of
servility, usually appears, something cold, calculating, lacking in
imagination.

But no one can go against the spirit of a country with
impunity and propaganda from the cradle to the grave can do a
lot.

This powerful statement stands at the centre of the story. It has
been prepared for by the account of Laura as outsider and victim,
and partly serves to describe her own condition. But it moves on to
become a savage indictment of the situation of all women,
including the two sisters. They too have regarded Laura as an
enemy because of her refusal to accept the inevitability of male
domination as they do. But they have enough of her in them, in
every sense, to feel her misery. Their failure to help her is seen as a
failure of sex loyalty as well as of kinship, since both turn against
her mainly under pressure from their husbands. So Laura's
thoughts are deeply relevant to them, and they are glimmeringly
alive to this. Mrs Hudson has 'moments' when she agrees with
Laura. Mrs Trant finds it 'nonsense', but her thoughts turn
anxiously to her favourite daughter, who not only liked Laura, but
opposed her father in standing up for her. Mrs Trant had taken the
slave's covert delight in any defiance of the master, but now feels
that it was bad: 'A girl ought to play safe, ought to go with the
tide, it was a bad sign when a girl liked unpopular people.' The
duty of young females to make themselves acceptable overcomes
her. She fearfully imagines Judy growing up to be unhappy
(another Laura, perhaps) and considers her sister a 'sterile old fool'
for offering the view that Judy is 'tough'. This further extension of
the web of hostility between women is not only Jean Rhys's way of
supporting and developing Laura's pronouncement. It also explains
why they cannot unite against the enemy in mutual help.

A final touch neatly catches up this aspect of the theme. The
'home', says Mrs Hudson, where Laura has gone, has a golf links
for the patients. '"But does she play golf?" said Mrs Trant. "Let's
hope," said Mrs Hudson, "let's hope" . . . ' The sentimentalist may
find in that a comforting reassurance of the unfailing warm concern

of the gentler sex for one another. It seems more likely, however, that it is intended to emphasise not only the hopelessness of Laura's fate, but also the dismal prospect for the women who 'survive'. Hope is all they have. It is standard currency among the hopeless. Jean Rhys invites us all to appreciate the joke.

In this suggestion that there is no real possibility of individual freedom for women, since they are moulded from their earliest years into conventionally acceptable forms, Jean Rhys touches a central nerve of much of women's writing in the twentieth century. Being dominated and manipulated by men, and being humiliated by this powerlessness, are themes which have been explored with a Rhys-like intensity by a number of different women. One common theme is the female's vulnerability through her body, especially in an age when every male is encouraged to feel entitled to a twenty-four-year-old Miss World as a sexual partner. Here Alison Lurie puts her self-styled 'respectable housewife' Janet through an ego-bruising encounter:

I did try to stop, though – several times. Once when he first reached inside my dress and I felt his fingers warm on my skin; and again later when he began to pull off my underpants. I gave another little yelp: 'Please! You mustn't do that!' I think I yelped.

Nick drew back from me at once and remarked flatly, 'So you're a tease too.'

I couldn't see his face in the dark, but there was so much bitterness in his voice, so much sour resignation (the slum child who's not really surprised when something is shown to him and then withdrawn), that I couldn't bear it. And I suppose I couldn't bear, either, being lumped with Anna May Mundy. And so I said, 'No, I'm not.'

The worst moment was when I'd finally taken everything off and Nick said suddenly, 'I want to look at you.' And before I could stop him he reached over me and turned on the light. The bulb glared out naked, and I grabbed for my clothes. I was abashed to expose all that soft, used forty-two-year-old flesh, creased in the corners like a pillowcase at the end of the week, and marked under the skin of the stomach and breasts with the irregular pale stretch marks of two pregnancies. I gave a cry and held my white dress to me, its sleeves dangling foolishly.

NICK: What's the matter? Come on. Put that thing down.
JANET: Don't look at me. I'm . . . too old. I feel ridiculous.
NICK: Oh, shut up. (*Real People*, 1969, p. 123)

But as Fay Weldon suggests in *Praxis* (1978, pp. 228–9), a woman does not need to get into a close sexual engagement with a man to be intimately humiliated by a man's routine, brutal exercise of his own sexuality:

> She was, astonishingly, forty. She knew, because men no longer whistled at her in the street, but otherwise she felt the same as usual. She felt rejected, and discarded, and humiliated when men at work or at home made lecherous remarks about other, younger, sexier women.
>
> 'If you live by your looks,' said Irma to her over the phone, 'you die by your looks. Come to a meeting.'
>
> But Praxis wouldn't. A meeting of all women! She felt she would be finally relegated, down among the women. A woman past her prime, taking comfort from the company of other rejected, ageing women. There was to her something infinitely depressing in the notion of any all-female group, which must lack the excitement and pleasure of mixed company.
>
> But the company of men was not what it was. The Deputy Creative Director took up with his young secretary, and Praxis suffered pangs of unreasoning jealousy. Phillip complained about her looks and her increasing lack of bosom. He would not do it directly; rather he let the implication be felt.
>
> 'I think you should stop using so much make-up. It's beginning to get in the cracks.' Or he'd point out a passing girl.
>
> 'God, what a figure. Look at those knockers!'

Yet the destruction of self-esteem is not the worst that women have to face from individual men. Marge Piercy's heroines have their existence right in the battle-lines of the war between the sexes, so that the most casual encounter with men can threaten verbal or physical violence, or both. In *Vida* (1980, p. 167), Eva and Vida are running two deserters up to Canada to help them out of reach of the law. But even in this situation the men are driven to try to dominate the women ideologically, and resort to man's most ancient recourse against them when they resist:

> . . . Eva and she had got in a furious argument with the two ex-soldiers about the women's movement and abortion. One of the guys had got so angry he had called them whores and murderers, and she knew he would have hit them if they had not been necessary to his safety. When they had finally let off the men, Eva was shaking. 'It's all theoretical for me. Women don't make you pregnant,' Eva had murmured. 'My hand's stiff and

sore from gripping the knife in my pocket. I was scared they'd attack us.' They had both been scared, but they did not say anything when they got back to Hardscrabble Hill. That was while Kevin still ruled, and neither Eva nor Vida would admit to anyone else being scared of two men.

In *Kinflicks* (1976, p. 104), Lisa Alther uses the character of Ginny to throw into relief the antics and attitudes taken by women in order to deflect men's hostility. Some are prepared to go to literally any lengths to 'make themselves attractive', denying their own physical reality through cosmetics, corsetry, surgery, even opthalmics, in the self-destructive urge to turn themselves into something a man would like:

Doreen threw open the cabinet doors so that Ginny could view her Isotoner Chin Strap and her Sauna girdle, her hair wax and deep cleanser and turtle oil moisturizer, several pairs of wash 'n' wear eyelashes, mud pack mix, six economy boxes of raspberry douche mix, depilatory cream, eyelash dye, every kind of hair roller, sixteen shades of nail polish, a Water Pik, tweezers, endless tubes and vials and bottles.

With renewed fascination, Ginny studied Doreen in the mirror. For an afternoon around the house, she had on blusher, eye liner, eye shadow, eyebrow pencil, mascara, lip gloss, and powder. Her pierced ear lobes sagged under gold filigree. She reeked of deodorant and perfume, and undoubtedly of raspberry douche if Ginny were to sniff up close. Her blond hair was impeccably dyed and teased and waxed and curled; pink nail polish, flawlessly unchipped; calves and armpits, satiny; chin, firm. She wore bright green contact lenses. Her E-cup breasts were artifically inflated, and an embryonic Oakland Raider inhabited her womb. What part of her body could she call her own?

Ginny's thoughts flashed briefly to her mother's black and blue swollen body. What was the point of Doreen's machinations? If she herself were in Doreen's rhinestone wedgies, as she might very well have been but for Clem Cloyd, would Ginny have gone this route, too? Or would she have vanished from Plantation Estates one dark November night and have turned up the next morning, corroded to death in the fetid Crockett River?

For as the last line with its chilling reminder of what men also do to women's bodies reminds us, all this effort is wasted in the face of men's deep anger against women, and the opportunities they have or make for expressing it. In a subtle, fluid vignette from *The Pure and the Impure* (1968 edition, p. 58), Colette penetrates the mask of the successful but hollow womaniser Damien to reveal the true nature of his preoccupation with the opposite sex:

> 'I hate women. They allow us to be their master in the sex act, but never their equal. That is what I cannot forgive them.'
> He took a deep breath, pleased at having so clearly rid himself of the essential motive of his long, low-voiced lament.

Angel Carter also sees men's basic weakness, rather than their much-discussed strength and 'aggression', as underlying their violence against women. Her strong man in *Nights at the Circus* (p. 276) expresses the contradiction between his outward toughness and his inner reality: 'All my life I have been strong and simple and – a coward, concealing the frailty of my spirit behind the strength of my body. I abused women and spoke ill of them, thinking myself superior to the entire sex on account of my muscle, although in reality I was too weak to bear the burden of any woman's love.' The urge to dominate and the compulsion to abuse seem to arise from the male's earliest days of sex consciousness, according to Michele Roberts's childhood scene in *The Visitation* (1983, pp. 10–11):

> – Watch me, he crows, watch me.
> He pulls down his shorts and pants and rotates gravely in front of her, his head flung back, his arms stretched out. . . . a temple dancer, a little god.
> – Now you. Go on, it's your turn.
> Helen sees him as her brother again because he has stopped dancing and has open, friendly eyes. She sees his small pink bum, the small pink penis dangling at his front. This item, long familiar from bathtimes, has never seemed significant. She shrugs, but pulls down her shorts and knickers and turns round and round in front of him, looking at him questioningly.
> – D'you see? Felix cries out in ecstasy: I've got a bum and a penis, and you've only got a bum. I've got two, and you've only got one. . . .
> They have been pirates, mothers, doctors, sheikhs, sailors and wild beasts. Always together. Identical. Equal. Now, tears rush into Helen's eyes and slide down her cheeks. She feels cold, and pulls up her clothes again.
> – You're horrible, she weeps furiously: I hate you, I'm not going to play with you any more . . . You're bad, she cries out in despair.

Clearly male chauvinists are both born and made. And their entry into the adult arena simply provides them with a wider stage on which to practise their anti-feminist drives. Of all Fay Weldon's gallery of woman-haters, persecutors, and destroyers, consider the compulsive Oliver, who cannot rest until he has destroyed the love his wife Chloe still miraculously feels for him by bullying her into a squalid sex threesome with their au pair. Here she depicts Oliver as a bastard still in the making, in his student days when the iron has not yet entered into his soul:

> And the girls! How he hates them, with their rounded vowels, their peeking bosoms, their Daddies and Mummies, their Aryan niceness. A proportion will even undermine him by obliging in bed, not wishing to be abused for purity or meanness – yet still, although on top of them he must plainly be victorious, they remain superior, kindly and patronising. It is he who cries out in his spasm: the most they do is moan agreeably and tell him they love him, which he knows to be untrue. He can make them smart, he can make them cry; yet twist their soft spiritual arms as he may, he cannot make them angry, or nasty.
>
> They are too nice. They are not human. Human beings rant and roister, fuck and feed, love and smother, shake their fists at the universe in thunder storms and defy a creator who is sure to get them with the next lightning bolt. These little English girls, with their soft, uncomplaining voices, and their docile hearts, whose worst crime has been a foul on the hockey pitch, are quite alien to him. He feels at liberty to behave with them as he pleases, and if in so doing he gets the better of the blond, smiling men, with their cool, intelligent, experienced ex-service eyes, so much the better. (*Female Friends*, 1974, p. 130)

As with the machinations of the organised masculine society, there is a profound importance in the naming of these acts of the individual male through their fictional representations. For Oliver is both an individual character, and a male type. His spiritual father is Lawrence in England and Portnoy in America, but he is very much *sui generis*, and a contemporary reality, alive and kicking. Man, the enemy who made Jean Rhys moan, though not in Norman Mailer's sense, all the way back in the 1920s, is still armed and dangerous all these decades later.

Yet as Fay Weldon herself does throughout her work, women writers have increasingly been using the form of the novel to question men's ultimate power of definition, showing that women too can take up these embattled attitudes and produce very similar

responses. The deceptively Jane Austenish Anita Brookner neatly
pins down a female version of the type in *Hotel du Lac* (1984):

> To Penelope, men were conquests, attributes, but they were also
> enemies; they belonged to the species that must never be granted
> more than the amount of time and attention she considered they
> deserved. Her tone with such men was flirtatious, mocking,
> never serious; she spread about her a propaganda of rapid
> affairs, rapidly consummated, with a laughing lack of commit-
> ment on both sides. She seemed to take a pride in the steady
> succession of names. She was, Edith saw, accomplished in
> venery . . . Yet she considered men to be a contemptible sex, and
> her eyes would sparkle when she recounted tales of conquest at
> the various committee meetings which were the very stuff of her
> social life. 'That dreadful little man,' she would say dismissively,
> of someone who did not know the rules of her game. (pp. 57–8)

Brookner's heroine, Edith, is a strong and astringent study of a
woman who cannot and will not play by the rules of this game,
which reduces women to gross devices of subservience and
collusion:

> Some women close ranks because they hate men and fear them.
> Oh, I know that this is obvious. What I'm really trying to say is
> that I dread such women's attempts to recruit me; to make me
> their accomplice. I'm not talking about the feminists. I can
> understand their position, although I'm not all that sympathetic
> to it. I'm talking about the ultra-feminine. I'm talking about the
> complacent consumers of men with their complicated but
> unwritten rules of what is due to them. Treats. Indulgences.
> Privileges. The right to make illogical fusses. The cult of
> themselves. Such women strike me as dishonourable. And
> terrifying . . .
>   'Above my head, I'm afraid,' said Monica, putting an end to
> her meditations. 'Anyway, you've got nothing to worry about, I
> should have thought. Our Mr Neville has taken quite a shine to
> you.'
>   'Monica,' said Edith wearily. 'That is not what I meant at all.
> I am not after Mr Neville or his money. I earn my own money.
> Money is what you earn when you grow up. I loathe the idea of
> women prospecting in this way.' (pp. 146–7)

But even without Edith 'prospecting', Mr Neville proposes. With
her habitual painful irony Anita Brookner deftly demonstrates how

well his proposal cues in with all Edith's fears about herself:

'I have watched you, trying to talk to those women. You are
desolate. And without the sort of self-love which I have been
urging on you, you are never going to learn the rules, or you are
going to learn them too late and become bitter. And when you
think you are alone, your expression is full of sorrow. You face a
life of exile of one sort or another.'
    'But why should you think me such a hopeless case?'
    'You are a lady, Edith. They are rather out of fashion these
days, as you may have noticed. As my wife, you will do very
well. Unmarried, I'm afraid you will soon look a bit of a
fool' . . . [Married] you will have a social position, which you
need. You will gain confidence, sophistication. And you will
have the satisfaction of knowing that you are doing me credit.
You are not the sort of woman of whom men are afraid, hysterics
who behave as though they are the constant object of scandal or
desire, who boast of their conquests and their performance, and
who think they can do anything so long as they entertain their
friends and keep a minimal bargain with their husbands.'
    'Women too are afraid of that sort of woman,' murmured
Edith.
    'No,' he said. 'Most women *are* that sort of woman.'
(pp. 164–5)

Edith, however, is not. It is a moment not unlike Nora's slamming
of the door in *The Doll's House* when Edith in her own understated
way slams the door on Mr Neville and his proposal. Edith is one of
a large band of women characters in the last twenty years or so,
who, their creators decided, should put their own interests as free
women above the social imperative to bond with men. And what
happened when women put themselves and their lives at the top of
their list for the first time in history has provided the impetus for a
radically new development of women's writing and of the novel at
large.

CHAPTER 9

Free women

. . . the burden and the complexity of womanhood were not
enough; she must reach beyond the sanctuary and pluck for
herself the strange bright fruits of art and knowledge. Clasping
them as few women have ever clasped them, she would not
renounce her own inheritance – the difference of view, the
difference of standard . . .

> Virginia Woolf, *Collected Essays* (1972), I, 204

I had a feeling that Pandora's box contained the mysteries of
woman's sensuality, so different from man's, and for which
man's language was inadequate. The language of sex had yet to
be invented. The language of the senses was yet to be explored.
Although women's attitude to sex was quite different from that
of men, we had not yet learned to write about it . . . I finally
decided to release the erotica for publication because it shows
the beginning efforts of a woman in a world that has been the
domain of men.

> Anais Nin, preface to *Delta of Venus* (1978), p. xiii

Impossible to avoid the conclusion. A few of the women were
writing in no way women had ever written before. . . . It was a
good style. At its best it read with the tension of an anger
profound enough to be kept under the skin. Every point was
made with a minimum of words, a mean style, no question of
that. It used obscenity with the same comfort a whore would
take with her towel.

> Norman Mailer, *The Prisoner of Sex* (1971), pp. 39–40

In recent decades one distinctive feature of modern fiction has been
the abandoning of the nineteenth-century concept of a female's
duty to maintain moral standards in society through her position in
the family ('The Angel in the House'). Women have been
relinquishing the unsatisfying and often delusory 'sphere of

influence' for that of direct involvement in action, especially sexual action. Any such effort is the natural opposite of that 'delicacy' which has for so long been a prerequisite of femininity. A new type of woman has emerged, putting a decisively new inflection on what Hardy called 'the ache of modernity'.

This newness does not lie wholly in the flexing of muscles not fully used before. Strong and capable women are nothing new; witness Charlotte Brontë's real-life and fictional definitions of woman's lot, or Jane Austen's Elinor Dashwood or Elizabeth Bennet. Even in Dickens, the daddy of all patriarchs in his preference for little-girl women, there are many examples of women who endure and who survive. This is also true of much other Victorian fiction; the two central female characters in Mrs Henry Wood's sensationally successful *East Lynne* (1861) are both tough and resourceful in their different ways. The best of the nineteenth-century literary heroines were never housebound and vapourish.

But the Victorian imagination in general was curiously attracted to the idea of the woman who expressed through her own weakness a tribute to the man's strength and competence. This in part accounts for the contemporary masculine fascination with 'green fruit', pre-pubescent girls (and boys), the ugly, cruel underbelly of the Victorian protective exaltation of the sexually immature. And the independence of nineteenth-century heroines, however real in the short term, usually assumed a return to the shelter of the man's cloak and comfort where it could be found and achieved – note the touching imagery of abandoned child, wandering orphan, lost bird or little animal that so frequently accompanies nineteenth-century fictional descriptions of women alone. Where the woman had to continue in her solitary state, this was frequently shown to be a punishment for some error or failing. Again, *East Lynne* is the classic example; the man's protection, the domestic reward, have been lost through female fault. In diametric contrast modern women writers have begun exploring oppositional versions of this experience, in which freedom from the ties of hearth and home are seen not as the punishment, but the prize. They seek independence, and wish to retain it.

This desire, often expressed with uncompromising directness, has naturally provoked some opposition and resentment. Norman Mailer described the devastating effect of the new women's writing upon men – 'A wind in this prose whistled up the skirts of male conceit. The basis of male conceit was that men could live with truths too unsentimental for women to support (hence the male mind was gifted with superior muscles just so much as the back).' Mary Ellmann, in *Thinking About Women*, also stressed the significance in literature of the new independence of women. As more and more made their way out of the doll's house, she observed that 'the old animal drama of male pursuit does not hold. Instead now, women tend to offer and men to refuse – or to be incapable of accepting, or to regret having accepted.'

The critic Jean Gagen has described a New Woman in Elizabethan and Jacobean drama in his book of that name; and more recently both Hardy and Ibsen have been accused of giving birth to New Women. But in the second half of the twentieth century the novel really has lived up to its name – women's new social freedoms, their adventures, mental, and especially physical, have provided totally novel material for writers. Doris Lessing acknowledges in herself 'whole areas of me made by the kind of experience women haven't had before', and shows a strong sense of her characters being a different breed. Her women are 'on some kind of frontier', and know it; see her ironic labelling of her heroines as 'free women' throughout *The Golden Notebook*.

Yet as we have seen, Doris Lessing's heroines, although struggling hard towards the various freedoms they can see on the horizon, do not regard themselves as truly free of their deep and humiliating dependence on men. It was left to the women writers of the next decade to produce in and through their fictions the female characters who were, externally at least, truly free. In Fay Weldon's *Praxis* (1978, pp. 13–14), an older woman vigorously defines the New Breed and some of her characteristics:

> The New Women! I could barely recognise them as being of the same sex as myself, their buttocks arrogant in tight jeans, openly inviting, breasts falling free and shameless and feeling no apparent obligation to smile, look pleasant or keep their voices low. And how they live! Just look at them to know how! If a man doesn't bring them to orgasm, they look for another who does. If by mistake they fall pregnant, they abort by vacuum aspiration. If they don't like the food, they push the plate away. If the job doesn't suit them, they hand in their notice. They are satiated by everything, hungry for nothing. They are what I wanted to be; they are what I worked for them to be: and now I see them, I hate them. They have found their own solution to the three-fold pain – one I never thought of. They do not try, as we did, to understand it and get the better of it. They simply wipe out the pain by doing away with its three centres – the heart, the soul and the mind. Brilliant! Heartless, soulless, mindless – free!

The New Woman of the post-sixties novel, free to range in

search of varities of sexual experience, and equally free to broadcast the results of her research, owes her existence to the breakdown of former notions of what was forbidden. The post-war world has seen a fracturing of literary, social, and personal taboos amounting in effect to a reassessment of the obscene. Previous constraints upon naturalistic treatment of sexual and excremental functions have been eroded to an unprecedented extent. This has inevitably brought with it certain problems, not least that of public response. As Havelock Ellis was concerned to stress in *The Revaluation of Obscenity* (1931), 'the taboo on the excremental obscene is only conventional and social, while that on the sexual obscene is regarded as also moral and religious'. We might add political too; the efforts of many women to redefine their sexual natures is explicitly linked with the examination of women's place in society at large, with a reconsideration of the female role in literature and life.

It is hard to overestimate the importance of this development for women writers. For what can compare with human sexuality as a tormenting paradox? In the words of John Bayley, 'Everyone recognises that – whatever you call it – sexual love is for most people the most interesting and memorable aspect of life' (*The Characters of Love*, 1960, p. 4). Rich with tensions and contrasts, this is at once an instinctual reflex carrying a humiliating reminder of our animal origins, and a primary expression of the highest spiritual impulse known to man, the love of a fellow creature. Alexander the Great described sex as an inescapable recollection of our mortality; yet poets down the centuries have insisted on what it is to be made immortal with a kiss. Sex travels so closely with love that many participants take or mistake the one to mean the other; it masquerades delusively as love, often claims to be or to serve in place of love; but life and literature alike offer countless examples of that sexual experience which leaves the partners in the roles of murderer and victim. Who is not, however dimly, haunted by a wraith of some such past encounter? For some, this aberration becomes the norm, and the promised closeness that sexual activity implies reveals itself to be a dreary repetitive act of apartness:

It was not so bad, she thought, when it was all over; not as bad as *that*. It meant nothing to her, nothing at all. Expecting outrage and imposition, she was relieved to find she felt nothing. She was able maternally to bestow the gift of herself on this humble stranger, and remain untouched. Women have an extraordinary ability to withdraw from the sexual relationship, to immunise themselves against it, in such a way that their men

can be left feeling let down and insulted without having anything
tangible to complain of. (Doris Lessing, *The Grass Is Singing*,
1950, p. 66)

The desolation suggested here, through the telling use of verbal
echoes ('not so bad . . . not as bad . . . nothing . . . nothing . . .
nothing . . . ') is not the worst that can be experienced in this area
of human behaviour; on the contrary it is in some ways the best
that anyone in this situation can hope for, so easily does this most
satisfactory become the least satisfactory of human contacts.

But sex activity is more than a perennially interesting theme. It
is a touchstone of sexual attitudes, demanding the cooperation of
the two sexes, whose culture and conditioning have rendered them
wary of if not hostile to each other. Each sex has continually to
cope with inherited notions of gender-appropriate behaviour,
fantasies, ideals and stereotypes which alternately welcome and
warn, beckon and threaten. Can any common ground be
discovered then between women writers in the treatment of sex?
Certainly large numbers of novelists, male and female, have made
the most of the recently acquired prerogative to mention the
unmentionable; and as female artists have for so long been denied
this outlet, it is hardly surprising that when the opportunity came
they burst out with some force.

Not that the subject was unthought of by former women writers.
That chastest of novelists, Virginia Woolf, in a description of her
own early career, adverted to the forbidden theme in these words:

The image that comes to my mind when I think of this girl is the
image of a fisherman lying sunk in dreams on the verge of a deep
lake with a rod held out over the water. She was letting her
imagination sweep unchecked round every rock and cranny of
the world that lies submerged in the depths of our unconscious
being. Now came the experience, the experience that I believe to
be far commoner with women writers than with men. The line
raced through the girl's fingers. Her imagination had rushed
away. It had sought the pools, the depths, the dark places where
the largest fish slumber. And then there was a smash. There was
an explosion. There was foam and confusion. The imagination
had dashed itself against something hard. The girl was roused
from her dream. She was indeed in a state of the most acute and
difficult distress. To speak without figure she had thought of
something, something about the body, about the passions which
it was unfitting for her as a woman to say. Men, her reason told
her, would be shocked. The consciousness of what men will say

of a woman who speaks the truth about her passions has roused
her from her artist's state of unconsciousness. She could write no
more. The trance was over. Her imagination could work no
longer. This I believe to be a very common experience with
women writers – they are impeded by the extreme conventionality
of the other sex. For though men sensibly allow themselves great
freedom in these respects, I doubt that they realise or can control
the extreme severity with which they condemn such freedom in
women.

In her private life Virginia Woolf was able to be more relaxed.
The accounts given by her friends, especially of her younger, less
troubled days, stress her relish of life, her sense of humour, her
enchanting gaiety, her love of new experience, and her ability to
adapt to it. This first-person anecdote, in Quentin Bell's admirable
Virginia Woolf: A Biography (1972, I, 124), gives some idea of the
Virginia her readers hardly ever see:

> Suddenly the door opened and the long and sinister figure of
> Mr Lytton Strachey stood on the threshold. He pointed his
> finger at a stain on Vanessa's white dress.
>   'Semen?' he said.
>   Can one really say it? I thought & we burst out laughing.
> With that one word all barriers of reticence and reserve went
> down. A flood of the sacred fluid seemed to overwhelm us. Sex
> permeated our conversation. The word bugger was never far
> from our lips. We discussed copulation with the same excitement
> and openness that we had discussed the nature of good.

Reflecting on this, Virginia Woolf concludes, 'telling the truth
about my own experiences as a body, I do not think I solved. I
doubt that any woman has solved it yet. The obstacles against her
are still immensely powerful – and yet they are very difficult to
define. Outwardly, what is simpler than to write books? Outwardly,
what obstacles are there for a woman rather than for a man?
Inwardly, I think, the case is very different; she has still many
ghosts to fight, many prejudices to overcome' ('Professions for
Women', *The Death of the Moth*, pp. 152–3).

Note the assumption that it would take time, but only time, for
the inner censor to be winkled out and sent packing. So it has
proved. Over the last twenty-five years, for the first time in the
history of fiction, women have been describing their experiences as
sexual beings. For the first time they have challenged the long-
undisturbed masculine versions of such events, like those of 'Fanny

Hill', Frank Harris, D. H. Lawrence, Henry Miller, or Norman
Mailer. Candid treatment of sexual topics is as old as man's sense
of himself. What was new in the 1960s was that women began
writing and publishing descriptions of sexual activity seen from the
woman's point of view. Additionally they were for the first time
able to explore all the specifically female areas of sensuality and
sexuality hitherto neglected, like childbirth, menstruation, masturbation, and lesbianism.

Few passages so clearly illustrate the historical movement
towards more and more exposure of body and of sensations than
this characteristically febrile extract from Rosamond Lehmann's
The Weather in the Streets (1936):

> Then it was afterwards. He said, whispering:
>   'I'm your lover. . . . '
> I thought about it. I had a lover. But nothing seemed
> changed. It wasn't disappointing exactly. . . . The word is:
> unmomentous. . . . Not wonderful – yet. . . . I couldn't quite look
> at him, but it was friendly and smiling. His cheek looked coarse-
> grained in the light of the lamp. I saw the hairs in his
> nostrils. . . . (1968 edition, p. 153)

In the context of this reticence, even the grain of Rollo's cheek and
the hairs of his nose assume the status of startling and abrasive
physical detail; but on the Virginia Woolf principle that 'stories
that follow people into their private rooms are difficult', the writer
takes us no further.

Virginia Woolf backs up this reference in *The Waves* with one of
those sequences, relatively rare in her work, in which she allowed
her gift of irony full play. Her description of the efforts of Bernard
to 'take the other boys into the private room' of Dr Crane, the
headmaster, and imagine the Cranes' sex life, has the quality
almost of prophetic warning as she parodies the dangers of the
revelatory style, the groping for the appropriately suggestive detail,
the grandiose fantasy, and the striking of attitudes, which are its
common features:

> The two rooms are united by a bridge of rosy light from the
> lamp at the bedside where Mrs Crane lies with her hair on the
> pillow reading a French memoir. As she reads, she sweeps her
> hand with an abandoned and despairing gesture over her
> forehead, and sighs, 'is this all?' comparing herself with some
> French duchess. (p. 36)

Seen in its comic aspect, sexual intercourse is not infrequently presented by Virginia Woolf as a coarse or low-class activity -- 'the growl of the bootboy making love to the tweeny among the gooseberry bushes'. The last phrase, with its joking reference to the time-honoured formula for evading sexual description, makes an ironic comment on the situation in itself, and illustrates the nature of Virginia Woolf's comic detachment.

This is, however, as far as she goes, at a time when even a masculine growl could be considered rather near the knuckle in polite fiction. By 1963, the defloration of Dottie, conducted amid the echoing shades of Krafft-Ebing, *A Midsummer Night's Dream*, and her lover's memories of previous lovers, could and did occupy an entire chapter in *The Group*. Mary McCarthy ironically relates every detail of tumescence and detumescence, and is sufficiently detached from her material to insist on its unromantic and even absurd aspects; the lover goes to sleep immediately after the intercourse, while Dottie is left wondering what's happening, and when he tells her 'get yourself a pessary', she thinks he says 'a peccary.'

Despite these unpromising circumstances, she has the surprise of her sheltered life with him. Orgasm succeeds orgasm as Dottie throws off the girlhood conditioning and restraints of social class (the lover nicknames her 'Boston') along with her clothes. Although the McCarthy irony is everywhere present, Dottie's feelings of adventure, excitement, pleasure, and eventually triumph, are faithfully recorded. The reader is asked to accept that in its modest way the liberation of Dottie is something of a success; here is a new type, the timid female freebooter embarked on the high seas of sexual discovery.

Mary McCarthy has been censured for her 'critical' method of novel-writing, which to some resembled the transfixing of the live butterfly for display; and Dottie may also be seen as one among many in the showcase of female folly which *The Group* offers its readers. But among fictional representations of women's sexuality, the astringent compares interestingly with the poetic. The modern mistress of this vein is Edna O'Brien. Here she describes her heroine's one-night stand with a man dimly remembered from a long-ago party who has stopped by, just temporarily, to take a break from his wife, his four children, his mistress, and his problems:

Relief. She thought, he means to stay until morning, and that pleased her as much as that he was going to sleep with her. She

remembered a man who got up and left after he came, while she
was still in the throes of desire.

  In bed she opened wide. And christened him foxglove because
it too grew high and purple in a dark secretive glade. He put the
bedside light on. She felt him harden and lengthen inside her like
a stalk. Soft and hard together. He loved her as no man had ever
done, not even the husband who first sundered her and started
off the whole cycle of longing and loving and pain and regret.
Because that kind of love is finally emptying.

  'You loved me lovely,' she said. His back was bathed in sweat.
He had laboured on her behalf and she was filled with the most
inordinate gratitude. (*August Is a Wicked Month*, 1965, ch. 2)

Not the stuff of which sexual adventuresses are made, you might
think. But this is to under-rate the manifold resorts of the heroine's
inertia and passivity. A new experience comes her way when she is
unable to resist the demands made by another casual lover that he
should immortalise the moment on film:

He crossed over and drew down one strap of her dress so that it
fell on her arm. The white sagging top of one breast came into
view. Above it was a line of raw pink where she had boiled in the
sun that morning in an effort to get a tan for him. He
photographed her like that and then with both straps down so
that the sag of both breasts was in view and then he brought her
dress down round her waist and photographed her naked top. It
had been too hot to put on a brassière. From his position,
stooped behind the camera, he indicated that she hold one
breast, perkily, as if she enjoyed showing it off. (Ch. 7)

This clearly is an example of what Doris Lessing had in mind
when she referred to 'the sort of experience women haven't had
before' (lady-novelist women, that is). Part of Edna O'Brien's
stylistic difficulty may be located in the novelty of her material – at
the time of writing there were few precedents to follow. If an
author chooses to do without the safeguard of deflationary humour
in the treatment of sexual themes in the way that Mary McCarthy
uses it, for example, then the discovery of the appropriate tone and
vocabulary presents enormous problems.

  Edna O'Brien made another effort to find a method adapted to
this material in the experimental *A Pagan Place* (1970). This novel
attempts to give a child's-eye view of sexual experience, both its
own and that of the adults around it. Here, in these desperately
impoverished and limited surroundings, the only diversions lie in

watching the village idiot or listening to visitors using the lavatory. Everyone is brought up among 'things to fear from the living and from the dead', and sexual exploration is the child's only entertainment.

To draw the reader into the young girl's experience, and to re-create the immediacy of the occasion, Edna O'Brien employs throughout her narrative the unusual second-person device. This combines with the equally esoteric nature of the material to produce some strange effects. What, one wonders, does Harold Pinter, the book's dedicatee, make of a line like this: 'You sat and put a doll's soft toe between your legs outside your knickers, and tickled yourself'? Readers who find this pawky and distasteful will not be won over by the sub-Joycean references to 'snot', and the pervasive use of infantile slang, 'diddies', 'number two', 'do pooly', for instance.

Whimsy like this is a more specialised taste than humour, and Edna O'Brien is on firmer ground when presenting her school-teacher, the 'brainy' Miss Davitt, who opines that 'toothpaste was probably of Greek origin, like all civilized things'. When cross with her pupils she sets them to write on 'A Day in the Life of a Penny'. There is much incidental pleasure, too, in some characteristically Irish witticisms and absurdities. One situation is laconically summed up in the observation that 'Hell hath no music like a woman playing second fiddle'. What Ivy Compton-Burnett calls 'the fine edge of family life' is also brought out by the use of humour. The youngest daughter is engrossed in First Love: 'You sent him a letter in secret. You wrote Remembrance is all I ask, but if remembrance should prove a task, Forget me. It seemed a bit extreme once you had posted it.'

Meanwhile, the elder and unmarried daughter's pregnancy has brought the doctor to condole with the father, who is reeling under the far more serious affliction of the death of the mare; and the doctor is understandably disturbed by the father's lamentation that 'her flesh was sold in France as a delicacy'. Finally, humour is significantly used in the presentation of the key sexual sequence, where the young girl is given her introduction to men by a young priest who is 'very partial to Mary Magdalene'. The girl is overwhelmed – 'It was an honour' – and in imagination clothes him in his vestments and cassock to sustain and intensify the effect. The climax is rendered with a refined sense of the ridiculous: 'Never had the corneas of eyes bulged so.'

There is a weakness, however, in the intermittent nature of the use of humour. Most of the young girl's feelings and observations about sex are set down with a leaden solemnity, as if sacrosanct.

The child's development pales, too, in comparison with the interest
of her mother. This characterisation is the true heart and real
strength of the book. It contains both the power of generalisation
and the acute particularity of fine writing; it could stand for any
Irish mother and yet is very evidently a portrait of a woman locked
in a precise situation. We see her domestic desperation, harassed
by money worries and a pig of a husband, whose joyless sexual
attentions are yet another anxiety to her, rather than a source of
any warmth or comfort. Her primitive efforts at contraception,
using the tissue from shoe-boxes, are vividly recalled by the child:
'Before she went across the landing she put tissue paper in the
inside of her pussy . . . over there she moaned and groaned. His
sinews crackled.' Her life is shadowed by the need to 'manage' her
bad-tempered and unreliable husband, and she shows a degraded
facility in various servile ruses and placatory devices to stop him
going off on drunken binges. Later there is a poignant episode
when she goes to the big city in search of a runaway daughter; we
see her frantically scouring the streets but pathetically bewildered
by urban life and unable even to use the telephone. The novel
closes with her, locked in her room, howling with grief as her
youngest child leaves home for the convent.

Like other women writers, Edna O'Brien made a number of
different attempts on this topic as her characters and viewpoint
shifted, and public tolerance increased. Doris Lessing is foremost
among women writers who have both helped to bring about and
benefited from the 'women's liberation' of the 1960s. In early
versions of the bedroom scene, she was forced by prevailing
conventions into the use of the 'and then it was afterwards'
formula. The autobiographical novel *Martha Quest* pushed as hard
as it could against the boundaries of the convention – the man is
described as undressing, down to the unromantic detail of
removing his shoes and placing them neatly together before getting
on to the bed. There is even reference to a condom (chastely
described as 'a packet'). But the main course of the action is
conducted within the safety of the romantic generalisation, and the
abstract or Latin term: 'the act'; 'the forms of sensitive experience',
'a drenching, saturating moment of illumination'. Not unnaturally
the lover fails to provide this, and suddenly it's all over; indeed
'then it was afterwards', in the time-honoured formula: 'and
afterwards she lay coiled meekly beside him like a woman in love,
for her mind had swallowed the moment of disappointment whole,
like a python. . . .'

Much had changed by the time Doris Lessing came to publish
The Golden Notebook in 1962; and much was changed as a result of

this brave book. Doris Lessing was unflinching in her confrontation
of the discrepancy between reality and romance in most women's
lives, and especially in their sexual experience. One aspect of
female behaviour which she illustrated more thoroughly than any
other women writer before her, is the ease with which a sexual
failure or disappointment becomes a continuing pattern of disaster,
until eventually, the woman is driven to seek only those encounters
which will fulfil her worst expectations.

Doris Lessing illustrates this by showing how one of her heroines
(all four of whom may plausibly be seen as different aspects of the
same female nature) approaches intercourse with a man who does
not attract her. Ella (*elle?*) works herself up to it by thinking that as
men can go to bed without scruples, women should be able to do so
too. Thus fortified, she is able to bring out 'Would you like to go to
bed with me?' After this venture into masculine assertiveness she
relapses into little servant girl: 'Well, now, *sir*, I think you should
set me at my ease, or something.' He tries, but it is a grisly
encounter:

> In bed, it was a delightful shock of warm tense flesh. (Ella was
> standing to one side, thinking ironically; Well, well!) He
> penetrated her almost at once, and came after a few seconds. She
> was about to console or be tactful, when he rolled on his back,
> flung up his arms, and exclaimed: 'Boy. Oh boy!'
> (At this point Ella became herself, one person, both of them
> thinking at one). She lay beside him, controlling physical
> disappointment, smiling. (p. 277)

All Doris Lessing's heroines are afflicted with this service
philosophy in their view of their own sex. They fear to make
demands of men, even those of common humanity, in case any
show of eagerness should frighten them off and nip the unfolding
'romance' in the bud. Taken to extremes, this becomes a kind of
masochism; Ella, here, in addition to bearing her own sexual
frustrations without reproach, schools herself to lie beside the over-
hasty ejaculator as he sentimentalises about his wonderful wife and
five kids. Even in longer-term relationships, Ella feels no
confidence, no security. She senses herself as entirely at the man's
mercy for sexual satisfaction, and believes that the quality of her
response must depend upon how much the man loves her at that
moment.

For in defiance of post-Freudian biological knowledge, Doris
Lessing in *The Golden Notebook* clings to the old notion of two types
of orgasm in female sexual response, the vaginal and the clitoral.

She also uses these terms in a highly idiosyncratic way, to differentiate the *emotional* stages of her heroine's love affairs. The vaginal orgasm is a sign to Ella that she really loves Paul – 'she could not have experienced it if she had not loved him. It is the orgasm that is created by the man's need for a woman, and his confidence in that need.' Again, in her relationship with Michael (it must be coincidental that these horribly unworthy males are named after saints), Ella is from the first dependent upon his attitude to her and his self-image for her orgasm. She cannot experience it if Michael is moody, withdrawn, or temporarily low in self-esteem. Later, as her love affair with Paul continues but fails to consolidate itself, he expresses his control over Ella by making sure that she does not have an orgasm. He is afraid of committing himself to her by releasing the 'emotion' that she sees it as:

> A vaginal orgasm is emotion and nothing else . . . the vaginal orgasm is a dissolving in a vague, dark, generalised sensation like being swirled in a warm whirlpool . . . there is only one real female orgasm and that is when a man, from the whole of his need and desire takes a woman and wants all her response. (p. 186)

In this, the ultimate expression of female dependence and submission, Doris Lessing has created a kind of super-orgasm which can only be achieved in order to satisfy the *man's* need, and in order to make it a fulfilling experience for *him*. The hysteria and uncertainty of the style here betray the writer's uneasy sense that she may be out on a limb. The prose is full of hocus-pocus, in which some portentous words and images ('emotion', 'dark', 'sensation', 'a warm whirlpool' – though note the telltale 'vague' and 'generalised') jostle furtively with the language and attitudes of True Love Romance – 'emotion and nothing else', the 'one real' moment, and the man with 'the whole of his need and desire' – a lighter and more irreverent writer would have perceived (and suppressed) the unfortunate pun in the last phrase.

In this strenuous contest the 'clitoral' orgasm is naturally presented as inferior. It is achieved through 'mechanical means'; this phrase alone shows Ella's dissociation from this part of the love-experience that she sees Paul's hand as a machine. When their love weakens, he 'began to rely on manipulating her externally' – again, the terminology suggests a bone-setter at the end of his resources rather than a loved partner. She resents what she feels is his denial of himself; she sees this orgasm as 'a substitute and a fake', and it is consistently opposed against the 'real' orgasm.

When the lover departs, he takes this with him, so that masturbation, the single woman's friend, is no satisfaction at all, but instead a humiliating reminder that the man has left her:

> She put herself to sleep, as always, by thinking of Paul. She had never, since he had left her, been able to achieve a vaginal orgasm; she was able to reach the sharp violence of the exterior orgasm, her hand becoming Paul's hand, mourning as she did so, the loss of her real self. She slept, overstimulated, nervous, exhausted, cheated. (p. 264)

Admittedly Doris Lessing makes some attempt to present a more objective assessment of the female's sex experience than this. At times the respecive merits of the two types of orgasm are discussed with chilling detachment – the 'clitoral' is 'very exciting', a more varied sensation than the 'vaginal' and more powerful. But the dualistic notion does not in any degree loosen its hold upon the writer's mind, and hence upon those of her characters. Paul at one stage asserts that 'there are eminent physiologists who say women have no basis for vaginal orgasm'. But Ella is not to be weaned away from her reliance upon the *idea* of 'the real thing', the irrational rejection of objective discussion in favour of 'intuition' – 'Then they don't know much, do they?' she says.

With these accounts of masturbation, hitherto the most private of private acts, Doris Lessing takes us well and truly into that area of life which was never extensively treated in literature outside pornography and other underground writing, before; that is, specifically female experiences set down and analysed by serious women writers for the general readership. It is rare in the history of art that a rich and previously untapped source of controversial material becomes available, and it is hardly surprising that writers of very different kinds have welcomed an opportunity which was not theirs before. In the free-floating yet direction-seeking 1960s, Margaret Drabble struck an important sexual nerve of the time when she became the first English woman to give voice to the delusive promise of the freedom and equality of university life, followed by the cold douche of matrimony and child-bearing. With a wholly idiosyncratic blend of cleverness and ordinariness, she captured the ear both of the women who had been to college and of those who would like to have been – not to mention the men who were getting, at last, an insight into the mentality and homelife of the bluestocking, with the reassurance that she really is like any other female, underneath.

This is not to underestimate Margaret Drabble's real talents as a

prosodist. She is an elegant and often witty writer, with a sharp eye
and a deftness at placing and pinning down her characters. But she
was hardly a great originator in subject-matter, which is how her
admirers saw her and how her public image had her. The clever
girl caught in the toils of the world, the flesh and the devil appears
throughout the fiction of the thirties and forties, and indeed
anywhere where clever girls have ever taken up their pens to obtain
their revenges or to have their heart's ease; the two Elizabeths,
Bowen and Jane Howard have already been discussed, and it
would not be going against the grain of her fiction to add Virginia
Woolf, too. The trials of unsupported motherhood (many considered
Drabble's pregnant, unmarried PhD in *The Millstone* to be her most
unusual creation, including the film company who bought the
rights to it), and the whole business of coping alone with an
unexpected pregnancy had been anticipated in Lynne Reid Banks's
The L-Shaped Room (1960).

Similarly the humiliation, frustration, and sheer backbreaking
work involved in the assorted processes of contraception, breast-
feeding, and child-rearing, as handled by Margaret Drabble in her
novels, especially *The Waterfall* (1969), had all been dealt with more
fully by Mary McCarthy in *The Group*. Consider this sequence on
the horrors entailed in the use and management of the Dutch cap:

When he wanted to revive within himself his tenderness for her,
and to make his own heart bleed, there was a string of incidents
which he would recall, which never failed to cause him an
intolerable barb of painful emotion. The first of these dated from
the second week of their marriage, when, after lying in bed
waiting for her, he had got out, finally, and gone to look for her.
He heard her before he saw her; she was in the living-room of
their small Paddington flat, and she was moaning softly and
rhythmically to herself. The light was off, and he did not dare to
put it on, but he found her, crouched in a corner behind the
armchair, her arms round her knees, wearing her smart
trousseau night shirt. Spread before her on the floor was a Durex
Dutch cap, an instruction leaflet, and various other accoutre-
ments of contraception. She was crying because she could not
manage them. She was too narrow, she said, or rather she did
not say, for she did not say such things, but this was what he
gathered, from her meaningless sobs. He tried to console her,
saying that he would occupy himself with such things, as he had
always done before their marriage, in their quite adequately
exciting courtship, but the sight of her, so reduced, had struck

him to the heart. And it was too late. Their first child was
conceived that week. (*Jerusalem the Golden*, 1967, p. 155)

Set that against the sister version of the Great Diaphragm
Disaster and note how the use of humour doesn't diminish but
increases the pathos and our sense of the woman's difficulty:

> Dottie did not mind the pelvic examination or the fitting. Her
> bad moment came when she was learning how to insert the
> pessary by herself. Though she was usually good with her hands
> and well co-ordinated, she felt suddenly unnerved by the
> scrutiny of the doctor and the nurse, so exploratory and
> impersonal, like the doctor's rubber glove. As she was trying to
> fold the pessary, the slippery thing, all covered with jelly,
> jumped out of her grasp and shot across the room and hit the
> steriliser. Dottie could have died. But apparently this was
> nothing new to the doctor and the nurse. 'Try again, Dorothy,'
> said the doctor calmly, selecting another diaphragm of the
> correct size from the drawer. And, as though to provide a
> distraction, she went on to give a little lecture on the history of
> the pessary, while watching Dottie's struggles out of the corner
> of her eye: how a medicated plug had been known to the Greeks
> and Jews and Egyptians, how Margaret Sanger had found the
> present diaphragm in Holland, how the long fight had been
> waged through the courts here. . . . (*The Group*, ch. 3)

Like many women writers, Margaret Drabble has not been well
served by her admirers. They have puffed her as the prophetess of
the new emancipated womanhood, when she is nothing of the sort.
Her cool, self-assured, often vinegarish heroines have more in
common with Emma Woodhouse than with Germaine Greer. Their
detachment, too, means that there is an oddly distant tone imposed
even on the closest fictional recordings of intimate events; they
forbid us to become engaged with, or even faintly warm about, the
events paraded before us. The effect, then, even when the material
is sexual in content, is resolutely asexual, even astringent. This
applies to episodes as diverse as the seduction scene in *The Garrick
Year* (1964) and the childbirth in *The Millstone* (1965). Sex without
tears, in brief; and without blood and sweat either, for that matter.
    Doris Lessing by contrast does not shrink from suggesting that
being female can be a grim business indeed. Through Anna in *The
Golden Notebook* she voices women's internalised physical disgust,
simultaneously making a calculatedly brutal attack upon an

assortment of literary and cultural prejudices with the exquisitely unfeminine line 'I stuff my vagina with a tampon of cotton wool'.

But this off-hand callousness towards what she elsewhere describes as 'the wound inside my body which I didn't choose to have' is misleading. Before setting out for the office the narrator, Anna, with a rooted though routine 'feeling of shame and modesty', hides her day's supply of tampons in the bottom of her handbag, concealing them under her handkerchief. She justifies, for herself and the reader, this departure from her self-imposed standards of honesty and clarity of behaviour:

> ... I read recently in some review, a man said he would be revolted by the description of a woman defecating. I resented this; because, of course, what he meant was he would not like to have that romantic image, a woman, made less romantic. But he was right, for all that. ... I have instantly to suppress distaste ... I begin to worry: Am I smelling? ... the faintly dubious, essentially stale smell of menstrual blood, I hate. And resent. It is a smell that I feel as strange even to me, as imposition from outside ... (p. 291)

The success of Anna's efforts to suppress distaste may be judged from an incident later on when she has to break off work to slip away and wash between her legs, even though she has already done so before she came out. Anna's experience here ties in with that attitude to menstruation which is indicated by its vernacular name, 'the curse'. Nevertheless, Anna's dislike is extreme, and verges on the neurotic. Perhaps most damaging is the association with defecation. But no less depressing is the self-punishing capitulation to the male viewpoint – 'he was right' – and the anxiety about smelling, the compulsion to make herself acceptable by the artificial standards of deodorant advertisements. Anna is not able to connect her menstruation in any way with human reproduction or with her own body, neither of which in any case seems at all natural and pleasant to her. Hence she greets it as a foreign thing, a painful external reminder of a reality which she has rejected. Doris Lessing never makes this connection, seeming concerned rather to treat this attitude of Anna sympathetically as the inevitable burden of the thinking woman. But it is hard for the reader to avoid linking Anna's withdrawal from her menstruation with her generally debilitated and impoverished emotional condition in the novel, her artistic block, her nightmares of aridity, and her fears for her survival as a person.

Not all women writers would agree with Doris Lessing when she

writes of her menstruation as 'my resentment against the wound
inside my body which I didn't choose to have'. In *The Woman
Warrior* Maxine Hong Kingston describes how, for her, menstruation was simply a part of life, and the badge of her womanhood:
'Menstrual days did not interrupt my training; I was as strong as
on any other day. "You're now an adult", explained the old
woman on the first one, " . . . you can have children".' Even more
commonplace is the matter-of-fact tone in which the characters
discuss the subject in Fay Weldon's *The President's Child* (1982,
pp. 33–4):

> 'Do you suffer much from pre-menstrual tension?' asked Bobby's
> mother.
> 'No,' said Isobel shortly.
> 'I never saw you hit Jason before. And he wasn't doing anything
> wrong, was he? I just thought it might be PMT. If men had to
> suffer from it they'd soon do something about it. I sometimes hit
> Bobby when I'm suffering. I'm sure most women do.'

This new frankness and freedom of familiarity with their own
bodies was very much the legacy of the taboo-breaking of the
1960s. Previous attempts by women writers to explore the intimate
nature of their sensuality and sexual experience had been confined
to private or surreptitious work like this erotic masturbation
fantasy of Anais Nin, originally produced as pornography for a
private buyer in her Paris girlhood:

> Then Mathilde wanted to know how she looked when Martinez
> told her to turn over. She lay on her left side and exposed her ass
> to the mirror. She could see her sex now from another side. She
> moved as she moved for Martinez. She saw her own hand
> appear over the little hill formed by the ass, which she began to
> stroke. Her other hand went between her legs and showed in the
> mirror from behind. This hand stroked her sex back and forth.
> Then a forefinger was inserted and she began to rub against it.
> Now she was taken with the desire to be taken from both sides,
> and she inserted her other forefinger into the ass hole. Now when
> she moved forwards she felt her finger in the front, and when she
> lurched back she felt the other finger, and she sometimes felt
> Martinez and a friend when they both caressed her at once. The
> approach of the orgasm excited her, she went into convulsive
> gestures, as if to pull away the ultimate fruit from a branch,
> pulling, pulling at the branch to bring down everything into a
> wild orgasm, which came while she watched herself in the

mirror, seeing the hands move, the honey shining, the whole sex and ass shining wet between the legs. (*Delta of Venus* written 1940–41, published 1978, p. 28)

Another essentially private female experience explored in the new freedom to deal intimately with bodily experience is that of abortion. An early account of Colette hints at the psychic pain of the women involved in this most lonely of actions:

> Married to a man she hated, my narrator had not dared to confess her despair when she fancied she was pregnant, except to an old footman, an ancient corrupter of princelings, a valet she feared.
>
> 'He brought me a concoction to drink,' she said, touched at the recollection, 'He and he alone in the world pitied me . . .
>
> What he gave me was pretty horrible . . . I remember that I wept . . . '
>
> 'With grief?'
>
> 'No. I cried because, while I swallowed that horror, the old fellow tried to hearten me by calling me niña and porbrecita, just as he had when I was a child'. (*The Pure and the Impure*, p. 79)

Later Marge Piercy was able to use the abortion itself as a metaphor of her heroine's condition: 'she was caught, she was stalled. She floated like an embryo in alcohol, that awful thing the Right to Life people had in that van on the street' (*Woman on the Edge of Time*, p. 20). Yet the woman trapped in an unwanted pregnancy was not always simply a victim:

> 'I'm going into hospital on Monday.' Dolly fluffed her hair. 'I persuaded him not to use that butcher on me. It costs a lot, but it will be a real hospital operation. Not with that butcher who does it all on the whores cheap.' Dolly spoke with pride.

The opposite experience, of the woman who has to carry out these abortions, is the focus of Fay Weldon's concern in *Praxis*:

> 'I expect you're right' [Mary writes to Praxis about the question of a woman's right to choose], 'but I feel you're wrong. I spent most of a year on a gynae ward. I was the one who got blood on my surgical gloves, remember, actually doing abortions. I'd do it happily for the older women who at least knew what was going on and were as distressed as I was, but I resented having to do it for the girls who used me as a last-ditch contraceptive because

they didn't want their holidays interfered with. (p. 255)

Provocatively, the 'right to life' argument is juxtaposed with an account straight from the heart of what it is to have to care for a newborn baby:

> The household was under considerable strain. Serena's baby had infantile eczema, and cried and cried, and scratched and scratched, and had to be fed on goat's milk, and dressed in muslin and receive Serena's full attention. Philip could not sleep. Work dried up again. Serena and the baby spent most of their nights in the spare room. The royal child, confused by the ups and downs in his life, wet his bed and soiled his pants. Serena, her eyes wide with strain and dismay, did her breathing exercises, started each day with a glassful of wine vinegar and honey, and achieved the lotus position, but little else.

Now, women could not only discover for themselves what such moments and episodes might mean, but with the freedom to publish came the even greater freedoms to share and compare these quintessentially female experiences with other writers and readers; and through their characters to create different and opposing versions of the same event. For Fay Weldon's Praxis, for instance, 'to lose one's virginity is not . . . an insignificant event. It is tremendous, momentous, and sets the pattern for an entire sexual life to come' (p. 35). In contrast, the heroine of Lisa Alther's *Kinflicks* speaks for all the women who find that on their first experience at least, the earth does not move:

> After all, this was it. This was the experience that people down the ages had sacrificed life and limb to achieve. Wars had been fought, kingdoms had fallen over the issue of who got to perform this act with whom. I wished Clem would get on with it . . .
> Get on with it Clem did, thrusting himself into me savagely time after time, like a murderer stabbing a still-stirring victim. This went on for quite a while. Finally, as I was mentally drumming my fingers on the platform, Clem stopped abruptly . . .
> I found it hard to believe that this was what Joe and Bob and I had spent almost two years building up to. 'You mean that's *it?*' I asked with dismay. It hadn't been exactly unpleasant, except for the first pain, but I couldn't exactly view it as the culmination of my womanhood. Frankly, the rupturing of my maidenhead had been just about as meaningful as the breaking of a paper Saniband on a motel toilet. (p. 127)

In her dry, witty tone vitalised by the background crackle of authentic indignation, Lisa Alther is very much the heir of Mary McCarthy here. The spirit of McCarthy also seems to hover over Ursula Bentley's wickedly funny treatment of sex in *The Natural Order* (1982), though Bentley's tone and material are very much her own. In the scene where the dreadful Mr Dacre pounces on the heroine-narrator, notions of sexual freedom and originality of comic invention are taken to new heights:

Within seconds his arm was around my waist and he was kissing me, though that is hardly the word. It was like being sucked into a turbo-jet: I thought half my face would be missing when I came up for air . . .

Mr Dacre had been going at me as though I were a thug resisting arrest. My hair had been pulled, my funny-bone banged and my knee squeezed until the patella was almost dislodged from its socket. In the space of five minutes my enthusiasm had plummeted, but Mr Dacre's had reached a peak. I wanted him to get on with it before I lost patience altogether. I knew there was no forgiveness for leaving a man standing in such condition, especially when it was all of my own doing. Speed was essential; with my now more objective eyes Mr Dacre's ridiculous earnestness, accentuated by his inept passion, struck me as of old.

He put the light out and threw himself on top of me in earnest. He had an *idée fixe* that ramming his knee into my groin was a *sine qua non*, and the rest of his technique consisted of biting any part of my face, ears, neck, shoulders and nose that proved receptive to his snapping jaws, all the while pinioning me to the floor by my hair.

It wouldn't go in. I was trying to simulate rapture – with difficulty. Mr Dacre was beginning to panic. His aim got more wildly optimistic. In between heart-felt moans which were meant, nevertheless, to be encouraging, I murmured discreet directions. 'Move to the left. No, not that far. Up a bit.' It was like guiding somebody into a parking space.

After five minutes or so of this, I sensed that all directions would be in vain. He had collapsed. (pp. 147–8)

Countless numbers of women writers, however, have maximised the recent freedoms to demonstrate again and again that there are other modes of writing about sexual experiences than the humorous and detached. Of a number of bold and strikingly written episodes in Michele Robert's *The Visitation*, this best illustrates her mastery of the theme:

> There are no words in the language to describe her embrace of him, and so they are forced to become poets, giggling, inventing new ones. This is what Helen's mother meant, then, when she used to say: it is very beautiful. When a man darts like a humming-bird and leaps like a salmon, and a woman flies up and out to meet him, and encloses him in mid-air, in the depths of streams. Only Helen, convinced she was a sinner, did not want to remember, did not want to know. But now there are words, and words, which flash across the darkness of her mind. Doors open, close, along the corridor. She is a violent, a blue flower, that beats its fleshy wings, that claps, she is a drum of blood, a shout, a city street. She presses down and down and down, as waves of blue sensation eddy up and up and up.
>
> Robert is letting her move him down strange paths, to places where they have not been together before. He lets her guide him, he listens to what her body says, he follows her slow dance, learning new steps very different from his former ones, a gentler rhythm. They let the body take over. Their bodies decline for them the verb to be: I am, you are, he is, she is. We are. And Helen comes, comes in response to him who responds to her, and is no longer frightened of you, me, and can let her body say with his: we are.

The heightened sensation of this experience leads Helen on into a transcendental apprehension of her deeper self:

> She is whole, she knows that now, and she can see all the different sides of herself; the masculine and the feminine; the productive and the reproductive; the receiving and the creative; the light and the dark; the rational and the irrational; the active and the passive. She needs to embrace all these parts of herself if she is to live without being maimed. Here are the twins after all; not, as she once thought, bright separate meteors flashing across the sky; not, as she once thought, warring archetypes exhausting her energy. The twins lodge simply, deep inside her, as images of different parts of herself, as needs for different sorts of activity. She begins to smile with delight at this recognition of what makes herself: wholeness dependent on twin capacities and twin needs. Out of the tension, the meeting between the two, she forms the synthesis of who she is today.

She cradles Robert's sleepy body in her arms. Do you know this already? she wants to ask him: have you also worked this out? Is it the same for men, or different? Tell me, please tell me.

– Let me live, she whispers: I want to create, wholly, with all of myself, not just half.

Robert in her arms shifts and grunts.

– I'm an honorary woman now, aren't I? he murmurs: wouldn't you say?

– I love you, she says, kissing him: I love you, I love you.

– Hmph, he mutters, and falls asleep, and begins to snore. (pp. 174–5)

With this new freedom have come new opportunities for women to be honest not only about their own experience of sex, but also to reveal the truth about their relations with men. In the 'anything goes' mode of the post-sixties revolt, these will not always be what a woman might expect:

Suddenly he reached between them and began to touch her clitoris as they were fucking, and she came in several moderate waves of electric pleasure.

'I've come,' she said. 'Now your turn.'

'Did you really?' He sounded suspicious. 'Take your time.'

'I came. Really and fully. Now you come.'

Suddenly he was soft in her. Yet she knew he had not climaxed. 'What's wrong, Joel?' She cradled him against her.

'Nothing. I don't think I can come.'

A man not going to come? This was a new one. 'Why not? Let me excite you.'

'No,' he said. 'Really, it's all right. Coming doesn't mean that much to me.'

Where have I heard that one? she thought. Me being polite.

His relaxed penis slid from her, and they curled side by side. 'You didn't really come, did you?' he said sulkily.

But this unpromising beginning develops into a moment of rare understanding for Marge Piercy's Vida as her lover begins to explore his own ignorance in the strange new world that men and women inhabit when the old rules no longer apply:

'I didn't think women came from fucking.'

'If it lasts long enough and if I'm excited first. A lot of women come more easily from being touched or eaten – but you're not in bed with most women, just with me. . . . Don't you give me a

hard time about that too. There have been times when other
women have made me feel like a fink, like a completely male-
identified counterrevolutionary sellout, because I have orgasms
from fucking.'

He laughed. 'Kiley told me fucking was oppressive to women.'

'Well, it has been a lot. Men call the shots. Their shots. A lot
of times you get into bed with a man and it's like he's fitting you
into how he wants it. He wants to fuck in position A-4 or B-12
and you're to put your legs up around him whether you like it or
not and he wants you to do X and not Y, and you say certain
words. Then he'll go on for as long as he needs to come, which
may be about ten seconds. That is oppressive. Also dull.'

'Did I do that?'

'Oh, Joel, not even slightly. My problem with you is that I
came and you didn't. That's more satisfying for me than it
would be for you. I want you to have pleasure too.' It all
sounded so exotic she felt like laughing and hugged him closer.
Sex role reversal, all right, and she found it delightful. 'What do
you need to come?'

'Nothing special. Just to be less nervous with you.' He grasped
her tightly. In a short while his breathing began to open into
sleep. She lay tangled with his strange pleasing body and smiled
at the invisible ceiling. She felt as if she had come upon a truly
new breed of human being, a man untouched by old macho
roles, vulnerable and open, gentle and emotional as a woman.
How dear he was, she thought, and stretched out relaxed under
the weight of his thigh dropped across her, thick and substantial
as a log. (pp. 76–7)

For some women writers, the challenge to write about sex
combines productively with the challenge to understand it. Lisa
Alther's heroine-narrator of *Kinflicks* has had something of a shock
when, responding to a friend's cry of 'Dear God, I'm dying!' she
bursts into the bedroom to find her 'locked in furious anal
intercourse' accompanied by screams of 'Yes! Mother of Jesus, *yes!*'
The narrator's subsequent determination to research 'Venous
Congestion and Edema as a Determining Factor in the Intensity of
Human Orgasm' leads to some interesting discoveries:

The thrust of the paper, as it were, was that blood was the key
factor in sexual response in humans. Blood, many ounces of it,
surged into the areas involved. Or as one of my sources put it
with regard to the female, 'The bulbous vestibule, plexus
pudendalis, plexus uterovaginalis, and, questionably, the

plexus vesicalis and plexus hemorrhoidalis externus are all involved in a fulminating vasocongestive reaction.' The tissues, engorged with blood, pinched the veins so that none of the blood being pumped in along the arteries could drain away. Being a corpuscle in such a situation was equivalent to being an MTA passenger on a platform during rush hour with no trains appearing; more corpuscles kept arriving but none could depart. This state of affairs continued until the distention reached its outer limits and triggered a reflex stretch mechanism in the neighboring muscles. These muscles then contracted in spasms, which expelled the blood along the pinched veins in spurts. The collective experience of the muscular spasms and the blood expulsion was referred to as 'orgasm.' The tissues and muscles involved in this female orgasm had their precise counterparts in the male.

In other words, the back-seat blue balls of high school days had been caused by the failure, for different sociocultural reasons, to trigger reflexive contractions of the bilateral bulbo-cavernosi, the transverse perineals, the external anal sphincter, the rectus abdominus, the levator ani, and the ischiocavernosi, which would have drained the congested venous erectile bodies of the corpora cavernosi of the penile shaft and the sinuslike cavities of the penile bulb, the glans, and the corpus spongiosum of the blood that had engorged them. This blood lingered on in oxygen-starved puddles. (Oh, Joe Bob, where are you now? I asked of the shelf of thirty-pound anatomy texts I was consulting.)

But why? What was the point of eternally filling those mysterious interconnected venous chambers with blood, and then pulling the plug and draining them – only to start filling them all over again almost immediately? It seemed like the task of Sisyphus. Luckily, I had learned from my philosophy paper about who made the world never to tack a 'why' on to the end of my topics. I now limited myself to the 'how.'

But this much I *did* know: Although my pudenda personally hadn't experienced much in the way of fulminating vasocongestion of the venous plexus, I had no intention of spending my life functioning as a hydraulic engineer. (pp. 196–7)

All this, of course, relates to conventional sexual intercourse. The 1970s in Britain and the US brought a number of fictional explorations of the less usual aspects of sexual activity. For the prostitute Elaine of Fay Weldon's *Praxis*, women give sex as a selfless act of therapy for men, because 'it's not as if most women enjoyed carnal knowledge, or got anything out of it . . . it's the peripheral bits of sex, not the sex itself, that women go for'. In her experience of this work, Praxis has plenty of opportunity to find out for herself the truth of this pronouncement:

> Sometimes fear, disgust, boredom or an acute sense of waste would intervene, and Praxis would elude her escort, or her trailer, or the drunken bumbler at her side – however he was best described – and slip off home, and bath, and wait for Mary to get back from school. But just as often and increasingly, she would complete the journey to the summer house, undress, display herself, watch her partner's mounting excitement, or if it did not mount, assist him as best she could, and do whatever was required of her: things she had never thought of, which Brighton wives were not required to do. To masturbate openly, suck and be sucked, spank and be spanked, be tied, tie up, bugger with dildo, be buggered herself; but mostly just to lie there in a fume of alcohol, her face wet with a stranger's tears, while he inexpertly plunged, lunged, failed, gave up, tried again, spoke his griefs and unburdened himself, via his ejaculation, of his troubles. (p. 131)

As this suggests, women writers are now boldly beginning to confront the implications of a situation in which a female character does not want sex or any kind of a relation with a man, but will submit to it anyway. Doris Lessing led the way in her exploration of this theme, as she did in so much else, making her heroine of *The Golden Notebook* declare, 'It was from Willi that I learned how many women like to be bullied' (p. 90). Earlier explorations of the idea that 'every woman adores a fascist', in Sylvia Plath's phrase, had necessarily been brief and veiled, or else confined to the underground world of the pornographer and his male readership. As a female writing pornography Anais Nin had given a powerful account of a female's masochistic impulse in *Delta of Venus*:

> Sometimes in the street or in a café, Elena was hypnotized by the *souteneur* face of a man, by a big workman with knee-deep boots, by a brutal, criminal head. She felt a sensual tremor of fear, an obscure attraction. The female in her was fascinated. For a second she felt as if she were a whore who expected a stab in the back for some infidelity. She felt anxiety. She was trapped. She forgot that she was free. A dark fungus layer was awakened, a subterranean primitivism, a desire to feel the brutality of man, the force which could break her open and sack her. To be

violated was a need of woman, a secret, erotic desire. She had to shake herself from the domination of these images. (p. 154)

The ramifications of a woman's urge to submit extend both mentally and physically. The former is movingly explored by Sibilla Aleramo in her suggestively entitled *A Woman* (1979, p. 37):

> As time went on I was taken over by a sort of lethargy. I seemed to do nothing except abandon myself completely to my new surroundings. As a result my body submitted to my husband's wishes, although I found him physically more and more repugnant.
>
> I put this down to my exhaustion, my tiredness. I never tried to overcome my frigidity. More demonstrative behaviour seemed inconceivable. My only pleasure was to feel desired: but even that disappeared when what I saw disgusted me and what I heard seemed brutal or senseless.

Two notable first novels which deal strongly with the physical as well as the mental implications of women's masochism interlocking with men's sadism are *The Killjoy* by Anne Fine and *Nothing Natural* by Jenny Diski (both 1986). In *The Killjoy* a young girl is drawn into the web of an older man, hideously deformed from a childhood accident. The story, interestingly, is told in the first person from the man's point of view, thereby tantalising the reader with its oblique glimpses of the woman's motivation. *Nothing Natural*, by contrast, centres firmly on Rachel, an independent woman who is drawn into a sado-masochistic relationship with Joshua. As Lisa Alther states in her response to this book, 'sexual sado-masochism is a theme feminist novelists have heretofore largely avoided'. Jenny Diski picks her way therefore through a political as well as an artistic minefield in her depiction of Rachel's growing passivity and dependence on Joshua, and even her attraction towards the buggery and brutality that he inflicts on her. Rachel finally recaptures her sense of self and regains the initiative in this unusual situation, in a dénouement that contradicts the notion that all women, necessarily and inevitably, want and need the domination of men, after the old Lawrentian formula.

These voyages into the largely uncharted waters of sexual experience are pioneering ventures, and it remains to be seen how far the hard-won freedoms of recent years may yet be still farther extended. The majority of women writers have contented themselves with dealing ever more confidently, and in a widening range of voices, with women's everyday experiences, and much interesting and rewarding work has been done in the interpretation of these themes and episodes for women readers, and for some men too. Of these writers, one voice soars distinctively above the rest. As the high priestess of the celebration of female sexuality, Erica Jong reigns alone. In her unique blend of romantic exhilaration with savage satiric bite, she has forged a language, indeed a lexicon, of the kind of women's experience that women themselves never knew they had before. Who has better expressed the age-old tension women feel between Just My Bill, the good old reliable husband, and Don Juan/Ivan the Terrible/Lord Byron, the Romantic Irresistible Sod?

> I was not against marriage. I believed in it in fact. It was necessary to have one best friend in a hostile world, one person you'd be loyal to no matter what, one person who'd always be loyal to you. But what about all those other longings which after a while marriage did nothing much to appease? The restlessness, the hunger, the thump in the gut, the thump in the cunt, the longing to be filled up, to be fucked through every hole, the yearning for dry champagne and wet kisses, for the smell of peonies in a penthouse on a June night, for the light at the end of the pier in *Gatsby* . . . (*Fear of Flying*, 1974, p. 17)

Yet in the superbly deflationary climax to Isadora's longing, Erica Jong's unrivalled comic skills and stylistic ability combine to create a Truly Memorable Moment:

> 'Madam, if you want to get laid, then you'll get laid.'
> . . . [But] what could be more poignant than a liberated woman eye to eye with a limp prick? . . .
> 'Do I scare you?' I asked Adrian . . .
> 'I do not have a potency problem – it's just that I am *awed* by your stupendous ass and I don't *feel* like fucking.'
> The ultimate sexist put-down: the prick that lies down on the job. The ultimate weapon in the war between the sexes: the limp prick. The banner of the enemy's encampment: the prick at half-mast. The symbol of the apocalypse: the atomic warhead prick which self-destructs. *That* was the basic inequity which could never be righted: not that the male had a wonderful added attraction called a penis, but that the female had a wonderful all-weather cunt. Neither storm nor sleet nor dark of night could faze it. It was always there, always ready. Quite terrifying when you think about it. No wonder men hated women. No wonder they invented the myth of female inadequacy. (pp. 88–9)

By an inevitable logic, we are back with the sex war, and man the enemy. Yet man the enemy is at the same time, for very many women writers and their readers, man, the woman's dearest friend. In an ideal world, the Free Woman meets the Free Man, the male strong enough not to be threatened by her hard-won autonomy, yet tender enough to arouse in her the kind of love that the old-style male never got anywhere near. As a novel of men and women wrestling with these issues in a post-liberation society, Marilyn French's *The Bleeding Heart* (1980) offers a more optimistic assessments of the prospects than her celebrated stark account in *The Women's Room* (1977). But like the heroines of Lessing, Rhys, Murdoch, and Jong, these women may be free of a number of trammelling conventions, but they are not and do not generally want to be, free of men. The choice of the women who do make this election has also been one of the freedoms that the contemporary novel has been able to explore.

CHAPTER 10

Loving women

There is a wide discrepancy in American culture between the
lives of women as conceived by men, and the lives of women as
lived by women.

Tillie Olsen, *Silences* (1978), p. 179

I mean the term *lesbian continuum* to include a range – through
each woman's life and throughout history – of woman-identified
experience; not simply the fact that a woman has had or
consciously desired genital sexual experience with another
woman. If we expand it to embrace many more forms of primary
intensity between and among women, including the sharing of a
rich inner life, the bonding against male tyranny, the giving and
receiving of practical and political support . . . we begin to grasp
breadths of female history and psychology which have lain out of
reach as a consequence of limited, most clinical, definitions of
'lesbianism'.

Adrienne Rich, 'Compulsory Heterosexuality and Lesbian
Existence', *Signs*, 5, 4 (1980), 648–9

It is becoming evident that many women writers, especially in
the twentieth century, can be understood only if the critic is
willing and able to adopt a lesbian point of view.

Bonnie Zimmerman (1985)

As the makers of the contemporary novel have explored the nature
of society and sexuality and their relation to each other, a solution
that has been emerging as more and more acceptable is the idea of
life without men. The lesbian alternative in fact implicitly offers a
radical critique of heterosexism, rejecting as it does the set of
values and structures that assumes heterosexuality to be the only
natural form of sexual and emotional expression, the old lie
insisting that women have only sought emotional and sexual
fulfilment through men – or not at all.

This alternative perspective has, however, been a long time coming. (See Jane Rule's scholarly and compelling *Lesbian Images*, 1975, and the fascinating *Lesbian Studies*, 1982, edited by Margaret Cruikshank.) Unspoken, unspeakable, underground, and invisible, lesbianism has been the perfect image of the love that dared not speak its name even more than male homosexuality. Pairs of women were invariably interpreted as friends in a passionless co-existence; woman-identified writers like Virginia Woolf, Emily Dickinson and Gertrude Stein were forced by a society at once homophobic and misogynist to adopt coded, oblique, or private languages. This in turn meant that lesbian women writers until very recently worked alone, cut off from their own history and tradition, and with little support or even hope of it from other lesbians, from other women, or from society at large. The lesbian in this situation thus became the perfect paradigm of the woman writer, suffering twice over the need to reinvent, imagine, discover, and verify everything for herself, devoid of signposts, milestones, and sustenance along the way. Our lesbian foremothers and the role-models they might have provided were not merely forgotten, but obliterated.

In these circumstances it is hardly surprising that women writers of the past often found it easier to deal with male homosexuality than with that expressed between the members of their own sex. There needed to be no breakdown of barriers here; this theme has had its place for many years unquestioned and unremarked, in the pages of some of our most austere and respected women writers. An interesting portrait in view of the author's lifelong attachment to a woman friend is that of the outrageous Julian in Ivy Compton-Burnett's *Brothers and Sisters* (1950). It is he, rather than the sister he lives with, who does the flowers and the catering, presides at tea-parties, and constantly invites attention to his delicate sensibilities; he sums it up himself in the sly comment, 'every little womanly touch in this cottage is mine'. He adores gossip, and revels in scandal, but on the credit side is quite without pomposity or pretensions to authority, and as a result is an extremely useful agent of the author in contrasting with and puncturing the attitudes of more orthodox male figures, like the clergyman, for instance.

Nevertheless, this is very much an exterior study, embodying some dated stereotyping, such as the belief that male homosexuals are inevitably effeminate. The same robustly denigratory view is expressed by Enid Bagnold in her presentation of Lewis Afric in *The Loved and the Envied* (1951). This character, whose real name (Snosvic) and nationality (Armenian) are chalked up against him as two black marks from the start, is pointedly made a woman's dress designer in the world of Paris fashion. In case the reader should fail to pick up this clue, he is later castigated in round terms as a 'pederast', a 'pansy', and 'one of those unhappy creatures'. The first term seems to be used very loosely, as Afric's lover is a man old enough to be a diplomat. But this is throughout a flippant and derisory use of the stereotype of the male homosexual. He is constantly made to seem pathetic and absurd, attempting to marry the heroine in an attempt to alleviate the punishing loneliness which is his unavoidable lot, and being edged out, virtually at the altar, by the handsome (straight) hero.

As an antidote to heartless or hostile treatments stands the work of Mary Renault, for many years virtually alone among women writers for her sympathetic and thoughtful studies of male homosexuality. Her special interest lay in the classical world; and in books like *The Last of the Wine* (1956), *The Mask of Apollo* (1966), *Fire from Heaven* (1970) and *The Praise Singer* (1980) she reworked and revitalised different tracts of Greek history and prehistory, each one seen through the perspective of a homosexual love affair. It has been argued that she glamorises and romanticises her subjects, choosing as her protagonists, for example, men of god-like stature or heroic attainment like Theseus and Alexander the Great. There is, too, a dangerous approximation to the conventions of Hollywood epic when historical personages like Alcibiades and Demosthenes casually wander across the action as extras. And Mary Renault throughout avoids confronting the physical reality of any overt sexual act by the use of such euphemisms as 'sharing a cloak'.

Against this, it is evident even from the partial and limited evidence remaining that the Greeks themselves found homosexual love just as capable of a romantic interpretation as heterosexual, thrilling as they did to accounts of the heroic demise of the Sacred Band of Thebes, when homosexual lovers, fighting side by side, the older and stronger protecting his younger lover, died as one man at the battle of Chaeronea. This was, even to those living through it, an age of gold, full of superhuman beings and achievements; and it is this quality that Mary Renault is at pains to convey, together with the personalities of those who made the epoch great, rather than any graphic exposé of the details of a homosexual relationship.

This is, in fact, a main clue to Mary Renault's angle and method. Her theme is essentially love, which she calls 'the most treacherous word in the language'. This phrase, from *The Charioteer* (1953), characterises one of her rare ventures into a twentieth-century setting for her homosexual lovers. This is a Second World

War story, in which she tries to trace and account for the
development of an ordinary little boy into an adult who can love
only those of his own sex. Some of the material is quite rigidly
schematised in line with contemporary psychological theorising on
the subject. There is the scene showing the departure of the central
character's father, which ensures that Laurie will henceforth be
brought up as a 'mummy's boy'. There is the public school
conditioning, the worshipping adoration experienced for the Head
of the House; and then, decisively, the Forces in wartime. Here
Laurie meets and falls in love with a boy whom he feels is too
young to be asked to admit 'the love that dare not speak its name',
either on his own or on another's account. While he is wrestling
with this difficulty, his Head of House, now a bronzed, blue-eyed
sea-captain, re-enters his life. The stage is set for an unorthodox
version of the Eternal Triangle.

In her picture of the unorthodox life of these eternal outsiders
(note that the novel was written years in advance of the Wolfenden
Report which finally paved the way in Britain for the repeal of the
punitive legislation against male homosexuals in the late 1960s),
Mary Renault is strong on the closely observed social detail of
homosexual domestic life, the flats, the odd parody of womanly
housekeeping, the parties, the 'marriages', the flirtations and
casual pickups. She introduces a wide range of men, from the calm
doctor, Alec, to the nauseous male whore Bunny, in an effort to
establish that masculine love breaches all divisions of class,
occupation, and educational background in its establishing of a
reassuring group, a defence against society. There are some
memorable moments which could only have occurred in a
homosexual setting, such as the portentous discussion of the
situation of homosexuals in relation to 'normal' people, which is
shattered by a truculent and drunken observation from one of the
party that 'a lot of bull is talked about Greece by people who'd just
have been a dirty laugh there'. But apart from Mary Renault, there
has been little overt interest from women writers in this subject.

If women writers have found it hard to deal genuinely and
responsively with male homosexuality, how much more difficult
has the subject proved when related to their own sex (is this
despite, or because of D. H. Lawrence's belief that consciously or
unconsciously, women are all lesbians?). Only one woman writer in
this century has seen it as her mission to attempt to tell the truth
about women's love for women. Radclyffe Hall established with
The Well of Loneliness in 1928 a reputation which even now has not
quite subsided; as late as 1974 this essentially harmless book was
still kept in the reserve stock of several provincial libraries. The

book has become, irrespective of literary merits, a classic statement
of this theme. In the furore which followed its publication
Radclyffe Hall was abused and obstracised, seriously impoverished
by the fight through the courts against charges of obscenity, and
finally driven from the country as an enemy of young girls, married
love, and the stability of the family. Her plea for an increased
understanding and tolerance of this sexual orientation was received
virtually as an attempt to subvert the state. These venomous and
hysterical reactions were based on a biased or incomplete reading
of the work. Few people, then or since, took pains to discover
Radclyffe Hall's attitudes or to analyse her work dispassionately.

Had this been done, there might have been some surprise at the
result. For it is one of literature's little ironies that the woman
writer who is commonly thought of as the voice of female
homosexuality should display in her work a sturdier set of
traditional sexual stereotypes than most heterosexual authors.
Even the writer who set out to reclaim and dignify this aspect of
human love, herself a homosexual, could not be free of the
countless other pressures which condition attitudes and behaviour.

A study of *A Saturday Life* (1925) shows clearly how Radclyffe
Hall's concept of sexuality is modified by her awareness of its
function in society. The novel is unmistakably homosexual in
theme, tone, and emotional colouring, yet its social and moral
values assert the supremacy of the 'straight' world. Homosexual
feeling is defined and limited by the 'normal' emotional modes, and
subordinated throughout to them. The norm in this case is that of
the independent, conservative middle class among which the action
takes place. As a result class emerges as a more significant agent in
the definition of personality than sex or sexual behaviour. The
satisfaction of class demands, the subtle, stringent exaction of
conformity, not only determine the heroine's ultimate fate but
precondition each stage of her career.

A Saturday Life tells the story of Sidonia from birth to marriage.
She is a difficult child whose management is largely left to Frances,
a friend of the family. Her restlessness leads her to experiment with
the dance, piano, art, singing, life in Italy, and personal
relationships (the novel's rather wilfully obscure title refers to an
Eastern belief concerning this sort of dilettante existence).
Radclyffe Hall constantly treats Sidonia's course as an emotional
pilgrimage of a purely artistic nature. This ignores the truth that it
is only made possible by the fact that Sidonia inhabits that social
class which can both afford the search for, and expect the reward
of, self-fulfilment. Similarly society requires and class describes the
final marriage, as Sidonia subsides into a woolly happiness that is

highly inartistic but predetermined by the fictional convention that follows the social so closely.

This failure to grasp or even to acknowledge in passing the interaction of the social and personal is related to a certain structural malfunction in the novel. Nominally its heroine is Sidonia, and her growing-up provides its subject and framework. But the emotional centre and motive force of the narrative is the homosexual woman, Frances. This character, whose name conveys the first intimation of her intersexuality, Radclyffe Hall projects as the type colloquially called 'butch lesbian' or 'dyke'. Her hair is touched at the temples with a 'gentlemanly greyness'; she wears an eyeglass, suit, shirt, and tie; she affects a no-nonsense attitude in emotional situations – 'You'll find the liver pills in the right-hand corner of the bathroom cupboard, I should take a dose' – or blows her nose gruffly when genuinely moved. She acts as the male partner to the feeble Lady Shore, Sidonia's mother, who literally weeps on her shoulder and turns to her in every crisis. Frances's spiritual retreat is her study, which, with its leather armchairs and ancestral portraits, is furnished to resemble as closely as possible 'the smoking room of a Piccadilly club'. Here Frances smokes, broods, twiddles her eyeglass, and reflects on the women in her life.

It is clearly stated that Frances never thinks of herself as a woman. With perverse logic, having cast herself as a man she assumes the traditional masculine superiority to women. She considers a thousand pounds a year enough for a woman to live on, though her income more than doubles that amount; she thinks in contemptuous generalisations of 'the average woman', 'the other female millions', that 'God intended them to marry and have nice babies'. Clearly Frances is the Radclyffe Hall figure. Her attitudes are her creator's, and this is especially remarkable in the handling of Sidonia's brief infatuation with her. Poised on the brink, this would-be wild adolescent is rather a nympholeptic projection than a real character, created to satisfy the imagination of a raffish but still deeply conformist female homosexual. (Radclyffe Hall's self-image emerges from Una Troubridge's *Life and Death of Radclyffe Hall*, 1961: her initial pose, 'How do I know if I will care for you in six months time?', gave way to a lifelong 'marriage'.)

Certainly the sequence reads like wish-fulfilment fantasy, employing the tone and vocabulary of standard romance, although with some homosexual colouring. Sidonia is boyish, tall and thin, but in case this sounds too austere, the author throws in a hint of fullness and sensuality with 'masses of auburn hair' and 'huge eyes'. In her admiration for Frances, Sidonia is rendered 'limp and adoring' like any pulp fiction romantic heroine. But the confusion of sexual roles in this courtship is indicated by Sidonia's opening gambit: 'If I were a man I'd marry you, Frances. I'd fall in love with you if you were a man.' A further layer of psychic insecurity is revealed when Sidonia adds demanding child to seductive woman as she makes her move proper:

> '. . . I need someone real, I need *you*! Why can't I have you? Aren't I younger than mother? Aren't I attractive? Don't I interest you enough? Frances' – she began to speak softly now – 'Frances, look at me! Don't you love me? Frances, won't you be my friend? I don't want to marry anyone, I tell you; I just want to work, and have you, all of you. . . . ' She laid her hand caressingly on Frances's arm. 'Frances, why won't you love me?' (p. 71)

Predictably, nothing comes of this. Frances, a sheep in wolf's clothing, disengages herself 'very gently' and leaves. The strangulation of the new love by the old forms, both social and artistic, is soon accomplished. Frances's efforts to find a husband for Sidonia give rise to some predictable man-baiting. All the suitors have weak chins, fishy eyes, and sheepish looks. But when one of more than average bone-headedness presents himself, his more than average wealth and social standing carry the day. Married, this man becomes even more bigoted and overbearing; Frances endures with gritted teeth repeated drenchings as he splashes about in the shallows of his ignorance. The novel ends with the birth of the first child. Frances accepts fairly happily Sidonia's pronouncement as she sums up her varied career and its climax in motherhood, 'I've a feeling that it's always ended like this.' But our sympathy and interest remain where they have been throughout, with Frances; and there is an unavoidable pathos, both within the terms of the novel and without, in the use of the homosexual woman to further, and finally to glorify, the conventional concept of undistinguished heterosexual romance.

Pathos there is again, and much more, in Radclyffe Hall's major work, *The Well of Loneliness*. This novel makes compulsive reading, despite the flaws of the style, alternating as it does between the florid and the flat. What gives the novel its massive drive and horsepower is the obsessive conviction of the writer which comes through on every page. Una Troubridge has related the way in which Radclyffe Hall undertook the first full-length and sympathetic study of female homosexuality in fiction as her special, divinely ordained task. That the novel is very substantially autobiographical makes its revelations even more arresting. It is clear that Radclyffe

Hall was not motivated by exhibitionism in her account. Only after much heart-searching did she decide to write a novel about the love of women, a subject which she believed had never before been treated seriously in fiction. To her it was 'a fact of nature' and she herself, as Michael Baker records in his sympathetic biography *Our Three Selves: A Life of Radclyffe Hall* (1985), was 'sick of ambiguities and only wished to dwell . . . in the palace of truth'.

Throughout *The Well of Loneliness*, therefore, the note that is sounded is that of the honest soul's duty to stand up and be counted. Much of the revelation springs from a disgusted refusal to tolerate any longer the hypocritical evasions and self-deceptions of regular members of society. These are the words with which the homosexual heroine of the novel, Stephen Gordon, is heartened to take up her burden of 'abnormality' by a sympathiser: ' . . . we're all part of nature. Some day the world will recognise this, but meanwhile there's plenty of work that's waiting. For the sake of all the others who are like you, but less strong and less gifted perhaps, many of them, it's up to you to have the courage to make good.' It is plain from her life as well as from her work that the writer herself felt much along this line.

And even today, after over half a century, the novel for which she was so reviled and humiliated at the time has lost little of its power to move and to disturb. It relates with a vivid sense of injury the various shattering stages by which Stephen is made aware that she is not like other women, and may not expect to live freely in her own mode of existence. She comes to regard her temperament as damned, herself as bearing the mark of Cain the outcast, and her whole existence as a supernal aberration, 'God's mistake'. In an era where even 'normal' behaviour was rigidly constrained by social and moral rules, such feelings of love as Stephen shyly nourishes are doomed from the start. Consequently her saga is one of inevitable disappointment or betrayal in love, since despite her painful longing to love and be loved in return, Stephen can never believe that she deserves or can retain any affection. She is not surprised that her first lover ruthlessly throws her over when self-interest dictates the move, and offers no reproach, but only the appallingly humble 'I'm just a poor, heart-broken freak of a creature who loves you'.

Later Stephen succeeds in achieving her dream of a deep and happy relationship with another woman. But she comes to feel that their love, at first mutually delightful, is having a damaging effect upon her lover. She sees Mary's personality coarsening and weakening under the strain of the hothouse lesbian life, cut off as they are from full membership of society. In addition, Stephen begins to be certain that in denying Mary a husband, children, security, and social acceptance, she is depriving her of more than she can offer her in devoted companionship, comfort, and protection. The more grimly she settles into seeing herself as a 'freak', the less is she able to forgive herself for dragging Mary down with her. In an apocalyptic conclusion Stephen nerves herself to kill Mary's love for her and to drive her away. Alone, almost maddened by her anguish, suffering 'rockets of pain, burning rockets of pain', Stephen sees armies of advancing shades, the accusing ghosts of all her 'sisters', who crowd in on her crying 'You dare not disown us!' On their behalf Stephen gasps out a plea for the basic right of survival. 'Acknowledge us, oh God, before the whole world. Give us also the right to our existence!'

A powerful novel of special advocacy, *The Well of Loneliness* nevertheless achieved an effect diametrically opposite to what its author had intended, in contributing heavily to the tradition which made a violent association of lesbianism with every form of deviancy, unhappiness, bitterness, and failure. The 'narrative of damnation' with an inescapable dying fall became the preferred form of lesbian fiction, outlining the lesbian's suffering as a lonely psychic outcast in the mould of Stephen Gordon. Djuna Barnes's *Nightwood* (1936), despite its brilliance, is another saga of sin and suffering, and like *The Well of Loneliness* again, was persecuted through the courts. In the years that followed, the love between women and its physical expression was treated lightly, mysteriously, or allusively where at all, as in the haunting symbolism of the swimming scene in *Two Serious Ladies* by Jane Bowles (1943):

> When at last Pacifica grew tired of splashing about in the water, she stood up and walked towards the beach. She took tremendous strides and her pubic hair hung between her legs sopping wet. Mrs. Copperfield looked a little embarrassed, but Pacifica plopped down beside her and asked her why she did not come in the water.
> 'I can't swim,' said Mrs. Copperfield . . .
> 'I will teach you' . . .
> Mrs. Copperfield undressed. She was very white and thin, and her spine was visible all the way along her back. Pacifica looked at her body without saying a word.
> 'I know I have an awful figure,' said Mrs. Copperfield.
> Pacifica did not answer. 'Come,' she said, getting up and putting her arm around Mrs. Copperfield's waist . . .
> Pacifica swam a little farther inland. Suddenly she stood up and placed both her hands firmly in the small of Mrs. Copperfield's

back. Mrs. Copperfield felt happy and sick at once. She turned her face and in so doing she brushed Pacifica's heavy stomach with her cheek. She held on hard to Pacifica's thigh with the strength of years of sorrow and frustration in her hand.

'Don't leave me,' she called out . . .

'Now,' said Pacifica, 'if you don't mind I will take one more swim by myself.' But first she helped Mrs. Copperfield to her feet and led her back to the beach, where Mrs. Copperfield collapsed on the sand and hung her head like a wilted flower. She was trembling and exhausted as one is after a love experience. She looked up at Pacifica, who noticed that her eyes were more luminous and softer than she had ever seen them before.

'You should go in the water more,' said Pacifica; 'you stay in the house too much.' (pp. 96–7)

In 1962 Adrienne Rich claimed that the greatest gains of feminist agitation were not the right to be educated or the right to vote, but rather the rights women now enjoyed 'for the first time / perhaps, to love each other'. To love each other openly, that is, without self-pity, apology or shame: 'neither as fellow-victims / nor as a temporary / shadow of something better' ('To Judith, Taking Leave', *Poems*, p. 133). Women were emerging, in Rich's analysis, for the first time as respected equals who rejected their historical isolation as a destructive separation from the pool of female energy and wisdom that can change their lives. Throughout Rich's poetry throbs the fear that women have not been able to avoid – 'We know we have always been in danger' – whether 'we' hide away, 'down in our separateness', or come forward to claim public space and attention. But 'now up here together' everything will be different, for 'till now / we had not touched our strength' ('Phantasia for Elvira Shatayer', *Amazon Poetry*, 1975, p. 42). Rich's message of women's secret source of communal strength was sorely needed and long overdue. But it was not until Mary McCarthy's portrait of Lakey in *The Group* (1963) that a novelist was able to show that a lesbian was acceptable: not damned and tortured, but glamorous, self-assured, and cosmopolitan, escaping both social stigma and self-contempt.

In the novels of the 1970s, the lesbian perspective seriously engaged for the first time with the conventional and commonly held notions of women's sexuality and the role of women in a patriarchal society. Colette, in *The Pure and the Impure*, besides giving a touching portrait of one woman's love for another ('There is not a single feature of her youthful face that I do not vividly recall') had offered an illuminating if partisan commentary on the needs of women for both emotional and sexual satisfaction through the character of La Chevalière:

> Restless and uncertain in her pursuit of love, she searched with her anxious eyes, so dark they were almost black beneath a low, white forehead, for what she never found: a settled and sentimental attachment. For more than forty years this woman with the bearing of a handsome boy endured the pride and punishment of never being able to establish a real and lasting affair with a woman. It was not for lack of trying, because she asked nothing better or worse. But the salacious expectations of women shocked her very natural platonic tendencies, which resembled more the suppressed excitement, the diffuse emotions of an adolescent, than a woman's explicit need. Twenty years ago she tried, with bitterness, to explain herself to me. 'I do not know anything about completeness in love,' she said, 'except the *idea* I have of it. But they, the women, have never allowed me to stop at that point . . . ' (p. 81)

As this suggests, lesbianism is not to be understood as an exclusively physical experience and phenomenon – it is both more and less than that – see Lillian Faderman's monumental and impressive *Surpassing the Love of Men* (1981). A good deal of energy in recent years has been devoted simply to understanding and discovering lesbian meanings, experiences, links. Maureen Brady's engrossing *Folly* (1982), raises a number of these questions that lesbians have only just learned openly to ask:

> Maybe they were just good friends, she thought. Maybe that was one way of being lesbian – having no use for men and pairing up with your best friend and helping each other out.
> Maybe Lenore wasn't a lesbian with Betsy, maybe it was with someone else. They couldn't have been lesbians when they were little girls . . .
> What I haven't figured out yet is whether they seem like lesbians because of the jobs they do, or whether they know jobs like welding and stuff because they're lesbians. (p. 20)

Above all, the lesbian seeker desperately needs to make the connections, between one woman and another, between her own experience and the legitimation of it:

Mary Lou's hand went to the last book on the shelf, pulled it out
and looked at the cover. 'Sappho was a Right-on Woman: A
Liberated View of Lesbianism': . . . she stuck it back on the shelf
as fast as she could without being conspicuous. Her hand felt as
if she had touched something red hot. She put it back in her
pocket. Wow, she thought, be cool. (p. 57)

These links take on an even greater significance if they can be
forged with another previously oppressed group to create a new
militancy and a new confidence:

Before Folly started dancing, she had been content to be
watching practically the whole room moving to the music, the
Black women and the white women dancing together . . . At the
factory they hung out in separate groups and barely knew each
other's names. Since the walk-out Folly had learned that the
Black women were more to be trusted than she had ever
realised – how they were less afraid to go against the man than
most of the white women, or if they were afraid, how they had
learned to contain their fear. (p. 87)

This passage indicates the ways in which lesbianism is almost
invariably feminist in its application if not in its original
orientation. The lesbian is gifted with a uniquely liberating, single
vantage point, from which to criticise and analyse the politics,
culture, and language of patriarchy. In personal terms too the
lesbian is liberated from the tyranny of a heterosexual union, seen
as a political institution rather than as an individual woman's
choice, since relations between men and women are both political
and institutionalised.
    These radical and separatist elements in lesbian thought and
practice account in part for the hostility felt and expressed towards
lesbians by men. But hostility is only half the picture. Male
attitudes to female homosexuality are deeply paradoxical, charac-
terised by the two simultaneous but distinct images of horror/
revulsion and attraction/compulsion. These are best expressed via
the image of the lesbian of popular culture, a 'bull dyke', clad in
dungarees and filthy from Greenham Common; and her direct
opposite, the fantasy duo, the lesbian couple beloved of pornography, two gorgous young women covered in baby oil and needing
only a man to come between them. The appropriation of
lesbianism by male heterosexual pornography constructs it simply
as an extension of male sexuality exploited as voyeurism. Yet as

Hilary Little stresses in 'Pornography: The Missing Link' (*Monitor*, 4, October 1986):

> Lesbianism is a form of sexual activity which excludes men, but the soft porn reader is actually so stupid that he doesn't know this. Blinded and deafened by his own arrogance he really is incapable of the thought that women have lives of their own and that yes, there are things he doesn't see.

The power of lesbians to live 'lives of their own' is now being explored and developed through a number of different women writers. Rita Mae Brown's semi-autobiographical *Rubyfruit Jungle* (1973) was one of the first novels to feature a strong lesbian who feels no need to dissimulate or apologise for her sexual preference. Molly Bolt grows up as a dirt-poor illegitimate Southern child who quickly learns that survival depends on her own feelings and assertive actions. One of the reasons why she makes out as a lesbian is that she refuses to accept the conventional limitations on being female.

But in her poetry, *The Hand That Cradles the Rock* (1971), Rita Mae Brown insisted that the rising strength of the individual woman is not the whole answer – only the sisterhood of women will bring about change. In 'Sappho's reply', she hears Sappho's voice as it 'rings down through thousands of years':

> Tremble to the cadence of my legacy,
> An army of lovers shall not fail . . .

The solidarity of women is a central theme of lesbian women's writing, since apart from anything else it usually offers the only way in which a woman can escape from the coils of an oppressive and inappropriate heterosexual union. In Marge Piercy's *Small Changes* (1973) a woman leaves her mother's domination for her husband's, and then finds herself trapped in an equally oppressive situation. She makes the break via a close personal friendship and a spell in a women's commune, moving through this on to a lesbian love relationship in which, despite the social difficulties, she finds personal fulfilment.

This imperative in fact dominates this recent work in the novel, as 'coming out' has come to seem the only honourable course for lesbians today. Elana Nachman's *Riverfinger Woman* (1974) is bristling with contempt for sexual role-playing:

We were too modern already to believe that one of us was the man and the other the woman. We felt like neither men nor women. We were females, we were queers . . . we knew we had the right to love whomever we loved. (p. 13)

In the interests of avoiding these misunderstandings and deceptions the heroine and her lover fantasise about enlightening the benighted world of heterosexuals; they will make a film 'so that people would see that lesbians are beautiful, that there is nothing at all unnatural about them, they too can have weddings and be in the movies' (p. 13). In *Lesbian Nation* (1973) Jill Johnston similarly celebrated the fact that 'that awful life of having to choose between being a criminal or going straight was over. We were going to have to legitimate ourselves as criminals' (p. 97). Among promising novels of self-legitimation came Bertha Harris's ambitious and ingenious *Lover* in 1976. Harris, the American equivalent of Monique Wittig, experiments with narrative pattern as an expression of her vision of sexuality. A modernist, she fragments and collapses characters, settings, chronology, and state of mind. The central consciousness of the novel appears and reappears in various different voices, and the preoccupation is as much with making a book, as with making a claim for lesbianism. But in its ingenious, sardonic, parodic tone and technique we see a brilliant comic intelligence with the confidence to joke.

This is not to suggest that women writers handling lesbian themes offer women's love as perfect or problem-free. On the contrary, the strength of the contemporary treatments lies in their authors' readiness to confront the awkwardnesses, uneasy compromises, and failures of lesbian relationships – their very normality, in fact. In *Other Women* (1984) Lisa Alther's wry, ironic tone signals both the pain of the lesbian lovers, and their down-to-earth, everyday acceptance of it:

Their relationship wasn't working, they finally concluded, because each had an equivalent need to be needed. In relationships with men, each had been exploited to her heart's content. But with each other life was a constant struggle to outnurture. The cabin filled up with their greeting cards. Banks of flowers were always dying on the tables. Each put on ten pounds from the candies and pastries the other brought home, which were dutifully devoured to please the donor. During lovemaking each would wait for the other to climax first, until both lost interest altogether. They fought over who got the most burnt toast, or the lukewarm second shower. They would have

fought to be the last off the *Titanic*, or the first off Noah's Ark.
Eventually they were compelled to address the issue of what to
do about two people in whom thoughtfulness had become a
disease. Diana felt the cure involved learning to do without
doing things for each other, including holding each other
through the night . . .
    . . . Caroline rested her chin atop Diana's head. Hard to
believe someone so small could trigger such overwhelming
feelings. But of course thousands had gone to their deaths for
Napoleon. She found herself studying Diana's large breasts,
which strained against the fabric of her uniform top. Off limits
now. How were you supposed to make that switch from one day
to the next?
    'You know,' said Caroline, 'I like celibacy fine. The only part
I don't like is not having any sex.' (pp. 21-2)

Yet despite the sadness here, this is not a negative presentation.
As with Bertha Harris, the keynote of the treatment is confidence
and strength. Lesbianism has become a positive image, in every
variation from Rita Mae Brown's ebullient attention-seeking,
to Alice Walker's wistful evocation of the love between women in
The Color Purple, and Jeanette Winterson's original, enchanting
Bildungsroman of a young lesbian in the prize-winning *Oranges Are
Not the Only Fruit* (1985). Winterson's heroine demonstrates in the
sharpest possible way that lesbian women will no longer tolerate
the ignorant, condescending judgment of the heterosexual world:

On Palm Sunday Melanie returned, beaming with an important
announcement. She was to be married that autumn to an army
man. To be fair he had given up the bad fight for the Good
Fight, but as far as I was concerned he was revolting. I had no
quarrel with men. At that time there was no reason that I
should. The women in our church were strong and organised. If
you want to talk in terms of power, I had enough to keep
Mussolini happy. So I didn't object to her getting married. I
objected to her getting married to *him*. And she was serene,
serene to the point of being bovine. I was so angry I tried to talk
to her about it, but she had left her brain in Bangor. She asked
me what I was doing.
    'Doing for what?'
    She blushed. . . .
    She left the day after, to stay with *him* and his parents. Just as
they were driving off . . . he patted my arm and told me he knew,

and forgave us both. There was only one thing I could do;
mustering all my spit, I did it. (p. 124)

'If you want to talk in terms of power' ... In that sentence
Jeanette Winterson economically sums up the growth of the lesbian
novel in the last twenty years – after centuries of denial and
repression, it has come into its own. As Adrienne Rich explains:

We're not trying to become part of the old order misnamed
'universal' which has tabooed us; we are transforming the
meaning of 'universality'. ('Compulsory Heterosexuality and
Lesbian Existence', 1980)

CHAPTER 11

Female, human, gifted, white and black

'This here is a riddle,' George said.
  'I listening.'
  'Two Indians was walking on a trail. The one in front was the son of the one behind, but the one behind was not his father. What kin was they?'
  'Less see. His stepfather.'
  George grinned at Portia with his little square, blue teeth.
  'His uncle, then.'
  'You can't guess. It was his mother. The trick is that you don't think about an Indian being a lady.'
  Carson McCullers, *The Heart Is a Lonely Hunter* (1943), pp. 270–1

One day the girl will be here, and the woman, whose name will no longer signify merely the opposite of masculinity, but something in itself, something which makes us think of no complement of limitation, but only of life and existence: the feminine human being. This step forward will (much against the wishes of the outstripped men to begin with) change the love experience that now is full of error, alter it fundamentally, refashion it into a relationship meant to be between one human being and another.
  Rainer Maria Rilke, *Selected Works* (1954), p. 106

It is the continuing paradox of women's writing from its very inception that while female writers were continually having to deny, disguise, justify, or apologise for their existence, they have quietly got on with the job of mastering the novel form and in doing so have made it very much their own. On any criteria of 'greatness' – enduring quality, human relevance, mythic resonance, capacity to delight – women have undoubtedly captured the heights with everything from *Evelina* (1778) to *The Color Purple* (1983). They have also explored all the highways and byways they thought attractive and appropriate, and while the numerous signs

193

declaring the novel territory for 'Men Only: No Trespassers Allowed' have undoubtedly deterred many women, it has never been possible for the border guards to keep all women writers at bay.

Now as the twentieth century draws towards its close it seems likely that women writers are at last not just making ground, but holding on to their gains and the ground that has been won. The cultural explosion of the 1960s blew a good deal of dated nonsense out of the window, and the tremendous progress on a number of fronts may be illustrated by this explanation by Elizabeth Hardwick in 1962, of why women writers could never expect to compete on equal terms with men:

> If women's writing seems somewhat limited, I don't think it is only due to these psychological failings. Women have much less experience of life than a man, as everyone knows. But in the end are they suited to the kind of experience men have? *Ulysses* is not just a work of genius, it is Dublin pubs, gross depravity, obscenity, brawls. Stendhal as a soldier in Napoleon's army, Tolstoy on his Cossack campaigns, Dostoevsky before the firing squad, Proust's obviously first-hand knowledge of vice, Conrad and Melville as sailors, Michelangelo's tortures on the scaffolding in the Sistine Chapel, Ben Jonson's drinking bouts, dueling, his ear burnt by the authorities because of a political indiscretion in a play – these horrors and the capacity to endure them are *experience*. Experience is something more than going to law school or having the nerve to say honestly what you think in a drawing room filled with men; it is the privilege as well to endure brutality, physical torture, unimaginable sordidness, and even the privilege to *want*, like Boswell, to grab a miserable tart under Westminster Bridge. . . . In the end, it is in the matter of experience that women's disadvantage is catastrophic. It is very difficult to know how this may be extraordinarily altered. (*A View of My Own*, pp. 180–1)

Old habits die hard, and after millennia of male-dominated culture, with both thought and thought-processes fashioned according to masculine habits of mind, it is hardly surprising that some of the old terms of the debate continue to hang on. One of these is the increasingly sterile discussion of 'masculine' and 'feminine' in literature. We have (most of us at least) moved away from the notion that all the vital powers of the mind, all the creative forces and shaping instincts are 'masculine', so described even when occurring in a woman. But a new dimension has been introduced into the discussion by the more recent attempts to address the question of the creative process in women writers as something *sui generis*. Set this in the wider context of the fact that it is only so recently in the history of human evolution that women have been able to speak in their own voices, publish under their own names, or 'tell it from within', and it becomes clear why it is difficult to abandon the fascinating topic of 'masculine' and 'feminine'.

Yet it is not hard to demonstrate how unhelpful, imprecise and even misleading they are, both as terms in literary criticism and as definitions of human characteristics, either in literature or in life itself. Both 'masculine' and 'feminine' in fact can mean anything that the individual speaker at the time wishes. Lisa Appignanesi has drawn attention to the overlapping and confusion which are inescapable adjuncts to the use of the concept:

> Literary critics repeatedly use the word 'feminine' to describe a writer, his vision, or his characters. It is often suggested that Henry James and Marcel Proust are 'feminine' writers, in contrast to the purely masculine Hemingway. Though George Eliot is personally said to have a strong 'masculine' side, yet her male characters are thought to be 'too feminine'. Wedekind's Lulu, Strindberg's Miss Julie, or Norman Mailer's 'Great Bitch' are all quoted as being embodiments of the 'feminine' principle, So too, somewhat paradoxically, are Dostoevsky's golden-haired whore, Sonya, in *Crime and Punishment* and Joyce's faithful-faithless Molly Bloom. (*Femininity and The Creative Imagination*, 1973, p. 1)

This confusion is neatly illustrated by the following remorselessly circular dialogue from Ivy Compton-Burnett's *The Mighty and Their Fall* (1961):

> 'Teresa writes like a man,' said Egbert, looking at the letter.
> 'I have noticed that,' said Selina. 'I have thought her a little like a man in herself.'
> 'I should have said she was the pure feminine,' said Lavinia. 'Herself and all to do with her. I don't remember her writing. I don't mean anything against her.'
> 'Why should you?' said Ninian. 'What are you but feminine yourself?'
> 'Oh, not purely, Father. Either in myself or as I have been influenced. It is quite a different thing.'
> 'Well, something is different.'

'We think of masculine women as tall and strong,' said
Egbert. 'Teresa is neither.'
'I did not mean masculine in that sense,' said Selina.

As this suggests, the use of these words places the speaker in the
position of one throwing a rope across a chasm and vainly hoping
that it will hold. Each speaker here uses the terms to mean 'What I
am not', 'What I disapprove of', or 'What I feel exists as a
quantity or entity but which I am under no obligation to link with
the sex whose name I have called it by'. Each of the characters is
also possessed by a patent assurance of his or her own uniqueness
and superiority to conventional sex typing. Possibly this is
something common to us all; in the grip of what Iris Murdoch has
called the 'fat relentless ego' we feel only our own dazzling
particularity, and readily resort to the comfort of generalisation
when it comes to any other, especially the other sex. Who has not
been guilty of some assumption like that of Cranford's Miss Pole:
'My father was a man, and I know the sex pretty well'?

Those who take on this pervasive and only half-conscious
process of generalisation find themselves striking at shadows.
When challenged, nobody uses these passwords. 'Masculine' and
'Feminine' may stand for such and such, or then again they may
not. The baffled may take refuge in Ninian's cautious platitude
above: 'Something is different.' But as psychology has been
struggling to assert, these words are in effect names for the
complementary functions of the personality, which are not
specifically or even necessarily related to physical sex difference.
Strong, weak, aggressive, submissive, analytical, intuitive; these are
all ways of being, of behaving, which all people, regardless of sex,
are potentially capable of.

The time is long overdue for criticism to abandon the use of
these inadequate and tendentious terms. Any assumption of the
existence of 'masculine' and 'feminine' must logically mean that
each should be largely if not wholly seen in the sex whose name it
carries. But can it in any way be shown that the intelligence of
male and female function differently? Do creative men and women
actually think and write differently? Do men and women write
differently from one another? Of course they do; but from one
another as individuals rather than as sexes. All writers who can
claim the title write differently from anyone else, that is all.

May criticism and literature at last be released from the tyranny
of the unbudging and reductive sexual classification? This
suggestion is hardly new or original. A number of writers have
made it their life's work to explore and establish the intersexuality

of much human behaviour through the discovery of the unsuspected fullness of the individual consciousness. James Joyce was the first of the modernists in this field, but he shares the fate of most of the greatest geniuses, and certainly of all great linguistic experimentalists, of proving to be a literary dead end; in the long run, the novel sank under him. Other writers in their own lives have shown how easily the sexual roles overlap; Scott Fitzgerald knew that his wife Zelda looked on him as the woman in the partnership, but he nevertheless regarded her as his child. In her adolescence Katherine Mansfield recorded in her journal, 'I am a child, a woman, and more than half man'; in her increasingly dreadful last years the 'man' in her took over, perhaps driven to it by the failure of the man in Middleton Murry to do any such thing, and she summoned her woman friend 'L.M.' to her side with the words 'I do love you and want you for my wife'.

Common usage of the terms 'masculine' and 'feminine' is not the result of any conscious critical activity in the minds of those who employ them. What they describe are socially directed sexual responses, descriptions of personalities cultured into complementary action. This in itself makes for territorial awareness in delineating male and female; both sexes display an uneasy half-consciousness that the areas of behaviour must be kept distinct in the service of some dim notion of the health of society. We must allow too for the constant and pervasive processes of sexual analogy. From this we find that male characters are presented and judged according to a set of criteria which includes strength, resource, initiative, while for women the prescription includes a greater degree of fragility, dependence, conventionality, and reliance upon external supports.

In the past, both male and female writers have united to support these social clichés of behaviour. In this way externally imposed patterns pass for sexual definitions informed by personal experience. Since the management of society has been largely in the hands of men, there is a case to be made out for regarding women as the products of men's imagination, conceived and shaped by men, the cultural a reversal of the biological sequence. A nineteenth-century novelist and feminist, Olive Schreiner, remarked from bitter personal discovery in her essay *Woman and Labour* (1911) that 'we all enter the world little plastic beings, with so much natural force, perhaps, but for the rest – blank; and the world tells us what we are to be, and shapes us by the ends it sets before us'.

Because in the past women writers have been shaped by the standards of androcentric cultures, and perceived and measured as writers by the standard of the 'real', male writer, it has usually been difficult or impossible for them to be entirely free of the widespread sense that, somehow or other, a 'woman writer' was second-class. In a 1984 article, 'Women Who Write Are Women', Elaine Showalter demonstrated how many twentieth-century women writers fight shy of the label itself. They are in fact unhappy with any sexual links between themselves and their work, equally unwilling to be associated with the woman reader too. Doris Lessing, for instance, 'has been outspoken for years about her wish to dissociate herself from her devoted female reading public', Showalter writes, while others lose no chance to protest that 'they are not "women writers" or "women's writers" (apparently worse), but *writers only*, less concerned with "female subjects" or "women's lot" than with the human predicament' (p. 1).

But this denial of their sex only serves to endorse the values of male-dominated societies which have for so long taught that only male experience is real experience, that only men's adventures and attitudes constitute 'the human predicament'; that women,'despite being in a majority of the human race, somehow don't count, are not fully human, or not fully equipped to express their humanity. So the male first-person narrator preferred by Iris Murdoch (why? we might ask – it would be interesting to know) is hailed as lending 'universal' significance to her work, even when as in *A Severed Head* (1961) he is a self-absorbed and hypochondriacal male of a particularly limited type. Doris Lessing's heroine-narrator by contrast, the 'I' of *The Golden Notebook*, as a female voice crying in the wilderness and insisting on the centrality of being a woman, was widely censured as creating a feminine 'ghetto', rather than seen as opening any doors of understanding of the largest sector of the population.

Doris Lessing has of course amply demonstrated her mastery of formal third-person narrative along with her continued determination to keep on tackling large, important, and socially central themes, in *The Good Terrorist* (1985). But her earlier work also indicates how inappropriate it is to cast her as the custodian/tenant of the Women's Room of the novel. Her fascinating *Briefing for a Descent into Hell* (1971) she describes as 'inner space fiction', but the novel has a wide applicability which is belied by this title. Its theme is that madness is the only form of sanity, a logical extension of her previous work with its attack upon the norm and the stresses that it imposes on the individual. As *The Golden Notebook* dealt with the sadness of separation from love, so here Doris Lessing hammered away at what she sees as a great loss in modern life: 'Some sort of divorce there has been somewhere along the long path of this race of man between the "I" and the "We", some sort of terrible falling away'.

In this work of extreme technical complexity, with its formal blending of stream-of-consciousness passages with letters, papers, hospital reports, snatches of poetry and narrative, Doris Lessing achieves an impressive synthesis of her varied material together with a passionate disgust which lends an impressive authority to her denunciation of human selfishness and separateness:

To celestial eyes, seen like a broth of microbes under a microscope, always at war and destruction, this scum of microbes thinks, it can see itself, it begins slowly to sense itself as one, a function, a note in the harmony, and this is its point and function, and where the scummy film transcends itself, here and here only and never where these mad microbes say I, I, I, I, I, for saying I, I, I, I, is their madness, this is where they have been struck lunatic, made moonmad, round the bend, crazy, for these microbes are a whole, they form a unity, they have a single mind, a single being, and never can they say I, I, without making the celestial watchers roll with laughter or weep with pity. (pp. 102–3)

Throughout this superbly exciting novel, as challenging stylistically as it is in form, content, and attitude, Doris Lessing urges human beings to look outward towards others, not inwards to loneliness and despair. Selfishness she sees as the modern madness, and the realisation of our common interests as the one true task of human life.

Yet whatever the authority of women's writing, its individual practitioners cannot always shake off the sense of strangeness with which their productions are likely to be greeted. It is as if there is some irreconcilable tension between the two realities of being a writer, and of being a woman. Alison Lurie's writer-heroine of *Real People* (1969) finds that only another woman writer is aware of and understands this:

I couldn't work at all this A.M., shut alone in my room with Wun [her dog], so I went out for a long walk through the woods. Coming back, I met H. H. Waters in the vegetable garden . . . it turned out well. One of the best conversations about writing I've ever had. Maybe because HHW (I still can't bring myself to call her 'Harmonia,' so I stupidly don't call her anything) knows what it's like to be a 'lady writer.'

I've complained of Clark that he thinks literature just a rather eccentric hobby for a housewife. But everyone here, even Kenneth, tends to speak of my life in Westford as if it were a

rather eccentric hobby for a writer. Since it seems to interfere
with my work, why don't I give it up? They don't see what
HHW sees at once, that it's the essential substance of my work,
without which there wouldn't be any Janet Belle Smith, or any
stories.

Really, most people don't like the idea of a serious woman
writer, or find it incongruous. They prefer to forget either that
you're a writer or that you're a woman – 'The usual choice, in
my case,' she said wryly. As a result, it's reported in interviews
that HHW can make peach pie, as if this were a most peculiar,
original circumstance. (pp. 82–3)

This concentration on the sex of a woman writer, with the
contingent but contradictory expectations it sets up, is still serving
to carry out one of its oldest and most important tasks, the
deflection of interest away from the writing and on to the
individual woman. As long as the cry is raised about each woman
as exceptional, strange, obscurely anomalous, it will be possible to
avoid dealing with the vast spread of women's achievement, the
whole development of a tradition parallel with and not inferior to
anything and everything written by men.

But recent developments in particular are becoming harder and
harder to sweep away, and they are attended too by encouraging
signs that women are now freer than they have ever been
historically to write what they want in the way that they want. The
upsurge of women's oppositional and counter-cultural writing
following on from the breakthrough of the 1960s has not only
favoured writings by lesbians and women of colour. Any and every
woman who finds herself out of step with her situation or society
can now use her writing as a form of resistance to whatever
constrains her, which is not necessarily a man, or an imposition of
a male-constructed society; many women's fictions are produced by
the tension between their secret inward vision of themselves and
the way they would like to live, and their personal inability to
bring this about, and such anger is as likely to be galvanic as
destructive. Carolyn Steedman's *Landscape for a Good Woman: A
Story of Two Lives* (1986) plays with the genre of autobiography to
interrogate her own experience and relate it outwards to the lives of
other women. *En route* she mounts a critique of contemporary
psychological and cultural theory without ever losing hold of her
analysis of the individual woman as her centre, in a sharp and
truly novel piece of writing.

It is interesting to observe how often women's writing as
resistance takes the form of a detailed survey of self and a

questioning of all the events, people, issues, and ideas that have gone into its formation. In a subtle and persuasive article 'On Female Identity' Judith Kegan Gardiner suggests why this should be so:

> To summarize, female identity is a process, and primary identity for women is more flexible and relational than for men. Female gender identity is more stable than male gender identity. Female infantile identifications are less predictable than male ones. Female social roles are more rigid and less varied than men's. And the female counterpart of the male identity crisis may occur more diffusely, at a different stage, or not at all. Cumulatively, we see a complex interplay between women's experiences of identity and men's paradigms for the human experience. It is not surprising, therefore, that the area of self-concept is especially troubled for women and that contemporary writing by women reflects these dissonances.
>
> Twentieth-century women writers express the experience of their own identity in what and how they write, often with a sense of urgency and excitement in the communication of truths just understood. Often they communicate a consciousness of their identity through paradoxes of sameness and difference – from other women, especially their mothers; from men; and from social injunctions for what women should be, including those inscribed in the literary canon.

This excitement of the discovery of identity, with its implicit sense both of the lonely self and the community of other women, is a task taken up in recent years by feminist criticism too. The work of Elaine Showalter, Josephine Donovan, and Cheri Register, among a number of others, develops the idea of the woman as writer at the centre of 'a female culture', which includes not only the individual's work and her relation to the literary heritage, but also her relations with other women: as mother and daughter, as sister, friend, lesbian lover, or colleague. This impetus is a welcome, if belated, response to Virginia Woolf's observation in *A Room of One's Own* that male authors so rarely show women in novels in relation to each other. Finally we seem to be in a position where the centrality and importance of women and women's lives and work, which includes their writing, are able to be acknowledged by both creative and critical literature.

In a sense, though, the hard work is only just beginning. The struggle to abandon the restrictive categories of 'masculine' and 'feminine', together with the pejorative associations of the label 'woman writer', has yet to be seriously engaged. But there has to be more in literature and criticism than the simple classification of authors by their sex. Compare 'woman writer' with other such trivialising subsections: regional novelist, Northern writer, dialectic poet, authoress. Its absurdity is revealed if we simply match 'lady novelist', a phrase still intermittently in use, with 'gentlemen novelist', or compare 'woman writer' with 'man writer'. For most women, creative or not, the fundamental choice is between sex and self, in Betty Friedan's phrase. Does she choose to live within her sex, undergoing all the personal, social, and educational restrictions that that can entail, or does she make the bid for full selfhood and equal partnership in human affairs?

For the artist, of either sex, the choice is between various modes, certain of which have been seen as 'masculine' or 'feminine', though these are not exclusively monopolised by, and may indeed have little direct relation to, individuals of either sex. But the creative choice is not as clear-cut as this. Like any of its members, the artist has to survive within society's framework of sexually determined stereotypes and agreed behavioural differences. These surround us from birth and exist at a level far below that of conscious attitude or decision. The creative task is to identify and resist them. Consequently where a writer or critic falls into any use of this category, there is inevitably a diminishing of the full artist, the full human being, and the full reader too. It reveals the adoption of a rigid posture, releasing irrational and inapposite associations into the critical atmosphere like a swarm of gnats: the response on learning that a writer is a man or a woman has been compared with finding out another's political convictions.

Like politics, sex is an unavoidable factor of human existence, and sex-based critical modes and the widespread use of sexual analogy have been deemed essential in the endless struggle to impose some significant distinctions on the eternal flux of human experience. Art and criticism alike find their primary work in the making of such distinctions. But there is also a vital sense in which the naming of anything alienates it from its true self, reduces its capacity by refusing to recognise its uniqueness, and renders it easier for society's consumption by asserting control over its real individuality. Something of this sort occurs every time the phrase 'woman writer' is used. It is, finally, the uncomprehending assault of the outsider on the mystery of the solitary artist; on all writers; and on all women.

For as Peter Schwenger insists in his provocative *Phallic Critiques: Masculinity and Twentieth-Century Literature* (1984) 'the massive problems of sex definition loom behind any analysis of masculine and feminine style. In a sense, however, the definition of sex *is* style' (p. 2). He amplifies this as follows:

> Similarities and differences must be held in the head simultaneously, resisting the temptation to exaggerate in either direction. This applies to men as a group; to men and women; to the individual and the whole of humanity. My preference is for differences, because they preserve the individual. (p. 157)

Yet a celebration of the difference must not be conducted in the spirit which has formed and deformed attitudes in the past. The examination of women as separate and different from men, the recognition of their own peculiar emotional processes and sensibilities, has led at times to an inability or refusal to see women in any other terms than these. This has also been responsible for two apparently unrelated modern phenomena, the derogation of 'romance' and women's writing in general and the sensational investigation of women's 'femininity' which concentrates entirely upon their sexuality.

Taken simply as individual females, rather than in relation to men and to society as in nineteenth-century fiction, women have not easily freed themselves from long centuries of fictional exploitation. The stress upon women's sexuality has in some cases become a way of obscuring or denying their full humanity. While their rational, creative, or administrative skills go largely unremarked, their bodies prove a goldmine for others, mainly men; both individuals and corporations have been making big money out of the partial and degraded representation of women as sexual creatures and sex objects in a series of developments not as far removed from the protected calm of the 'lady novelist's' study as many like to think. This degradation of women is further accomplished in the contemporary cult of brutalism, with its vaunting of masculine aggression, hostility, and violence. When women writers acquiesce in this disparagement of their sex, or lend themselves to lowering it further, then the result is particularly depressing. It is admittedly the artist's duty to know herself before she can know anything else. But women writers must, as Doris Lessing has, learn to look outside as well as in.

For there is much to be done that only women can do, in the recognition and weeding out of some continuing notions, in the readjustment, where possible, of the historical bias against women. As long as the accepted mode of society remains masculine in its orientation, then the general consciousness will continue to be influenced by attitudes inherited from the pursuit of two world wars and the virtually unchanged possession by males of all property, authority, and power. In this situation the position of women as both subjects and authors of fiction, will inevitably remain 'special', anomalous, and disadvantaged. It is significant that even in the most futuristic avenues of the so-called 'apocalyptic' novel in America or in that odd sport of fiction, the sci-fi novel, there are few real advances posited for the female of the species. Writers who are capable of dreaming up horrendous changes affecting total environment, technology, and personality, still see change as affecting every area of experience other than this one. Female characters continue to meander through the unimaginable timescapes of the future, still 'emotional', still in need of masculine domination, and still unable to understand the internal combustion engine or even to use a screwdriver.

To work against this is still the major task for writers as women. They have also their duty to themselves as writers. It seems that they must still learn to avoid being ghettoised as female, as George Eliot did. As creative artists they must endeavour to widen their field of vision and experience, not narrow the focus so that only one limited area comes into view. It is only by developing a sense of others, and of the ways in which individuals interact within society, that women writers will be able to free themselves and their sisters from the constrictions of sex-typing and sex-based writing in general. This emancipation will never be achieved by a narrow concentration upon the minutiae of women's lives, the emphasis on domestic difficulties and sexual sorrows. The sheer parochialism of much women's writing has sounded its deathknell; to take an admonition from a writer who succeeded in the artistic obligation to turn personal preoccupations into universal truths, Dostoevsky: 'Arid observations of everyday trivialities I have long ceased to regard as realism – it is quite the reverse.' But to make the particular the general, to assert the power of the female's full and compelling humanity: that is the task and the obligation.

To go outward; to develop a sense of community; to look to the moral rather than to the purely emotional dimension; to make the right choice and to make it work; these are not only the tasks of women, but of all writers. In addition, it is the duty of the novel to be novel – that is, to keep up with, to record, and to comment upon the contemporary. The trials of modern life are very specialised. Our age, with its increased social, educational, and emotional mobility has seen many casualties, and not all female. We have come, too, to a fuller acquaintance with the problems of internal migration, awkward transitions of personality which may ruin formerly stable relationships or at best render them obsolete. We have needed our fiction-makers to observe and relate all this, to give a name to every one of the processes of alienation which permeate personality and destroy the capacity for warm and secure loving.

This need becomes more urgent every day as the strains of urban life and a runaway technology bite more deeply. But the challenges of modern fiction to watch, shape up, and recount all this for those of us who are living through it, must be faced in a forward-thinking way. Much previously necessary assimilation in fiction of the disruptive events of life itself has now become outmoded. So, too, have some of the techniques whereby this is carried out, the use of sexual stereotypes and the clichés of sex definition. Every time that a writer capitalises on or even connives at the transmission of these clichés, then she or he is ensuring their perpetuation.

For the novel does not only reflect and record experience; it defines and delineates it too. Writers need to be constantly on the alert for the dangerous encroachments of these belittling assumptions, must resist the temptation of the creeping suggestive generalisation. The use of these will not only betray their own limitations, but will be responsible for the imposition of these limitations upon others. Twentieth-century fiction must make an effort to shake off the rags and tatters of nineteenth-century thinking which hang about it still. It should seek to assist psychology and sociology in their discovering and developing ways for human beings to live together, free and equal. Then, and only then, will we have the novels that will make 'woman's novel' a fatuous and superannuated phrase.

As to the women themselves, they see different scenarios for the future of the novel, and the freedom of the women writing within it. Bertha Harris, author of the experimental lesbian novel *Lover* (1976), envisaged a future free of the sex war, free of man the enemy, because free of man:

> There is not a literature that is not based on the pervasive sexuality of its time; and as that which is male disappears (sinks slowly in the west) and as the original all-female world reasserts itself by making love to itself, the primary gesture leading to the making at last of a decent literature out of a decent world might simply be a woman like myself following a woman like Djuna Barnes [author of the lesbian novel *Nightwood*] and all she might represent down a single street on a particular afternoon. (*Amazon Expedition: A Lesbian Feminist Anthology*, 1973)

Yet other women writers feel strongly about the work that is still to be done in the world of men, much of it because men are unable or unwilling to confront it themselves. As the black woman writer Alexis De Veaux explained to Claudia Tate:

> Men are more afraid because of the way they are taught to experience themselves, and because they have such a heavy burden to live up to in terms of what they think manhood is . . . Women have a certain primary sense of things like blood, which is life . . . Men also seem more conservative in their treatment of 'taboo' themes. Women tend to explore subjects that are not 'taken seriously' by male writers, or that are far less concerned with bravado and being number one, and some other mythologies created by their male experience . . . male writers are less inclined to want to explore new themes, new images of themselves. (In Claudia Tate (ed.), *Black Women Writers at Work*, 1985)

'New themes, new images', women's versions of the world where men and women will live together, free and equal – these have the gleam of tremendous promise. So too does the idea of a female culture acting as an intellectual centre and emotional base for all women writers to draw on and come home to at need. The female culture will only be fostered and allowed to grow by a renewed and sustained attention to women's experience in its every manifestation. Yet this is not without its problems and traps. The radical separatist feminist demand that would tie women to writing only of the world of women would not seem a wholly fulfilling direction for either women writers or the novel to take. On the other hand, any denial of the validity of women's lives and experience – *any* denial – is inescapably the same old misogyny rising up from the primeval swamp, whether expressed by a man or, as frequently happens, a woman. This denial can take many forms, can even come on in the guise of 'encouragement' to women writers to 'realise their potential'. Something of this sort seems to be at work in the often-expressed desire for women writers to transcend their sexual identity and become 'writers only', dealing with 'the real business of the world'. Has anyone ever expected Tolstoy, Dickens, Hardy, Lawrence, Scott Fitzgerald or Hemingway to make this transcendence? Although espoused by a number of writers and critics, of whom the most distinguished remains Virginia Woolf, this theory of the woman writer aspiring to an androgynous nirvana where she is neither male nor female was, is, and always will be inescapably derogatory to the individual woman, to the work she has produced, and the whole of the female tradition that lies behind her.

For the assumption at the root of this is that women writers are not there yet – that they still have journeys to make, distances to travel, changes to undergo before they arrive as novelists. George Eliot, while considering that women had the potential to write great novels – 'we have only to pour in the right elements: genuine observation, humour and passion' – seems to have been sublimely unaware that she herself had raised the novel to heights previously unattained and not subsequently exceeded. Virginia Woolf also pinned her hopes on the future; on the famous five hundred a year and a room of one's own, on 'the habit of freedom and the courage to write exactly what we think':

> Then the opportunity will come and the dead poet who was Shakespeare's sister will put on the body she has so often laid down. (*A Room of One's Own*, 1929)

Even Elaine Showalter in her impressive study of women writers strikes at last the part-visionary, part-hopeless note of 'next year in Jerusalem':

> If contact with a female tradition and a female culture is a center; if women take strength in their independence to act in the world, then Shakespeare's sister, whose coming Woolf asked us to await in patience and humility may appear at last. Beyond fantasy, beyond androgyny, beyond assimilation, the female tradition holds the promise of an art that may yet fulfill the hopes of Eliot and Woolf. (*A Literature of Their Own*, 1977, p. 319)

'May yet?' Along with the 'patience and humility' recommended above, this apologetic timidity is exactly what has prevented women novelists and critics from laying claim to the multiple greatnesses women have achieved. Always the expectation of women's fulfilling the promise of the novel is set somewhere in the future – yet from the moment when women first picked up the pen, the target has mysteriously and steadily receded before them. Even the women who by any standards were conquering the heights, were still led to believe that they were merely toiling away in the foothills – that somewhere in the future lay the woman writer, the woman's novel, that would justify the effort and existence of all.

In the past, carrying the innumerable chains and scars of their subordination which they struggled with mixed success to cast off, women writers had a double task. They had both to write the novels, and continuously to negotiate their right and space to do so. Small wonder that they could take nothing for granted, not even their own individual successes as the bench-mark of their worth. Criticism can now right the centuries-old historical wrong that has been done to generations of women writers and assert that from its foundation the novel has been and remains *the* female form.

Bibliography

All books are published in London unless otherwise stated.

Non-fiction

Abel, Elizabeth (ed.), *Writing and Sexual Difference* (1982).
Abel, E., Hirsch, M., and Langland, E., *The Voyage In: Fictions of Female Development* (Hanover, NH, 1983).
Allott, Miriam K., *Novelists on the Novel* (1959).
Anderson, Rachel, *The Purple Heart Throbs: The Sub-Literature of Love* (1974).
Angelou, Maya, *I Know Why the Caged Bird Sings* (1969).
———— *Gather Together in My Name* (1974).
———— *Singin' and Swillin' and Gettin' Merry Like Christmas* (1976).
Angier, Carole, *Jean Rhys* (1985).
Appignanesi, Lisa, *Femininity and the Creative Imagination: A Study of Henry James, Robert Musil and Marcel Proust* (1973).
Austen-Leigh, James, *Memoir of Jane Austen* (1870).
Baker, Michael, *Our Three Selves: A Life of Radclyffe Hall* (1985).
Bald, Marjory, *Women-Writers of the Nineteenth Century* (Cambridge, 1923).
Bargainnier, Earl F. (ed.), *Ten Women of Mystery* (Bowling Green, Ohio, 1981).
Barthes, Roland, *Mythologies* (1972).
Bayley, John, *The Characters of Love: A Study in the Literature of Personality* (1960).
Beauvoir, Simone de, *The Second Sex* (1952).
Beer, Patricia, *Reader, I Married Him* (1974).
Bell, Quentin, *Virginia Woolf: A Biography* (2 vols, 1972).
Bennett, Joan, *Virginia Woolf, Her Art as a Novelist* (Cambridge, 1945).
Bergonzi, Bernard, *The Situation of the Novel* (1970).
Boyers, Robert, *Atrocity and Amnesia: The Political Novel Since 1945* (Oxford, 1985).
Burgess, Anthony, *The Novel Now* (1967).
Byatt, A. S., *Degrees of Freedom* (1965).
Charney, Maurice, *Sexual Fiction* (1981).
Chisholm, Shirley, *Unbought and Unbossed* (1970).
Cixous, Hélène, 'The Laugh of the Medusa', tr. Keith and Paula Cohen, *Signs: Journal of Women in Culture and Society*, 1 (1976), 875–93.
Colby, Vineta, *The Singular Anomaly: Women Novelists of the Nineteenth Century*

(New York and London, 1970).

Courtney, W. L., *The Feminine Note in Fiction* (1904).

Cox, C. B., *The Free Spirit* (Oxford, 1963).

Cruickshank, Margaret, *Lesbian Studies: Present and Future* (New York, 1982).

Cunningham, Gail, *The New Woman and the Victorian Novel* (1978).

Daiches, David, *Virginia Woolf* (1945).

Damon, G. (alias Grier, B.), Watson, Jan, and Jordan, Robin, *The Lesbian in Literature: A Bibliography* (Reno, Nevada, 1975).

DeVeaux, Alexis, *Spirits in the Streets* (1973).

———— *Don't Explain: A Song of Billie Holiday* (1980).

Dick, Kay, *Ivy and Stevie* (1971).

Donovan, Josephine, *Feminist Literary Criticism: Explorations in Theory* (Lexington, Kentucky, 1975).

Edel, Leon, *The Psychological Novel 1900–1950* (1955).

Egan, Michael, *Henry James: The Ibsen Years* (1972).

Ellis, Havelock, *The Revaluation of Obscenity* (1931).

Ellis, Sarah Stickney, *The Women of England: Their Social Duties and Domestic Habits* (1839).

Ellmann, Mary, *Thinking About Women* (1968).

Evans, Mari (ed.), *Black Women Writers* (New York, 1984).

Ewbank, Inga-Stina, *Their Proper Sphere: A Study of the Brontë Sisters as Early-Victorian Female Novelists* (1966).

Faderman, Lillian, *Surpassing the Love of Men: Romantic Friendship and Love Between Women from the Renaissance to the Present* (New York, 1981).

Fallon, Eileen, *Words of Love: A Complete Guide to Romance Fiction* (New York and London, 1984).

Figes, Eva, *Sex and Subterfuge: Women Novelists to 1850* (1982).

Firestone, Shulamith, *The Dialectic of Sex* (1971).

Forman, A., *Femininity as Alienation: Women and the Family in Marxism and Psychoanalysis* (1977).

Foster, Jeanette, *Sex-Variant Women in Literature: A Historical and Quantitative Survey* (New York, 1956).

Friedan, Betty, *The Feminine Mystique* (1963).

Gallop, Jane, *Feminism and Psychoanalysis: The Daughter's Seduction* (1982).

Gardiner, Judith Kegan, 'On Female Identity', in Abel, Elizabeth (q.v.).

Gass, William, *Fiction and the Figures of Life* (1971).

Gilbert, Sandra M., and Gubal, Susan, *The Madwoman in the Attic: The Woman Writer and the Nineteenth-Century Literary Imagination* (New Haven, 1979).

Greene, Gayle, and Kahn, Coppelia (eds), *Making a Difference: Feminist Literary Criticism* (1985).

Greer, Germaine, *The Female Eunuch* (1970).

Hardwick, Elizabeth, 'The Subjection of Women' in *A View of My Own* (New York, 1962).

———— *Seduction and Betrayal: Women and Literature* (1974).

Harris, Bertha, 'The More Profound Nationality of their Lesbianism: Lesbian Society in Paris in the 1920s', in *Amazon Expedition: A Lesbian*

Feminist Anthology, ed. Phyllis Birkby *et al.* (Washington, NJ, 1973).

Heilbrun, Carolyn G., *Reinventing Womanhood* (New York, 1979).

Homans, Margaret, *Women Writers and Poetic Identity* (Princeton, 1980).

Hull, Gloria T., Scott, P. B., and Smith, B., (eds), *All the Women Are White, All the Men Are Black, But Some of Us Are Brave: Black Women's Studies* (Old Westbury, NY, 1982).

Jacobus, Mary (ed.), *Women Writing and Writing About Women* (New York, 1979).

James, Selma, *Jean Rhys: The Ladies and the Mammies* (1983).

Johnson, Barbara, *The Critical Difference* (Baltimore, 1981).

Johnson, R. Brimley, *Some Contemporary Novelists, Women* (1920).

Johnston, Jill, *A Place for Us* (1969).

—————— *Lesbian Nation: The Feminist Solution* (New York, 1973).

Jones, Ernest, *Sigmund Freud, Life and Work* (3 vols, 1953–7).

Jones, Phyllis M. (ed.), *English Critical Essays, Twentieth Century* (1933).

Jong, Erica, 'The Artist as Housewife', in Russ (q.v.), p. 90.

Kaplan, Sydney Janet, *Feminine Consciousness in the Modern British Novel* (Urbana and London, 1975).

Kermode, Frank, *Lawrence* (1973).

—————— *Essays on Fiction 1971–82* (1983).

Kingston, Maxine Hong, *The Woman Warrior: Memoirs of a Girlhood Among Ghosts* (New York, 1975).

Kramarae, C., and Treichler, P., *A Feminist Dictionary* (1985).

Kroeber, Karl, *Styles in Fictional Structure* (Princeton, 1971).

Lerner, Gerda, *Black Women in White America* (1972).

Lewes, G. H., 'The Lady Novelists', *Westminster Review*, n.s. 11 (1852).

Little, Hilary, 'Pornography: the Missing Link', in *Monitor* 4 (October 1985).

Lodge, David, *The Language of Fiction* (1966).

McCarthy, Mary, *Memories of a Catholic Girlhood* (1957).

—————— *On the Contrary* (1962).

Mailer, Norman, *Cannibals and Christians* (1967).

—————— *The Prisoner of Sex* (1971).

Mainiero, Lina (ed.), *American Women Writers: A Critical Reference Guide from Colonial Times to the Present* (4 vols, New York, 1979–81).

Mann, Jessica, *Deadlier than the Male: An Investigation into Feminine Crime Writing* (1981).

Mantz, Ruth Elvish, *The Critical Bibliography of Katherine Mansfield* (1931).

Mews, Hazel, *Frail Vessels* (1969).

Milford, Nancy, *Zelda Fitzgerald: A Biography* (1970).

Miller, Jane, *Women Writing About Men* (1986).

Millett, Kate, *Sexual Politics* (1969).

Mitchell, Juliet, *Psychoanalysis and Feminism: Freud, Reich, Lang and Women* (1975).

—————— *Women, the Longest Revolution: Essays on Feminism, Literature and Psychoanalysis* (1984).

Mitchell, Juliet, *et al.*, *Feminine Sexuality* (1982).

Moers, Ellen, *Literary Women: The Great Writers* (1977).

Moi, Toril, *Sexual/Textual Politics: Feminist Literary Theory* (1985).

Morgan, Fidelis, *The Female Wits 1660–1720* (1981).

Murdoch, Iris, *The Sovereignty of Good* (1970).

Murry, John Middleton (ed.), *Katherine Mansfield's Letters to John Middleton Murry, 1913–1922* (1951).

Newton, Judith Lowder, *Women, Power and Subversion: Social Strategies in British Fiction 1778–1860* (New York and London, 1985).

Olsen, Tillie, *Silences* (New York, 1978).

Orr, John, *Tragic Realism and Modern Society: Studies in the Sociology of the Novel* (1977).

Plath, Aurelia Schober (ed.), *Letters Home, Sylvia Plath: Correspondence 1950–63* (1975).

Radway, Janice E., *Reading the Romance: Women, Patriarchy and Popular Literature* (Chapel Hill and London, 1984).

Register, Cheri, 'Review Essay: Literary Criticism', *Signs: Journal of Women in Culture and Society* 6, 2 (1980), 268–82.

Rhys, Jean, *Smile Please: An Unfinished Autobiography* (1979).

Rich, Adrienne, 'Compulsory Heterosexuality and Lesbian Existence', in *Signs: Journal of Women in Culture and Society* 5, 4 (1980), 648–9.

Rigney, Barbara Hill, *Madness and Sexual Politics in the Feminist Novel* (Madison, Wisconsin, 1978).

Roberts, J. R., *Black Lesbians: An Annotated Bibliography* (Tallahassee, 1981).

Rogers, Katharine, *The Troublesome Helpmate: A History of Misogyny in Literature* (1966).

Rule, Jane, *Lesbian Images* (New York, 1975).

Ruskin, John, *The Ethics of the Dust, Ten Lectures to Little Housewives on the Elements of Crystallisation* (1866).

Russ, Joanna, *How to Suppress Women's Writing* (Texas, 1983).

Savage, D. S., *The Withered Branch: Six Studies in the Modern Novel* (1950).

Schorer, Mark, *The World We Imagine* (1969).

Schreiner, Olive, *Woman and Labour* (1911).

Schultz, Elizabeth, 'Free in Fact and at Last: The Image of the Black Woman in Black American Literature', in *What Manner of Woman: Essays on English and American Life and Literature*, ed. Marlene Springer (New York, 1977).

Schwenger, Peter, *Phallic Critiques: Masculinity and Twentieth-Century Literature* (1984).

Shange, Ntozake, in Tate, Claudia (q.v.).

Showalter, Elaine, *A Literature of Their Own: British Women Novelists from Brontë to Lessing* (Princeton, 1977).

——— 'Feminist Criticism in the Wilderness', in Abel, Elizabeth (q.v.).

——— 'Women Who Write Are Women', *New York Times Book Review* 16 December 1984.

Smith, Martin Seymour, *Fifty European Novels: A Reader's Guide* (1980).

Spacks, Patricia Meyer, *The Female Imagination* (New York, 1975).

——— (ed.), *Contemporary Women Novelists: A Collection of Critical Essays* (Englewood Cliffs, NJ, 1977).

Spender, Dale, *Mothers of the Novel* (1986).

Sprigge, Elizabeth, *The Life of Ivy Compton-Burnett* (1973).
Spurling, Hilary, *Secrets of a Woman's Heart: The Later Life of Ivy Compton-Burnett* (1984).
Staicar, Tom, *The Feminine Eye: Science Fiction and the Women Who Write It* (New York, 1982).
Staley, Thomas F. (ed.), *Jean Rhys: A Critical Study* (1979).
—— *Twentieth-Century Women Writers* (1982).
Stead, C. K. (ed.), *Katherine Mansfield: Letters and Journals* (1981).
Stimpson, Catherine, 'Zero Degree Deviancy: The Lesbian Novel in English', *Critical Inquiry*, 2 (1981), 364.
Stubbs, Patricia, *Women and Fiction: Feminism and the Novel 1880 to 1920* (1979).
Tate, Claudia (ed.), *Black Women Writers at Work* (1985).
Todd, Janet, *Dictionary of British and American Women Writers 1660–1800* (1984).
Washington, Mary Helen (ed.), *Midnight Birds: Stories by Contemporary Black Women Writers* (New York, 1980).
Wilson, Colin, *The Craft of the Novel* (1975).
Wise, T. J., and Symington, J. A. (eds), *The Brontës: Their Lives, Friendships and Correspondence* (The Shakespeare Head Brontë) (4 vols, Oxford, 1932).
—— *The Shakespeare Head Brontë* (19 vols, Oxford, 1931–8).
Wittig, Monique, *The Lesbian Body* (1975).
Woolf, Virginia, *A Room of One's Own* (1929).
—— *Three Guineas* (1938).
—— *The Death of the Moth* (1942).
—— *A Writer's Diary* (1953).
—— *Collected Essays*, ed. Leonard Woolf (4 vols, 1972).
Zimmerman, Bonnie, 'Lesbian Feminist Criticism', in Greene and Kahn, (q.v.).

Fiction, drama and poetry
Al-Shaykh, Hanan, *The Story of Zahra* (1986).
Aleramo, Sibilla, *A Woman* (1979).
Alther, Lisa, *Kinflicks* (New York, 1976).
—— *Other Women* (New York, 1984).
Amis, Kingsley, *Lucky Jim* (1954).
—— *Stanley and the Women* (1984).
Amis, Martin, *The Rachel Papers* (1973).
Aristophanes, *Lysistrata* (411 BC).
Atwood, Margaret, *Survival* (1972).
—— *Surfacing* (Toronto, 1972).
—— *Bodily Harm* (Toronto, 1982).
Austen, Jane, *Pride and Prejudice* (1813).
—— *Mansfield Park* (1814).
—— *Emma* (1815).
—— *Persuasion* (1818).
Bagnold, Enid, *The Loved and the Envied* (1951).

Ballard, J. G. *Crash* (1973).

Banks, Lynne Reid, *The L-Shaped Room* (1960).

Barnes, Djuna, *Nightwood* (1936).

Baum, Vicki, *Grand Hotel* (1930).

Bedford, Sybille, *A Favourite of the Gods* (1963).

—— *A Compass Error* (1968).

—— *A Legacy* (1973).

Bentley, Ursula, *The Natural Order* (1982).

Bowen, Elizabeth, *The House in Paris* (1935).

—— *The Heat of the Day* (1949).

Bowles, Jane, *Two Serious Ladies* (New York, 1943).

Brady, Maureen, *Folly* (1982).

Braine, John, *Room at the Top* (1957).

Brontë, Charlotte, *Jane Eyre* (1847).

—— *Shirley* (1849).

—— *Villette* (1853).

Brook-Rose, Christine, *Xorander* (1986).

Brookner, Anita, *Hotel du Lac* (1984).

Brown, Rita Mae, *The Hand That Cradles the Rock* (1971).

—— *Rubyfruit Jungle* (1973).

—— *Six of One* (1978).

Browning, Elizabeth Barrett, *Complete Works*, ed. Charlotte Porter and Helen A. Clarke (6 vols, New York, 1900).

Burgess, Anthony, *A Clockwork Orange* (1962).

Burney, Fanny, *Evelina* (1778).

Burroughs, William S., *The Wild Boys* (1972).

Byatt, A. S., *The Game* (1967).

Cardinal, Marie, *The Words to Say It* (1985).

Carter, Angela, *Nights at the Circus* (1984).

Chase, Joan, *During the Reign of the Queen of Persia* (1983).

Chopin, Kate, *The Awakening* (1899).

Christie, Agatha, *The Murder of Roger Ackroyd* (1926).

Cixous, Hélène, *The Laugh of the Medusa* (1976).

Cliff, Michelle, *Abeng* (1984).

Colette, *The Pure and the Impure* (1932).

Compton-Burnett, Ivy, *Pastors and Masters* (1925).

—— *Men and Wives* (1931).

—— *A House and Its Head* (1935).

—— *Brothers and Sisters* (1950).

—— *A Father and His Fate* (1957).

—— *The Mighty and Their Fall* (1961).

Congreve, William, *The Way of the World* (1700).

Conrad, Joseph, *Typhoon* (1903).

Dawson, Jennifer, *The Ha-Ha* (1961).

Dickens, Charles, *Martin Chuzzlewit* (1844).

—— *Bleak House* (1853).

Diski, Jenny, *Nothing Natural* (1986).

Dostoevsky, Fyodor, *The Idiot* (1886).

Drabble, Margaret, *The Garrick Year* (1964).
—— *The Millstone* (1965).
—— *Jerusalem the Golden* (1967).
—— *The Waterfall* (1969).
—— *The Needle's Eye* (1972).
Duffy, Maureen, *That's How It Was* (1962).
—— *Wounds* (1969).
—— *Capital: A Fiction* (1975).
Eliot, George, *Adam Bede* (1859).
—— *Middlemarch* (1871–2).
—— *Daniel Deronda* (1874–6).
Emecheta, Buchi, *The Wrestling Match* (1980).
—— *Double Yoke* (1982).
Emerson, Sally, *Listeners* (1983).
Fine, Anne, *The Killjoy* (1986).
Fitzgerald, F. Scott, *The Great Gatsby* (1925).
Fitzgerald, Zelda, *Save Me the Waltz* (1932).
French, Marilyn, *The Women's Room* (1977).
—— *The Bleeding Heart* (1980).
Gaskell, Elizabeth, *Ruth* (1853).
Gasner, Beverley, *Girls' Rules* (1969).
Gilman, Charlotte Perkins, *The Yellow Wallpaper* (1892).
Gordimer, Nadine, *The Conservationist* (1974).
—— *The Burger's Daughter* (1979).
Guy, Rosa, *Bird at My Window* (1966).
Hall, Radclyffe, *A Saturday Life* (1925).
—— *The Well of Loneliness* (1928).
Hansberry, Lorraine, *To Be Young, Gifted and Black* (1969).
Hardy, Thomas, *The Return of the Native* (1878).
—— *The Woodlanders* (1887).
Harris, Bertha, *Lover* (1976).
Harrison, Sarah, *Hot Breath* (1985).
Hemingway, Ernest, *The Sun Also Rises* (1926).
—— *Men Without Women* (1927).
—— *To Have and Have Not* (1937).
—— *The Snows of Kilimanjaro* (1938).
—— *The Short Happy Life of Francis Macomber* (1938).
—— *Across the River and Into the Trees* (1950).
—— *The Garden of Eden* (New York, 1986).
Hill, Susan, *Strange Meeting* (1971).
Holtby, Winifred, *South Riding* (1936).
Hospital, Janette Turner, *Borderline* (1985).
Howard, Elizabeth Jane, *The Sea Change* (1959).
Hulme, Keri, *The Bone People* (1985).
James, Henry, *Daisy Miller* (1879).
Jenkins, Elizabeth, *Honey* (1968).
Jong, Erica, *Fear of Flying* (1974).
Joyce, James, *Ulysses* (1922).

Kaufman, Sue, *Diary of a Mad Housewife* (1971).
Keane, Molly, *Good Behaviour* (1981).
Kincaid, Jamaica, *Annie John* (1986).
Lawrence, D. H., *The Rainbow* (1915).
────── *Women in Love* (1921).
────── *The Man Who Loved Islands* (1927).
Lehmann, Rosamond, *The Weather in the Streets* (1936).
Lessing, Doris, *The Grass Is Singing* (1950).
────── *Martha Quest* (1952).
────── *The Golden Notebook* (1962).
────── *Briefing for a Descent into Hell* (1971).
────── *Memoirs of a Survivor* (1971).
────── *The Good Terrorist* (1985).
Linton, Eliza Lynn, *The One Too Many* (1894).
────── *The Marriage of William Ashe* (1905).
Livia, Anna, *Accommodation Offered* (1985).
Lurie, Alison, *Real People* (1969).
McCarthy, Mary, *The Group* (1963).
McCullers, Carson, *Reflections in a Golden Eye* (1941).
────── *The Heart Is a Lonely Hunter* (1943).
────── *The Member of the Wedding* (1947).
Miller, Henry, *Tropic of Cancer* (1964).
Miller, Isabel, *A Place for Us* (1969; republished as *Patience and Sarah*, 1972).
Mitchell, Margaret, *Gone with the Wind* (1936).
Morrison, Toni, *The Bluest Eye* (New York, 1972).
────── *Sula* (New York, 1974).
────── *Song of Solomon* (New York, 1978).
Mortimer, Penelope, *The Pumpkin Eater* (1962).
────── *The Home* (1971).
Murdoch, Iris, *Under the Net* (1954).
────── *The Flight from the Enchanter* (1956).
────── *The Sandcastle* (1957).
────── *The Bell* (1958).
────── *A Severed Head* (1961).
────── *An Unofficial Rose* (1962).
────── *The Italian Girl* (1964).
────── *The Red and the Green* (1965).
────── *The Time of the Angels* (1966).
────── *The Nice and the Good* (1968).
────── *The Unicorn* (1969).
────── *Bruno's Dream* (1969).
────── *A Fairly Honourable Defeat* (1970).
────── *An Accidental Man* (1971).
────── *The Black Prince* (1973).
────── *The Sacred and Profane Love Machine* (1974).
────── *A Word Child* (1975).
────── *The Sea, the Sea* (1978).

—— *Nuns and Soldiers* (1980).
—— *The Philosopher's Pupil* (1983).
—— *The Good Apprentice* (1985).
Nachman, Elana, *Riverfinger Woman* (Plainfield, Vermont, 1974).
Nichols, Grace, *Whole of a Morning Sky* (1986).
Nin, Anaïs, *Delta of Venus* (1978).
Oates, Joyce Carol, *With Shuddering Fall* (1964).
O'Brien, Edna, *Girls in their Married Bliss* (1964).
—— *August Is a Wicked Month* (1965).
—— *A Pagan Place*(1970).
—— *Johnny, I Hardly Knew You* (1977).
Piercy, Marge, *Going Down Fast* (1969).
—— *Small Changes* (1973).
—— *Woman on the Edge of Time* (1976).
—— *Vida* (1980).
Plath, Sylvia, *The Bell Jar* (1963).
Rawlinson, Jane, *The Lion and the Lizard* (1986).
Renault, Mary, *The Charioteer* (1953).
—— *The Last of the Wine* (1956).
—— *The Mask of Apollo* (1966).
—— *Fire from Heaven* (1970).
—— *The Praise Singer* (1980).
—— *Funeral Games* (1981).
Rhys, Jean, *Left Bank* (1927).
—— *Postures* (1928; republished in 1969 as *Quartet*)
—— *Good Morning Midnight* (1939).
—— *Wide Sargasso Sea* (1966).
—— *Quartet* (1969).
—— *Sleep It Off, Lady* (1979).
Rich, Adrienne, *Poems* (New York, 1962).
—— *Amazon Poetry* (New York, 1975).
Richardson, Dorothy, *Pilgrimage* (12 vols, 1915–38).
Rilke, Rainer Maria, *Selected Works*, tr. G. Craig Houston, introd.
   J. B. Leishman (2 vols, 1954).
Roberts, Michele, *A Piece of the Night* (1978).
—— *The Visitation* (1983).
Ros, Amanda M'Kittrick, *Irene Iddesleigh* (1897).
Roth, Philip, *Portnoy's Complaint* (1967).
Rubens, Bernice, *Mr Wakefield's Crusade* (1985).
Sackville-West, Vita, *All Passion Spent* (1931).
Shange, Ntozake, *For Colored Girls Who Have Considered Suicide When the Rainbow is Enuf* (1976).
—— *Sassafrass, Indigo, Cyprus* (1982).
—— *Betsey Brown* (1985).
Slaughter, Carolyn, *Dreams of the Kalahari* (1981).
Solzhenitsyn, Alexander, *The Love Girl and the Innocent* (1969).
Soueif, Ahdaf, *Aisha* (1983).
Spark, Muriel, *The Driver's Seat* (1970).

Steedman, Carolyn, *Landscape for a Good Woman: A Story of Two Lives*
  (1986).
Stendhal, *The Charterhouse of Parma* (1839).
Strindberg, August, *The Father* (1887).
———— *The Stronger* (1888).
———— *The Dance of Death* (1901).
Tey, Josephine, *The Daughter of Time* (1951).
Thomas, D. M., *The White Hotel* (1981).
Undset, Sigrid, *Kristin Lavransdatter* (1920–2).
Walker, Alice, *The Third Life of Grange Copeland* (1970).
———— *The Color Purple* (1983).
Walker, Margaret, *Jubilee* (1965).
Ward, Mrs Humphry, *The History of David Grieve* (1892).
———— *The Marriage of William Ashe* (1905).
Weldon, Fay, *Female Friends* (1974).
———— *Praxis* (1978).
———— *The President's Child* (1982).
———— *The Shrapnel Academy* (1986).
Wells, H. G., *Love and Mr Lewisham* (1900).
———— *The History of Mr Polly* (1910).
Wesley, Mary, *The Vacillations of Poppy Carew* (1986).
Winterson, Jeanette, *Oranges Are Not the Only Fruit* (1985).
Wollstonecraft, Mary, *Mary, a Fiction* (1788).
Wood, Mrs Henry, *East Lynne* (1861).
Woolf, Virginia, *To the Lighthouse* (1927).
———— *The Waves* (1931).
———— *Between the Acts* (1941).

Index

Accidental Man, An, 96, 98, 100, 101
Across the River and into the Trees, 68
Adam Bede, 47
Aisha, 127
Al-Shaykh, Hanan, 126–7
Albee, Edward, 14
Alchemist, The, 3
Alcibiades, 179
Aleramo, Sibilla, 174
Alexander the Great, 151, 179
All Passion Spent, 52–5
Alther, Lisa, 143, 167, 168, 171,
    174, 190
Amazon Expedition, a Lesbian Feminist
    Mythology, 205
American Women Writers, 6
Amis, Kingsley, 81, 82, 86–7
Amis, Martin, 86
Angelou, Maya, 104, 109
Angier, Carole, 136
Annie, John, 104
Appignanesi, Lisa, 17, 195
'Artist as Housewife, The', 88
Atherton, Gertrude, 37
Atrocity and Amnesia: The Political
    Novel since 1945, 92
Atwood, Margaret, 126
Aubrey, John, 65
August Is a Wicked Month, 155–6
Austen, Jane, 1, 5, 7, 8, 9–10, 12,
    21, 23, 43–6, 57, 64, 113, 146,
    149
Austen-Leigh, James, 21, 45
Awakening, The, 112

Backwater, 51

Bagnold, Enid, 31, 178
Bailey, Hilary, 7
Baker, Michael, 184
Bald, Marjory, 10
Ballard, J. G., 59
Banks, Lynn Reid, 162
Barnes, Djuna, 24, 185, 205
Barstow, Stan, 81
Barthes, Roland, 5, 91
Basu, Rekha, 130
Bayley, John, 99, 151
Beauvoir, Simone de, 111
Beerbohm, Max, 7
Behn, Aphra, 1, 3, 36
Bell, Quentin, 153
Bell, The, 98
Bell Jar, The, 124
Bennett, Joan, 55
Bentley, Ursula, 168
Bergman, Ingmar, 126
Bergonzi, Bernard, 79
Betsey Brown, 104
Between the Acts, 56
Billy Liar, 81
Bird at My Window, 129
Black, Hermina, 27
Black Prince, The, 71, 98, 101
Black Women in White America, 130
Black Women Writers at Work, 20, 206
Bleak House, 66–7
Bleeding Heart, The, 176
Bluest Eye, The, 109
Boswell, James, 194
Bowen, Elizabeth, 18, 23, 30, 31,
    62, 89, 162
Bowles, Jane, 185

Boyers, Robert, 92
Brady, Maureen, 129, 187
Braine, John, 81
Briefing for a Descent into Hell, 51, 198–9
Brontë, Anne, 23
Brontë, Charlotte, 9, 19, 22, 23, 27, 34, 38–42, 46, 47, 49, 64, 149
Brontë, Emily, 2, 23, 39
Brontës: Their Lives, Friendships and Correspondence, The, 38, 49
Brookner, Anita, 12, 23, 146
Brophy, Brigid, 14
Brothers and Sisters, 113, 116, 178
Brown, Rita Mae, 110, 189, 191
Browning, Elizabeth Barrett, 132
Bruno's Dream, 98
Buck, Pearl, 29
Burger's Daughter, 92
Burgess, Anthony, 7, 12–14, 84–6, 123
Burney, Fanny, 1, 20–1
Burroughs, William, 59
Byatt, A. S., 42–3
Byron, George Gordon, Lord, 31, 175

Camus, Albert, 134
Cannibals and Christians, 7, 13
Cardinal, Marie, 126
Carr, E. H., 94
Carter, Angela, 103, 111, 128, 144
Cartland, Barbara, 42
Cather, Willa, 23
Cecil, Lord David, 141
Chaeronea, battle of, 179
Characters of Love, The, 99, 151
'Charge of the Light Brigade, The', 58
Charioteer, The, 179
Charterhouse of Parma, The, 89
Chaucer, Geoffrey, 65
Chisholm, Shirley, 108
Chopin, Kate, 112
Churchill, Caryl, 3
Cixous, Hélène, 19
Clarke, Helen A., 132
Clear Horizon, 51

Clockwork Orange, A, 84–6
Clytemnestra, 80
Colby, Vineta, 10
Colette, 144, 166, 187
Color Purple, The, 104, 109, 191, 193
Complete Works of Elizabeth Barrett Browning, The 132
Compton-Burnett, Ivy, 8, 9, 16, 22, 23, 24, 112–17, 132, 157, 178, 195
'Compulsory Heterosexuality and Lesbian Existence', 177, 192
Conrad, Joseph, 67, 194
Conservationist, The, 92
Contemporary Women Novelists, 9, 14
Corelli, Marie, 28
Country Wife, The, 119
Courtney, W. L., 11–12
Cox, C. B., 67
Craft of the Novel, The, 64
Craig, Isa, 47
Cranford, 57, 72, 196
Crash, 59
Crime and Punishment, 195
Critical Bibliography of Katherine Mansfield, 61
Critical Differences, The, 1
Cronos, 59
Cruikshank, Margaret, 178
Cymbeline, 65

Daiches, David, 15, 56
Daisy Miller, 46
Dance of Death, The, 137
Daniel Deronda, 38, 123
Daughter of Time, The, 90
Daughters of England, 48
Dawn's Left Hand, 51
Dawson, Jennifer, 124
De Jongh, Nicholas, 41
De Veaux, Alexis, 206
Deadlock, 51
Death of the Moth, The, 1, 56, 153
Defoe, Daniel, 72
Degrees of Freedom, 43
Delaney, Shelagh, 3
Delta of Venus, 148, 166, 173–4
Demosthenes, 179
Derrida, Jacques, 13

Deutsch, Helene, 80
Dialectic of Sex, The, 67
Dick, Kay, 16, 115, 117
Dickens, Charles, 6, 14, 66–7, 72, 73, 94, 149, 206
Dickinson, Emily, 2, 178
Dictionary of British and American Women Writers, 6
Dimple Hill, 51
Dinesen, Isak, 23
Diski, Jenny, 174
Disraeli, Benjamin, 114
Diving into the Wreck, 19
Doll's House, The, 147
Don Quixote, 94
Donovan, Josephine, 201
Dos Passos, John, 18
Dostoevsky, Fyodor, 93, 94, 98, 194, 195, 204
Dostoevsky 1821–1881, 94
Drabble, Margaret, 24, 25, 124, 161–3
Dreams of the Kalahari, 128
Driver's Seat, The, 79
Du Maurier, Daphne, 64
Dutrueil, Nicole, 64

East Lynne, 47, 149
Edel, Leon, 62, 73
Eliot, George, 1, 6, 10, 23, 37–8, 42, 51, 55, 195, 204, 207
Ellis, Havelock, 151
Ellis, Mrs Sarah Stickney, 48
Ellmann, Mary, 9, 16–17, 57, 149
Emerson, Sally, 132
Emma, 44
English Critical Essays: Twentieth Century, 7
Erinnyes, the, 80
Essays on Fiction 1971–82, 65
Ethics of the Dust, 48
Euripides, 57
Evelina, 21, 193
Ewbank, Inga-Stina, 2

Faderman, Lillian, 187
Fairly Honourable Defeat, A, 99, 100, 101

Fallon, Eileen, 34
Fame Is the Spur, 51
Fanny Hill, 153–4
Farnol, Jeffery, 64
Farrell, James T., 18
Father, The, 137
Father and His Fate, A, 114
Fear of Flying, 175
Female Eunuch, The, 73
Female Friends, 74, 145
Female Wits, The, 3
Feminine Consciousness in the Modern British Novel, 18
Feminine Mystique, The, 73
Feminine Note in Fiction, The, 11
Femininity and the Creative Imagination, 17, 195
'Fiction and the Analogical Matrix', 43
Fiction and the Figures of Life, 13
Fifty European Novels: A Reader's Guide, 65
Fine, Anne, 174
Fire from Heaven, 179
Firestone, Shulamith, 67
Fitzgerald, F. Scott, 22–3, 32, 197, 206
Fitzgerald, Zelda, 22–3, 197
Flight from the Enchanter, The, 95, 96, 101, 117
Folly, 129, 187–8
Ford, Ford Madox, 132
Forster, E. M., 18, 89
Frail Vessels, 15, 66
Frame, Janet, 24
Free Spirit, The, 67
French, Marilyn, 8, 176
Friedan, Betty, 73, 202
Freud, Sigmund, 68, 73–4, 78, 79, 159
Fulbrook, Kate, 62

Gagen, Jean, 150
Garden of Eden, The, 68
Gardiner, Judith Kegan, 201
Garrick Year, The, 163
Gaskell, Mrs Elizabeth, 21, 46
Gasner, Beverley, 120

Gass, William, 13
Gems, Pam, 3
Gilbert, W. S., 6
Girl's Rules, 120
Glasgow, Ellen, 23
Glaspell, Susan, 23
Glyn, Elinor, 28
Goldberg, Philip, 6
Golden Notebook, The, 13–14, 111, 121–3, 137, 150, 158–61, 163–4, 173, 198
Gone with the Wind, 88
Good Behaviour, 74
Good Morning Midnight, 134, 135–6
Good Terrorist, The, 198
Gordimer, Nadine, 92
Gracchi, the, 5
Grand Hotel, 90
Grass Is Singing, The, 105–7, 152
Great Gatsby, The, 32, 175
Green, Hannah, 24
Greer, Germaine, 73, 163
Grey, Marina, 5
Group, The, 155, 162, 163, 186
Guardian, 7, 42
Guy, Rosa, 129

Ha-Ha, The, 124
Hall, Radclyffe, 180–5
Hall, Willis, 81
Hand That Cradles the Rock, The, 189
Hansberry, Lorraine, 24
Hardwick, Elizabeth, 194
Hardy, Thomas, 14, 29, 149, 150, 206
Harris, Bertha, 190, 191, 205
Harris, Frank, 154
Harrison, Sarah, 25
Heart Is a Lonely Hunter, The, 90–1, 108, 193
Heat of the Day, The, 89
Hellman, Lillian, 3, 24
Hemingway, Ernest, 18, 55, 64, 68–70, 75, 81, 195, 206
Herbst, Josephine, 24
Hill, Susan, 24, 89
History of David Grieve, The, 46
Hobbes, John Oliver, 7

Holtby, Winifred, 89–90
Homans, Margaret, 2, 35
Home, The, 125
Honey, 32
Honeycomb, 51
Hot Breath, 25
Hotel du Lac, 146
House and Its Head, A, 114, 116
House in Paris, The, 30
How to Suppress Women's Writing, 24
Howard, Elizabeth Jane, 31–2, 162
Hulme, Keri, 12
Hurston, Zora Neale, 24

I Know Why the Caged Bird Sings, 104, 109
Ibsen, Henrik, 53, 78, 150
Idiot, The, 93
Interim, 50, 51
Iphigenia, 80
Irene Iddesleigh, 28
Italian Girl, The, 95, 100
Ivy and Stevie, 16, 115

James, Henry, 46, 195
Jameson, Mrs Anna, 47
Jane Eyre, 34, 39–42, 47, 124
Jean Rhys, 136
Jellicoe, Ann, 3
Jenkins, Elizabeth, 32
Jerusalem the Golden, 163
Jones, Ernest, 74
Jones, Phyllis M., 7
Johnson, R. Brimley, 11
Johnson, Samuel, 138
Johnston, Jill, 190
Jong, Erica, 88, 175–6
Jonson, Barbara, 1
Jonson, Ben, 3, 194
Joyce, James, 25, 27, 157, 197
Jubilee, 24

Kafka, Franz, 134
Kaplan, Sydney Janet, 17–18
Katherine Mansfield, 62
Katherine Mansfield: The Memories of L. M., 24

Katherine Mansfield: Letters and Journals, 22
Katherine Mansfield's Letters to John Middleton Murry 1913–1922, 60
Keane, Molly, 74
Keats, John, 30
Kermode, Frank, 65, 76
Killjoy, The, 174
Kincaid, Jamaica, 104
Kinflicks, 143, 167, 171–2
Kingston, Maxine Hong, 4, 126, 165
Krafft-Ebing, Richard, 155
Kristin Lavransdatter, 65
Kroeber, Karl, 41

'L. M.', 24, 197
L-Shaped Room, The, 162
'Lady Novelists, The', 50
Landscape for a Good Woman: A Story of Two Lives, 200
Language of Fiction, The, 13
Last of the Wine, The, 179
'Laugh of the Medusa, The', 19
Lawrence, D. H., 12, 42, 55, 56, 69, 75–80, 82, 128, 145, 154, 174, 180, 206
Lawrence, 76
Left Bank, 132–3
Lehmann, Rosamond, 31, 62, 154
Lenoir, Jacqueline, 5
Lerner, Gerda, 129
Lesbian Images, 178
Lesbian Nation, 190
Lesbian Studies: Present and Future, 178
Lessing, Doris, 13–14, 19, 25, 26, 51, 74, 105–7, 111, 121–3, 137, 150, 152, 156, 158–61, 163–4, 173, 176, 198–9, 203
Letters Home, Sylvia Plath, 20
Lewes, George Henry, 23, 48–9, 50
Life and Death of Radclyffe Hall, The, 182
Life of Ivy Compton-Burnett, The, 9
Lind, Sylvia, 61
Linton, Mrs Eliza Lynn, 46, 47
Listeners, 132

Literary Women, 2
Literature of Their Own, A, 19, 35, 36, 207
Little, Hilary, 189
Lodge, David, 13
Love-Girl and the Innocent, The, 66
Loved and the Envied, The, 31, 178
Lover, 190, 205
Lucky Jim, 81, 82
Lurie, Alison, 15, 141, 199
Lysistrata, 80

McCarthy, Mary, 4, 7, 18, 23, 25, 61, 81, 93, 116, 155, 156, 162, 168, 186
McCullers, Carson, 23, 24, 25, 90–1, 102–3, 107, 193
McEwan, Christian, 7
McGonagall, William, 28
Mackenzie, Compton, 78
Mahy, Margaret, 88
Mailer, Norman, 7, 13, 18, 62, 84, 128, 145, 148, 149, 154, 195
Mainiero, Lina, 6
Malet, Lucas, 37
'Man in the Brooks Brothers Shirt, The', 25
Man Who Loved Islands, The, 78
Mansfield, Katherine, 18, 21–2, 23, 24, 60–1, 62, 78, 197
Mansfield Park, 9–10, 123
Mantz, Ruth Elvish, 61
Marriage of William Ashe, The, 46
Martha Quest, 25, 26, 158
Martin Chuzzlewit, 67
Martineau, Harriet, 1, 47
Mary, 111
Masefield, Muriel, 10
Mask of Apollo, The, 179
Maybury, Anne, 27
Medusa, 80
Melville, Herman, 194
Member of the Wedding, The, 102–3, 108
Memoir of Jane Austen, A, 45
Memories of a Catholic Girlhood, 4
Men and Wives, 8, 22
Men Without Women, 68

Mews, Hazel, 15, 39
Middlemarch, 37, 40
Midsummer Night's Dream, A, 155
Mighty and Their Fall, The, 117, 195
Mikado, The, 6
Milford, Nancy, 22
Miller, Henry, 84, 128, 154
Millett, Kate, 73, 76
Millstone, The, 163
Mitchell, Juliet, 73
Mitchell, Margaret, 88
Moers, Ellen, 2
'Morality and the Novel', 75
Morgan, Fidelis, 3
Morgan, Lady (Sydney Owenson),
   47
Morrison, Toni, 109
Mortimer, Penelope, 124–5
Mothers of England, 48
Mothers of the Novel, 5
Murder of Roger Ackroyd, The, 90
Murdoch, Iris, 12, 23, 24, 71–2, 89,
   93, 94–102, 117, 119, 176, 196,
   198
Murry, John Middleton, 21–2, 60,
   78, 197
Mythologies, 5

Nachman, Elana, 189
Natural Order, The, 168
Needle's Eye, The, 124
Nice and the Good, The, 94
Nichols, Grace, 103
Nicholson, Nigel, 53
Nights at the Circus, 103, 111, 128,
   144
Nightwood, 185, 205
Nin, Anais, 4, 24, 148, 165, 193–4
Nothing Natural, 174
Novel Now, The, 7, 12
Nuns and Soldiers, 98

Oates, Joyce Carol, 24, 125
Oberland, 51
O'Brien, Edna, 155–8
O'Connor, Flannery, 24
Olsen, Tillie, 23, 177
On Female Identity, 201

On the Contrary, 18, 61
One Too Many, The, 46
Oranges Are Not the Only Fruit, 191
Orr, John, 65
Osborne, John, 81
Other Women, 190
Ouida, 7, 28
*Our Three Sisters: A Life of Radclyffe
   Hall*, 184

Pagan Place, A, 156–8
Page, Louise, 3
Pankhurst, Sylvia, 47
Parker, Dorothy, 23, 37
Paston Women, The, 26
Pastors and Masters, 116
Penelope, 80
Persuasion, 44–5, 64, 66
*Phallic Critiques: Masculinity and
   Twentieth Century Criticism*, 202
Piercy, Marge, 92, 126, 142, 166,
   170–1, 189
'Pig's-Eye View of Literature, A',
   37
Pilgrimage, 51
Pinter, Harold, 157
Plath, Aurelia Schober, 20
Plath, Sylvia, 20, 124, 173
Pointed Roofs, 51
Pornography: The Missing Link, 189
Porter, Charlotte, 132
Porter, Katherine Anne, 23
Portnoy's Complaint, 82–4, 145
Portrait of a Marriage, 53
Postures, 133
Praise Singer, The, 179
Praxis, 121, 142, 150, 166–7, 172–3
President's Child, The, 131, 165
Pride and Prejudice, 44, 57
Prisoner of Sex, The, 7, 148
Proust, Marcel, 25, 194, 195
Psychoanalysis and Feminism, 73
Psychological Novel 1900–1950, The, 73
Pumpkin Eater, The, 124
Pure and the Impure, The, 144, 166,
   187

Quartet, 133

Rabelais, François, 65
Rachel Papers, The, 86
Radway, Janice, 33
Rainbow, The, 76
Reading the Romance, 33
Real People, 15, 141, 199–200
Red and the Green, The, 89
Register, Cheri, 201
Renault, Mary, 179–80
Return of the Native, The, 29
Revaluation of Obscenity, The, 151
Revolving Lights, 51
Rhys, Jean, 40–1, 74, 132–41, 145, 176
Rich, Adrienne, 19, 177, 186, 192
Richardson, Dorothy, 18, 23, 50–1, 61, 62
Richardson, Henry Handel, 23
Richardson, Samuel, 72
Rilke, Rainer Maria, 193
Riverfinger Woman, 189
Roberts, Elizabeth Madox, 24
Roberts, Michele, 128, 144, 169
Rogers, Katharine, 14, 65–6
Room at the Top, 81
Room of One's Own, A, 3, 24, 25, 56, 81, 201, 207
Ros, Amanda M'Kittrick, 28
Roth, Philip, 82–4
Rover, The, 3
Rubyfruit Jungle, 109, 189
Ruck, Bertha, 29
Rule, Jane, 178
Ruskin, John, 48
Russ, Joanna, 24
Ruth, 46

Sackville-West, Vita, 52–5
Sandcastle, The, 95, 97, 98
Sarton, May, 24
Saturday Life, A, 181
Savage, D. S., 60, 61
Save Me the Waltz, 22
Scenes from Clerical Life, 6
Schorer, Mark, 43, 69
Schreiner, Olive, 197
Schwenger, Peter, 202
Sea Change, The, 32

Sea, the Sea, The, 95
Second Sex, The, 111
Secrets of a Woman's Heart, 9
Severed Head, A, 101, 198
'Sexual Imperialism: The Case of Indian Women in Britain', 130
Sexual Politics, 73
Shakespeare, William, 1, 3, 7, 42, 58, 65, 66, 72, 95, 207
Shange, Ntozake, 20, 104, 105
Shirley, 39, 40
Short Happy Life of Francis Macomber, The, 69–70
Showalter, Elaine, 19, 35, 36, 198, 201, 207
Shrapnel Academy, The, 88
Sidney, Sir Philip, 42
Sigmund Freud: Life and Work, 74
Silences, 23, 177
Sillitoe, Alan, 81
'Silly Novels by Lady Novelists', 38
Simenon, Georges, 64
Singular Anomaly, The, 10, 66
Situation of the Novel, The, 79
Slaughter, Carolyn, 128
Small Changes, 189
Smith, Lillian, 24
Smith, Martin Seymour, 65
Smith, Stevie, 10, 23
Snows of Kilimanjaro, The, 69
Solzhenitsyn, Alexander, 66
Some Contemporary Novelists (Women), 11
Sophocles, 57
Soueif, Ahdaf, 127
South Riding, 89–90
Southey, Robert, 64
Sovereignty of Good, The, 101
Spacks, Patricia Meyer, 9, 14
Spark, Muriel, 79
Spender, Dale, 5–6, 62
Spenser, Edmund, 42
Sprigge, Elizabeth, 9
Spring, Howard, 51
Spurling, Hilary, 9
Stafford, Jean, 24
Stanley and the Women, 86–7
Stead, C. K., 22

Stead, Christina, 24
Steedham, Carolyn, 200
Stein, Gertrude, 23, 187
Stendhal, 89, 194
Story of Zahra, The, 126
Stowe, Harriet Beecher, 37
Strachey, Lytton, 153
Strange Meeting, 89
Strindberg, August, 137, 195
Stronger, The, 137
Suffragette, The, 47
Suffragette Movement, The, 47
Sula, 109
Sun Also Rises, The, 68, 69
Surfacing, 126
*Surpassing the Love of Men: Romantic
    Friendship and Love Between Women,
    from the Renaissance to the Present*,
    187
Survival, 126
Sybil, 114
Symington, J. A., 38

Tate, Claudia, 20, 206
Tennant, Emma, 8
Thebes, Sacred Band of, 179
Their Proper Sphere, 2, 149
Thesus, 179
Thinking About Women, 9, 149
Third Life of Grange Copeland, The,
    109
Thomas, D. M., 59
Thomas, Dylan, 25
Three Guineas, 52, 56
Thurber, James, 64
Time of the Angels, The, 96, 97
To Have and Have Not, 70
To the Lighthouse, 57, 58–9
Todd, Janet, 6
Tolkien, J. R. R., 64
Tolstoy, Leo, 14, 194, 206
Tragic Realism and Modern Society, 65
Trap, The, 51
Trollope, Anthony, 36
Trollope, Mrs Frances, 36-7
Tropic of Cancer, 72
Troublesome Helpmate, The, 14, 66
Troubridge, Una, 182

Tunnel, The, 51
Two Serious Ladies, 185
Typhoon, 67

Ulysses, 27, 194
Unbought and Unbossed, 108
Under the Net, 96
Undset, Sigrid, 64
Unicorn, The, 94
Unofficial Rose, An, 96, 98
Uranus, 59

Vacillations of Poppy Carew, The, 33
Vida, 92, 142, 170–1
View of My Own, A, 194
Villette, 39, 41
Vindication of the Rights of Woman, A,
    15
Virginia Woolf, 56
Virginia Woolf: A Biography, 153
Virginia Woolf: Collected Essays, 121,
    148
Virginia Woolf: Her Art as a Novelist,
    55
Visitation, The, 128, 144, 169
Voynich, 37

Wain, John, 81
Walker, Alice, 12, 74, 104, 108, 109
Walker, Margaret, 24, 191
Wallace-Dunlop, Marion, 47
War and Peace, 64
Ward, Mrs Humphry, 21, 46, 47
Waterfall, The, 162
Waterhouse, Keith, 81
Waves, The, 57
Way of the World, The, 80
Weather in the Streets, The, 31, 154
Wedekind, Frank, 195
Weiner, Gaby, 7
Weldon, Fay, 74, 88, 121, 130–1,
    142, 145, 150, 165, 166–7, 172–3
Well of Loneliness, The, 183–5
Welty, Eudora, 24
Wesley, Mary, 33
West, Jessamyn, 24
West, Rebecca, 62
Wharton, Edith, 23

Wheatley, Phillis, 105
White Hotel, The, 59
Whole of the Morning Sky, 103
Wide Sargasso Sea, 40–1, 136
Wild Boys, The, 59
Wilde, Oscar, 71
Wilkins, Miss Mary, 37
Williams, Raymond, 37
Wilson, Colin, 64–5
Wilson, Edmund, 23
Winter's Tale, The, 72
Winterson, Jeanette, 191
Wise, T. J., 38
With Shuddering Fall, 125
Withered Branch, The, 60
Wittig, Monique, 190
Wives of England, 48
Wollstonecraft, Mary, 15, 111
Woman, A, 174
Woman and Labour, 197
Woman on the Edge of Time, 126, 166
Woman Warrior, The: Memoirs of a Girlhood Among Ghosts, 4, 126, 165

Women in Love, 77, 78
Women Novelists from Fanny Burney to George Eliot, 10
Women of England, 48
Women Writers and Poetic Identity, 2, 35
Women Writers of the Nineteenth Century, 10
Women's Room, The, 176
Wood, Mrs Henry, 149
Woodlanders, The, 29
Woolf, Leonard, 23
Woolf, Virginia, 1, 3, 10, 14, 15, 17, 18, 21, 23, 24, 25, 26, 51–2, 55, 56–63, 81, 121, 148, 152–3, 154–5, 162, 178, 201, 206
Words of Love, 34
Words to Say It, The, 126
World We Imagine, The, 43, 69
Writer's Diary, A, 52, 58

Zelda Fitzgerald: A Biography, 22
Zimmerman, Bonnie, 177

→ Pg 206 Androgeny